A Prince's Passion The Life
of the Royal Pavilion

Jessica Rutherford

The Grand-Signior retiring.

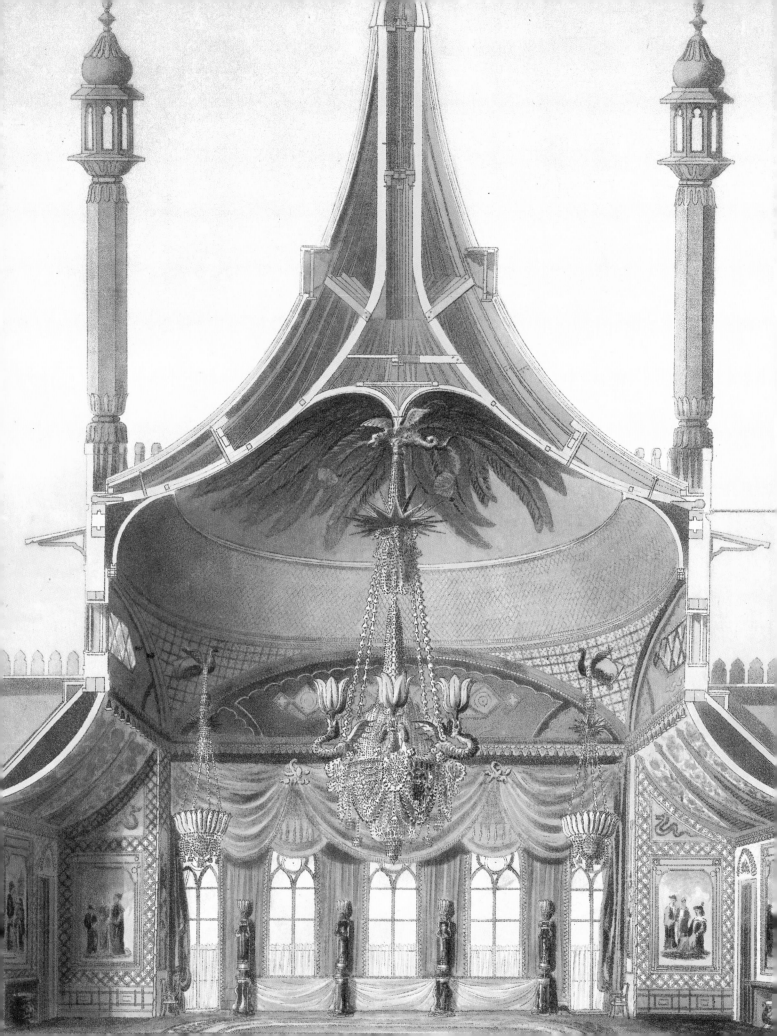

A Prince's Passion The Life of the Royal Pavilion

Jessica Rutherford

Published by the Royal Pavilion, Libraries & Museums (Brighton & Hove City Council)
with the support of the Friends of the Royal Pavilion, Art Gallery & Museums, 2003

British Library Cataloguing In Publication Data
A catalogue record for this book is available from the British Library

©Jessica Rutherford 2003

Designed by Nigel Cunningham

Printed by B A S Printers, Salisbury

ISBN: 0 948723 54 8

Front jacket: illustration from *THE GEWGAW: or BRIGHTON TOY, a caricature poem in one canto* by Peter Broadgrin,
London n.d. A gewgaw is a gaudy ornament or bauble. Reproduced by courtesy of Henry Smith Esq.

Back jacket: The North Front of the Pavilion from Nash's *Views* (detail).

Endpapers: detail of the dragon wallpaper designed by Robert Jones for the Royal Pavilion and block-printed in several
colours including chrome yellow, red lake and green. One complete repeat of the complex design of dragons, dolphins
with a giant sunflower and phoenix required thirty blocks, with an additional eight for the dado.

Half-title: *The Grand Signior retiring*, published 25 May 1796. The Prince of Wales enters the bedroom of his mistress,
Lady Jersey. On the door is a map of the Channel Islands, showing 'the road into the harbour of Jersey'.

Frontispiece: the Great kitchen and Banqueting Room from the cross-section (detail) in Nash's *Views*.

Brighton & Hove

Contents

Preface

In the early 1880s the American writer Moncure Daniel Conway described the Royal Pavilion in Brighton as a barbaric and tasteless 'temple of vanity', the 'physiognomical monument of George IV – his cerebral interior projected into stone and decoration'.

That was mild compared to some of the opprobrium heaped on this extraordinary and fascinating building since it first emerged from scaffolding in 1818, although it also had its share of fervent supporters. Even today, love it or hate it, few are indifferent to this unique building.

The story of its evolution is inextricably linked to the character, taste and obsessions of its patron, George IV. It embodies his personality and Regency social conventions. In its final incarnation, it met the King's every need and whim – whether social, physical, culinary or aesthetic. The magnificent and luxurious public and private rooms were furnished to new standards of comfort and convenience with the application of the most modern technology available.

For those of us who work in the Pavilion this weird and wonderful creation can become all consuming. Two centuries on, it still continues to reveal its complex past - for it also carries the imprint of two successive monarchs, 150 years of municipal management as a former royal palace and the city of Brighton's changing attitudes towards its role and value.

After the purchase of the Pavilion Estate by the town in 1850 large parts of the complex were demolished. All the ancillary kitchens, the courtyard with its clock tower, the servants' quarters and the Royal Chapel disappeared as well as the South Gate, dormitories and servants' accommodation built by William IV. The interior architecture of the Pavilion and the configuration of rooms on the ground and first floors were altered, in some cases irrevocably, to accommodate its new civic uses. No longer an occupied royal palace, its meaning as a living, inhabited residence was lost.

Decades of restoration and the reinstatement of the original interior architecture as well as the original fittings, furniture and decorative schemes have gradually re-established its Regency character and grandeur. Much has been written on its architecture and design, but little on its social evolution, how it functioned as a royal palace and the role of the Royal Household.

This book is written in the hope that with a better understanding of the social and cultural context of the Pavilion and how it was used and managed in George IV's time, we may, at least in our imagination, appreciate and enjoy it even more.

Acknowledgements

Amongst the many people who have helped with this book I would particularly like to mention Jackie Frisby, who tragically died in May 2000. She researched various aspects of the Pavilion, but was particularly interested in George IV's private band and its leader, Christian Kramer. Some of her research has been included in chapter 3. We would like to record her exceptional contribution to the Royal Pavilion, Libraries & Museums here in Brighton and Hove.

I should like to thank personally a number of people for their help and advice: David Anderson, Andrew Barlow, David Beevers, Stella Beddoe, Sir Geoffrey de Bellaigue, Sue Berry, Sally Blann, Jackie Lewis and the staff of the Brighton History Centre, Jan Cadge, Leslie Caron, Patrick Conner, Mark Easton, Elaine Fayers, Gordon Grant, Deborah Grubb, Peter Guttridge, The Rt Hon. Lord Healey, Michael Jones, Celia Kendall, Jenny Knight, Marie Leahy, Gerald Legg, Neil MacGregor, Samantha McNeilly, Sandy Nairne, Rebecca Quinton, Sir Hugh Roberts, Henry Smith, Matthew Winterbottom and Pam Woolicroft.

All illustrations are from the collections of the Royal Pavilion, Libraries & Museums (© Brighton & Hove City Council) unless otherwise acknowledged. When illustrations are credited as Nash's *Views*, these come from *Views of the Royal Pavilion* by John Nash (1826), dedicated to George IV. The majority of the plates were based on watercolours by A. C. Pugin, assisted by James Stephanoff, who contributed the figures.

We are particularly grateful to Her Majesty Queen Elizabeth II for permission to reproduce pictures from the Royal Collection and to refer to documents held in the Royal Archives, Windsor Castle, and the Royal Collection. We should also like to thank the British Museum, the British Library, the Chicago Institute of Art, the National Portrait Gallery, *The Times*, *Vogue*, The National Trust, the House of Lords Library, The National Archives and Spode Museum Trust for their generous support and for their permission to reproduce material from their collections. I should also like to thank Jim Watts of The National Trust for his photograph of the ice house at Felbrigg Hall (National Trust).

The book could not have been published without support from the Friends of the Royal Pavilion, Art Gallery & Museums, chaired by the Rt Hon. Lord Briggs.

But most of all I should like to thank Maureen Simmonds for her encouragement and patient support with numerous drafts and her comments and suggestions, as well as her knowledge. Without her I would have given up.

Jessica Rutherford

1 George, Prince of Wales, and the town of Brighton

Introduction: 'The King is to this town what the sun is to our hemisphere'[1]

1. (left) George, Prince of Wales, *as a young man, 1780–1782, watercolour on ivory by Richard Cosway. By courtesy of the National Portrait Gallery, London.*

Regency Brighton, rich in temptations for the vain and greedy, provided the perfect setting for a contemporary moral tale designed to improve the minds of impressionable young ladies and gentlemen. In *Sketches of Young People or a Visit to Brighton*, the anonymous author described the effete, simpering young men, encased in tight stays and fashionable dress, with pencilled eyebrows, curled mustachios and curled hair, strolling pretentiously along the Steine amidst the bustle, bands, performers and promenading society. He added that they were all observed from life – as if his reader would not believe such a description. These 'dandies' provided an exemplar of vanity, idleness and self-obsession. But the author's young heroine, Caroline, was able to extol the pleasures of exercise and sea air and the cultural benefits of subscribing to a private library rather than vainly frittering money on smuggled silks or laces in Brighton's tempting shops.[2]

2. (right) Beauties of BRIGHTON, *by George Cruikshank, 1826. A satire on Brighton's fashionable society, pretentiously parading in front of the Royal Pavilion with its equally exaggerated skyline.*

Beauties of BRIGHTON

This racy image of Brighton contrasted singularly with the image of Weymouth, the only other south-coast resort patronised by the Royal Family, and in particular by the Prince of Wales's[3] father, George III. During the period 1789–1805 he regularly visited Weymouth, for four to six weeks in August and September. The King loved the bathing, yachting, horse-riding and parades and also reviewing the local regiments. These gave little pleasure to Queen Charlotte, who found some relief in visits to the theatre, concerts and social occasions.

Though physically removed from the constraints of court life in London, the King still insisted on all court protocol; even walks on Weymouth promenade retained a certain formality. The annual visit was a family affair. The King and Queen were accompanied by the young Princesses and occasionally, and with reluctance, by their sons. Ernest made it clear that he would have preferred to pass the time with his elder brother George, the Prince of Wales, in Brighton. He considered Weymouth not very amusing, 'humdrum', even 'terrible'. As the years passed the Princesses, although loyal to their father and indulgent of his routines, found Weymouth increasingly tedious. As Princess Mary wrote to her brother George in 1798: 'this place is more dull & stupid than I can find words to express'.[4]

George, Prince of Wales, was born on 12 August 1762, the first of fifteen children borne by Queen Charlotte, the wife of George III. He was brought up in a cultured environment, but one imbued with the importance of public duty, moral rectitude and personal discipline. By the time he celebrated his eighteenth birthday in 1780, Brighton was already an established fashionable seaside resort. It was easily accessible from London and favoured by George III's brothers, the Duke of York, the Duke of Cumberland and the Duke of Gloucester. At eighteen the Prince was granted his own establishment by his father. This was, however, accompanied by various rules and regulations designed to limit his extravagant behaviour. One condition prohibited him from visiting the Dukes of Cumberland and Gloucester, partly because the King considered them a disruptive influence and partly because he believed (with some justification) that the Duchess of Cumberland was 'procuring' women for the young Prince. Once he was twenty-one (in 1783) the Prince could please himself and a few weeks after his birthday he came to stay for a short period in Brighton with his uncle, the Duke of Cumberland, at Grove House, later known as Marlborough House.[5] The following year, apparently on the advice of his physicians, George returned in late July.

Georgiana, Duchess of Devonshire, an intimate friend of the young Prince, described him in her private papers in 1782 when he was aged just twenty. As these papers were not intended for public reading they probably give a fair and accurate portrait of George as a young man:

> The Prince of Wales is rather tall and has a figure which tho' striking is not perfect. He is inclined to be too fat and looks too much like a woman in men's cloaths [sic], but the gracefulness of his manner and his height certainly make him a pleasing figure. His face is very handsome and he is fond of dress even to a tawdry degree, which, young as he is, will soon wear off. (fig.1)

3. (right) The Prince of Wales, c. 1795, by William Beechey. In January 1793 the King agreed to appoint the Prince of Wales to the position of Colonel Commandant of the 10th (or Prince of Wales) Own Light Dragoons. He was thrilled by the splendid uniform of his new regiment, which is displayed to its best advantage in this romantic portrait. The Royal Collection © 2003 Her Majesty Queen Elizabeth II.

As for his character:

> he is goodnatur'd and rather extravagant … But he certainly does not want for understanding, and his jokes sometimes have an appearance of wit … He is suppos'd to be capricious in his tastes and inclinations, but this more so than he really is … He shew'd very early his taste for dress and amusement.[6]

The life of this vain but cultured and well-educated young man revolved around banquets, horse racing, hunting, gambling, boxing, theatre and his love affairs. The mornings were generally devoted to riding and the afternoons to cricket, and the evenings were occupied with dancing, dining, music, theatre, balls and gambling.

George, like sovereigns' eldest sons before him, held the title of Prince of Wales but was not entrusted with a constitutional or military role, or with significant social duties. He was educated to become king, a role he only finally took on as he approached the age of 60. Without a stable and supportive family life to sustain him, he obsessively indulged his own whims and passions.

No other monarch, apart perhaps from Charles I, took such a close interest in the visual arts and architecture. Carlton House in London, the Pavilion in Brighton, Buckingham Palace and Windsor Castle were all transformed through his royal patronage. The Royal Pavilion is one of the most extraordinary and distinctive buildings in the Western world – an oriental caprice, evoking fantasies of both China and India, and of a generalised, largely mythical Orient. It is a building which could only have been created for an individual who had great confidence in his own taste and was mostly indifferent to the opinion of others.

As a collector his enthusiasm ranged from seventeenth-century Dutch and Flemish painting to French eighteenth-century decorative arts. In architecture he enjoyed oriental styles as well as French neo-classicism and gothic. His residences in London and Windsor were like immaculate sets to show off his superb collections. They were a visible testament to his own good judgement and artistic pre-eminence. The Royal Pavilion – subsequently furnished with exquisite French, English and Chinese export furniture and objects – was an object in itself, a complete work of art. All surfaces were lavishly decorated to create unique and consistent interiors, housed in equally unique and flamboyant architecture. In matters artistic, George had both the vision and the power to ensure that his architectural ambitions were realised.

The Prince's patronage of the small resort town of Brighton endured for over forty years, from 1783 to his final visit in 1827. The transformation of Henry Holland's modest Marine Pavilion (1787) into Nash's structure of oriental splendour (1815–1822) mirrored George's change in status from Prince of Wales to Prince Regent (1811–1820) and to King George IV (1820–1830). Arguably because of his presence the population of Brighton grew significantly, from some 3,620 inhabitants in 1786 to 7,339 in 1801, 24,429 in 1821 and 40,634 in 1831. Further stimulus to the town's growth was given by the opening of the London to Brighton railway in 1841: the official census of 1851 records 65,569 inhabitants.

4. The Race Ground, by Thomas Rowlandson, c. 1789. A key attraction in Brighton for residents and visitors, it was patronised by both a fashionable and a disreputable clientele.

His importance to the prosperity and social development of Brighton from the 1780s should not be underestimated. Holland and Nash's rebuilding of the Prince's home provided work for local tradesmen, labourers and craftsmen. The presence of the King, his guests, members of society and the Royal Household provided invaluable business for the local builders and tradesmen and the service industries. For example a quarterly account for linen washed for His Majesty's household in 1821, which included 487 pairs of sheets and 644 pillowcases, gives an indication of the extensive support required by the King's household alone. This single laundry bill for £85 17s. 1¾d. was equal to two years' salary for a housemaid in the Pavilion's service. *Baxter's Stranger in Brighton and Directory* (1824) lists the numerous local suppliers of goods to George IV; these included butchers, perfumers, chemists, bakers, poulterers, grocers, wine merchants, saddlers and boot and shoe makers, who also provided goods and services to the *haut ton* or fashionable society that followed the King to the town.

Brighton and the impact of war with France

For over a century England had turned to France for guidance in taste and fashion, and the Prince of Wales, in his love of the arts (both decorative and culinary), was a committed francophile. He both spoke and wrote French, often peppering his personal letters with French quotations and phrases.

In the years prior to the French Revolution, Brighton played host to the Prince's illustrious guests from the French court, visiting England to enjoy the races in Brighton, Lewes and Newmarket, as well as the dinners and balls held in their honour. In August 1784 the Duc de Chartres, the Marquis de Conflans and the Comte de Ségur arrived via Dover with a party of French nobility. The local paper, overwhelmed by the influx of French aristocracy, delighted in describing the town as 'the Paris of the day'.

Following the outbreak of war in 1793 personal contact with France became extremely difficult; peace in 1803 briefly allowed Continental travel, but contact was broken again by the renewal of war in 1804. During this period there was understandable sympathy (and empathy) amongst the English nobility for the French aristocracy, and many *émigrés* and exiles were welcomed into English society. As the situation worsened in Paris in the early 1790s, members of the French aristocracy escaped from Dieppe by boat to Brighton. In August 1792 the Comtesse de Noailles crossed the Channel and was welcomed by the Prince and his great love and companion Mrs Maria Fitzherbert. The Comtesse had travelled by boat disguised as a man, concealed in a giant coil of cable for fourteen hours. Mrs Fitzherbert took her in and gave her suitable clothes. Over a period of a few days some five hundred French immigrants, including many priests, arrived on the Dieppe packet or by fishing boat. In January 1804 the Prince hosted a splendid ball and supper in Brighton. The ball, which commenced at 10.00 p.m., was opened by the Duc d'Orléans (the dissipated companion of the Prince) and Lady Caroline Wrottesley. Other guests included the Dukes of Clarence, Richmond and Norfolk, the Ambassadors Baron Starembergh and Count de Lima, and Lord Egremont.

After England's declaration of war against France in 1793, temporary encampments were established along the south coast as military training zones and defence posts against possible French invasion. The first camp in Brighton comprised some ten thousand troops. It was located between the East and West Batteries, with a large encampment in the area near Regency Square and extending westward. *The Times* on 5 August reported on the preparations for this encampment 'in a delightful spot by the sea-side'. The Prince of Wales's Own Regiment of Light Dragoons (the 10th), whose officers were almost entirely George's personal friends, were due to arrive that day. A large temporary building was prepared as a mess room for the Prince and the regiment.

FRENCH INVASION OR BRIGHTON IN A BUSTLE.

5. French Invasion or Brighton in a Bustle, *published 1 March 1794. Fear of invasion was a reality for the people of Brighton. Here soldiers and local people defend themselves, the latter with any implement available – brushes, pitchforks and staves.*

As might be expected, the Prince's quarters were lavish in their furnishing, with a superb bed with 'hangings of a very delicate chintz, a white ground with a lilac and green cloud'. The fringes, tassels and other ornaments were very rich and beautiful, the four bed corners ornamented with the Prince's feathers and motto. The tent even had a state room and the chairs were said to cost £1,000. The rest of the furniture for the tent was equally elegant. In early December the attractive young Lady Webster (subsequently Elizabeth, Lady Holland) visited the Prince. He treated her with great courtesy and gave her breakfast in his tent and showed her his regiment, of which she recalled he was 'extremely vain'.[7] The Prince revelled in his ceremonial military role, in the uniforms, the pageantry and the feeling of regimental comradeship.

Despite the costs of the war to the country and his own debts, the Prince of Wales still managed to concern himself with the niceties of life and his own personal comfort. In late August 1793 the *St James's Chronicle* reported: 'The Prince of Wales has just built a long carriage for travelling – it is so constructed, that, in a few moments, it forms a neat chamber, with a handsome bed, and every other convenience for passing the night in it, on the road, or in a camp.'

The presence of the Prince's own regiment, the most popular in the army for fashionable gentlemen, added to the attractions of the town. 'In Lydia's imagination', wrote the young Jane Austen in 1796,[8] 'a visit to Brighton comprised every possibility of earthly paradise. She saw with the creative eye of fancy, the streets of the gay bathing-place covered with officers … the glories of the camp – its tents stretched forth in beauteous uniformity of lines, crowded with the young and gay, and dazzling with scarlet.'

Though the Prince was very conscious of his military responsibilities as Colonel-in-Chief, the regiment in subsequent years became part of the town's seasonal entertainments. Parades, grand reviews, mock battles and displays took place, the excuse usually being George's birthday on 12 August. The military became a permanent feature of Brighton. The infantrymen based at the Church Street Barracks not only mounted a guard at access points to the Prince's estate as part of their regular duties, but also assisted in the construction of the Royal Stables complex (now the Dome and Corn Exchange).

The image of Regency Brighton: 'Piccadilly by the sea-side'

The local papers revelled in the notoriety and publicity the King brought to the town. In 1822 the *Brighton Gazette* reported:

> Gay and fashionable equipages are daily pouring into the town, and every thing gives
> promise of a brilliant and prosperous winter season. Many large houses on the Cliffs,
> Marine Parade, &c have been engaged for Noblemen within the last fortnight … Who
> indeed would not fly the dirt and smoke of the crowded metropolis for a place like
> Brighton, where he may at once enjoy the pure and healthful breezes of the occean [*sic*],
> and a salubrious climate, without being subjected to the dreary *ennui* of a country life?

The benefits were listed – 'here are to be found all the advantages of a capital, without its inconvenience and discomforts, – all the pleasures of the *beau monde*, combined with all the attractions of a favourite and distinguished watering place. Who would not then come to Brighton?'[9]

William Wilberforce, who famously said of the Pavilion that 'it looks as if St Paul's had come down to the sea and left behind a litter of cupolas', described Brighton, after a visit in 1815, as 'Piccadilly by the sea-side'. Piccadilly in London (extending from Piccadilly Circus to Hyde Park Corner) had become one of the most fashionable and sought-after residential areas. It housed Georgiana, Duchess of Devonshire, Lord Byron and the Duke of Wellington, all of whom were frequent visitors to Brighton.

KICKING·SETT.   ACTIVE·SETT.   PASSIVE·SETT.

Capt. J. Merce fina.

Morning Promenade upon the Cliff, Brighton.

Published Jan. 24th 1806. by H. Humphrey 27 S. J.

6. Morning
Promenade upon the
Cliff, Brighton, *by*
James Gillray,
published
24 January 1806.
Donkeys were
renowned for their
unpredictable
behaviour. This new
craze amongst
fashionable ladies
provided a constant
source of amusement
to onlookers.

According to one contemporary commentator, after the end of the London season (which ran from April to June) the rich and fashionable fled, and the city became 'a mere blank after the 4th of June. *Nobody* remains in *Town*; it is too hot, too suffocating! *Every body* therefore retires to their seats, *if they have them*; and *the rest* fly to *Margate, Ramsgate*, and *Brighton*, those *capacious* receptacles.'[10]

The dashing rogue and gifted writer the German Prince Pückler-Muskau, in search of a new and wealthy wife, visited Brighton several times during his tour of England in 1826–1828. He also noted the similarities between the capital and the seaside resort, observing that 'in Brighton we find the copy of London in little'.[11] As in London, the most fashionable ladies, the 'Patronesses' of Almack's, dominated Brighton's social life. Almack's was an exclusive social club, dominated by a group of the most influential ladies in society who ensured unsuitable people were excluded. Private balls and suppers were organised and the Patronesses distributed tickets to those deemed socially acceptable. The favoured guests had to pay for the privilege of attending these overcrowded events where 'hundreds are here packed like negro slaves',[12] as Pückler-Muskau recalled. Despite the discomfort and inadequate facilities (which made dances such as quadrilles almost impossible) such events were *de rigueur* for high society.

Brighton offered to visitors an endless succession of balls, concerts, soirées, private dinners, theatrical events and promenades, interspersed with vigorous riding or restorative vapour-bath treatments. The town had many privately run subscription libraries designed to attract 'the young, the cheerful, and the gay'. And here in elegant rooms assembled and loitered 'the beauty and fashion of the town, to see and be seen'.[13] Libraries in the 1820s were a focus for social life, for both residents and fashionable visitors. They provided coffee rooms and lounges for conversation, reading, musical events and card games, as well as lending books, music sheets and – in some instances – musical instruments.

Other leisure options included sea excursions in sail or rowboats, or the more traditional dip in the sea from the bathing machines, which were segregated on the seafront into male and female zones. Riding donkeys or using them to pull a buggy or curricle was a fashionable activity amongst female society. (fig.6) This fad was scorned by one resident, who observed how ludicrous it was to see two corpulent women drawn in a vehicle by two or four donkeys. He added wryly, 'the *Sans Culotte* appearance of the postillions will always excite a smile'.[14]

As the 1820s progressed, the King's visits to Brighton became more infrequent, but when he came he usually spent between two and four months during the winter and spring at the Pavilion. The town awaited his visits with eagerness and anticipation; rumour of delay or cancellation caused anxiety. Much depended on the monarch's patronage. Builders continued to speculate on the need for houses to let to the fashionable world that followed the King, numerous traders and shopkeepers relied on the influx of visitors to the town. Indeed the Brighton Gas Light & Coke Company established itself here in 1816 with the hope of obtaining royal patronage.

The King's departure caused distress, as the local newspaper lamented:

> The pecuniary injury which the town must suffer from the regretted absence of the
> Monarch, is incalculable … trade of all descriptions must suffer in the consequent
> decrease of our fashionable population, and the tenantless state of our best houses. Many
> noble families, who … would have enlivened the place with their presence … have now
> entirely changed their intentions, and postponed their visits *sine die*.[15]

The Prince's popularity amongst Brighton residents was enhanced by his generosity. At Christmas, dinners were distributed to some three thousand needy people in the town. Annually the Household servants were permitted to enjoy the King's magnificent palace: 'On Tuesday evening, the upper class of domestics on the Royal establishment, the Pages, etc the same as last year, were allowed to entertain their friends with a supper and ball at the Palace', reported the *Sussex Weekly Advertiser*, 'and on Thursday, the second class of servants were similarly indulged. The entertainments were equally sumptuous, and made happy all participators.'[16]

MERMAIDS at BRIGHTON

7. Mermaids at Brighton, by William Heath, c. 1829. Horse-drawn bathing machines carried the bathers into the shallow waters. Men and women had to bathe from different parts of the shore; here professional 'dippers' help the apprehensive women, clad in flannel gowns and caps, from the bathing machines into the sea water.

In addition to these regular entertainments special balls were organised for younger members of society. On one occasion it was observed that 'the juvenile branches of nobility and fashion were on the light fantastic for a cheerful succession of hours. His Majesty contemplated the interesting and lively throng with feelings of delight.' [17]

When, in January 1823, the King was in residence, the *Brighton Gazette* joyously noted 'Brighton is now gay, crowded and fashionable', but later that year there was anxiety about rumours that the King would abandon 'his favourite residence'. With confidence, the *Gazette* stated in September 1823: 'Windsor will be the future residence of His Majesty during Summer and Autumn; the Spring and Winter will be passed in London and Brighton.'

The town's reliance on the King's presence was poetically proclaimed by the *Sussex Weekly Advertiser* on 24 April 1820: 'the King is to this town what the sun is to our hemisphere – universal cheerfulness is presented when the rays of Royalty sparkle upon the picture of our local sociabilities and interests'. For the King's visit in December 1823 a magnificent display (paid for by local townsmen and visitors) was mounted; illuminations decorated the Chain Pier and a brilliant firework entertainment including 30-foot (9 m) 'superb Chinese pagodas' was created by a Mr Jones, 'Artist in Fireworks'. The bands of the 7th Hussars and the 58th Regiment of Infantry concluded the

festivities with 'God save the King'. The theatre was opened free of charge, and 'everything in short contributed to shew [*sic*] the happiness of the inhabitants of Brighton at being again honoured with the presence of their King'.[18]

Much like the *paparazzi* of today, journalists hung around the Royal Pavilion Estate, noting the coming and going of visitors and tradesmen. Whilst the King was away they constantly looked for signs to indicate an imminent royal visit, which were duly reported in detail in the local papers. The King did not spend the Christmas of 1825 or 1826 in Brighton, but in late December 1826 four carriages, each carrying a pianoforte, were observed arriving at the Pavilion. So was Sake Deen Mahomed,[19] the King's Superintendent of the Royal Baths, who was spotted entering the building on several days, presumably to prepare bathing facilities for his master. As the years passed, George resented intrusions into his private life in the Pavilion by the press, and in 1827 a request was made to *The Times* to cease publishing accounts of his private life at Brighton.[20]

In January 1824 the King held a court and Privy Council in the Pavilion. After the completion of business the court was invited to dinner. The centrepiece, displayed on the Banqueting Room table, was an illuminated model of the Royal Lodge in Windsor Great Park. The King had moved on to new architectural projects. This small cottage, lavishly transformed by John Nash and then Jeffry Wyatville, was contemptuously referred to by some as the King's 'Thatched Palace'.

8. (above)
2, 3, 5 and 8, *or* A Summer's Evening at the Royal Marine Library, *by C. W. Wing, 1830. Libraries were important social and cultural centres, providing refreshments, entertainments and musical events as well as lending books and music sheets. In the 1820s there were nine private libraries in Brighton.*

9. Brighton Picture Gallery, from R. Sickelmore's The History of Brighton, *1823. The Picture Gallery on Grand Parade in the centre of Brighton was available to subscribers at an annual fee of one guinea. It boasted an unrivalled regional collection including pictures by Caravaggio, Claude, Poussin, Raphael, Hogarth and Gainsborough; daily papers, reviews and magazines were provided for clients.*

In the spring of 1826 further anxiety was caused by a report in the newspapers that some thirty or forty casks of strong ale had been removed from the royal cellars in the Pavilion for consumption elsewhere. This did not bode well for a lengthy return by the monarch and indeed the King was to spend more and more time in the quiet seclusion of Windsor. The local paper noted 'the King visits Windsor for the sake of taking exercise in the park, where he can be more private than at Brighton'. The writer continued a little waspishly, 'we trust that the dampness of the atmosphere, arising from the frequent floods in the adjacent country, will not prove unfavourable to his Majesty's health'.[21] The King's health was a concern, but so too was the economic health of Brighton. Now absorbed by new building projects at Windsor, he was to return only once more to Brighton. After his final visit to the Pavilion in early 1827, he used Windsor as his private residence until his death in 1830.

Few mourned him. The press and politicians eagerly welcomed the new King, his younger brother, William IV. If George was remembered, it was usually as a subject of ridicule or contempt. Princess Lieven, a close and consistent friend of the King for some twenty years, was genuinely saddened by his death, perceptively noting that what a nation appreciates in its sovereign is domestic virtue – a quality much lacking in George IV. This had overshadowed 'much that was striking and brilliant in his reign'. She added, 'his glory is forgotten, and his vices exaggerated'.[22]

2 'Life's a Bumper' – The young Prince's first Brighton residence

The Marine Pavilion

In the mid-1780s the Prince rented a small farmhouse in the fashionable centre of Brighton. He had by then met the woman who became the most significant influence in his life. Mrs Maria Fitzherbert – a Catholic, twice widowed, attractive and of independent means – was (as so often was the case with George's companions and mistresses) some six years his senior. Their notorious secret marriage took place in December 1785. The Prince, overwhelmed by personal debts, sold his racehorses and stopped work on his London residence, Carlton House. The following year, depleted of funds, they both retired to a quiet and frugal life in Brighton, where for several years Mrs Fitzherbert had taken lodgings to escape the pressures of London.

2. (right) The Marine Pavilion, *c. 1787, by*
Samuel Hieronymus
Grimm. The
watercolour shows the
east front of Henry
Holland's Marine
Pavilion under
construction.
© The British Library.

In 1787, after much pleading and promises on the part of the Prince of Wales, the House of Commons agreed to clear his debts and increase his income. He was now able to engage his Carlton House architect, Henry Holland, to transform his Brighton farmhouse into a modest villa, which became known as the Marine Pavilion.[23] The exterior of the neo-classical building was decorated with Holland's favourite cream-glazed Hampshire tiles. Holland's design, in the process of being completed, was recorded by Samuel H. Grimm in two watercolours, now in the British Library. (fig.2)

The east face of the new building overlooked the Steine, an open area where fishermen used to dry their nets, a traditional activity soon to be displaced by the promenading of the fashionable world. Together with the Duke of Marlborough, the Prince contributed to draining this area, which was prone to flooding, with a wooden sewer that took excess water to the sea. In the summer evenings all society converged on the Steine, where bands played popular melodies and hopeful young ladies displayed themselves to advantage in the latest fashions. Such a scene delighted the Prince, who was observed to be 'much gratified with the sight of so many beautiful women that crowded around him, and whose eyes are directed towards him in all directions, irradiating with their lustre the finest features in the world'.[24]

The Prince's apartments were located in the south wing flanking the rotunda or Saloon, overlooking the Steine, with a glimpse of the sea. The ground-floor breakfast room and anteroom were linked to a central staircase which led to the Prince's first-floor

3. View of the West Front of the Pavilion towards the Garden, 1808, by Humphry Repton, from Designs for the Pavillon [sic] at Brighton, 1808. *Repton has deliberately depicted the west front in a manner that ensures the Marine Pavilion is totally dwarfed by Porden's new stable complex on the left.*

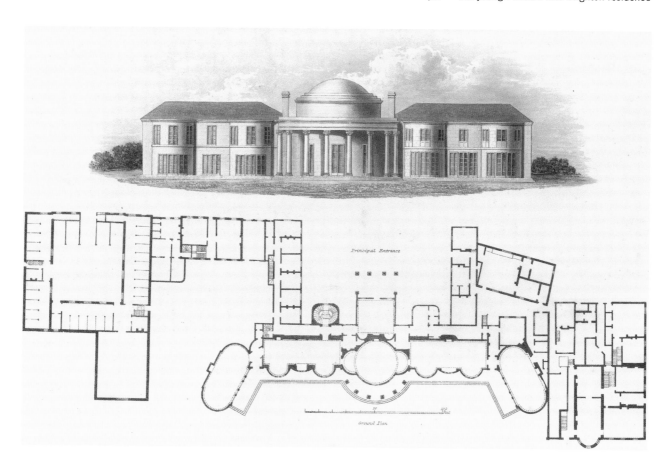

4. Elevation and ground plan of the Marine Pavilion, *from Nash's* Views. *On the left (south) are the stables, with Marlborough House on the right (north).*

bedroom and dressing room, with a page's room adjacent. To the north were the columned eating room and the library. The modest kitchens, kitchen court and ancillary offices were located in a block to the west, with servants' accommodation adjacent in the flanking wing. The stables and stable yard were to the south beyond the house of George's faithful servant and general factotum, Louis Weltje. (fig.4)

In 1801–1802, the Marine Pavilion was enlarged by Holland's office, with two angled ground-floor wings providing a new eating room and conservatory. The ground-floor rooms flanking the Saloon were combined into two large galleries with a new staircase off the adjacent Long Gallery. During this period, the interior was furnished for the first time with Chinese papers, furniture and objects, mostly supplied by the Crace firm of decorators.[25]

Carlton House in Pall Mall, London, had been granted to the Prince as his first independent residence in 1783. At considerable expense the building was partly rebuilt and lavishly refurbished by Holland.[26] Both John Crace and his son Frederick had worked for the Prince at Carlton House before commencing their redecoration of Holland's Marine Pavilion in the Chinese style in 1802–1804.

As well as designing and executing elaborate decorative interiors, the Craces also worked as agents for their patron, acquiring large quantities of porcelain, bamboo and lacquer furniture and objects to complement their own designs. They superintended the packing and collection of objects, including clearing goods through customs. The

5. The Gallery as it was, *from Nash's* Views *(detail)*. On the left can be seen one of the life-size Chinese mandarin figures, clad in real robes, made by Crace in 1803. The figures, nearly 6 feet (1.8 m) tall, were subsequently displayed on the north staircase ledge and removed by William IV in 1831.

accounts record the purchase of china, cabinets, bamboo furniture and quantities of 'Fine India paper'. These 'India' papers (so called because they were imported by the East India Company) were hand-painted decorative Chinese papers and came with strips of borders and birds and insects. The motifs were cut out and glued to the paper to conceal defects or improve the overall composition. The hanging of these papers was directed by the Prince himself, and he presumably chose where the different patterns should be hung.

'Chinoiserie' or the decorative style inspired by China was at its most fashionable in the mid-eighteenth century, appearing in the bedrooms and drawing rooms of numerous grand country houses. In the early decades of the nineteenth century the Pavilion's interiors would not have been viewed as of high fashion or trend setting. Rather they reflect the Prince's own eclectic and idiosyncratic taste, developed to its full in the subsequent decorations of Nash's new Pavilion.

6. The Saloon, from a watercolour by A. C. Pugin, c. 1817, showing an early chinoiserie scheme designed by Crace.

Other items supplied by Crace included objects of curiosity, such as a set of chopsticks, parasols, shoes, and Chinese tobacco, pouches and pipes. Clay mandarin figures were purchased to furnish the Gallery, and the Craces also crafted Chinese figures 'as large as Life' in painted wood, dressed in real clothes for display in the Marine Pavilion.[27] (fig.5)

The firm undertook responsibility for day-to-day maintenance and repair of the interiors, furnishings and furniture, including washing and dusting. They also prepared rooms for balls and evening entertainments by removing all the furniture and china, chalking the floors with designs for dancing, and lighting all the lamps and lanterns. At such events both John and Frederick Crace were required to attend the Prince for the entire night. The Crace firm remained in the Prince's employment until the early 1820s.

Marriage, mistresses and birthday celebrations

The Prince's favoured consort, at any given time, reigned as mistress of the Marine Pavilion. Despite declarations of eternal love, the Prince of Wales had, by 1794, replaced Mrs Maria Fitzherbert in his affections with the notorious schemer Lady Jersey. However, the separation of George and Maria lasted but a few years and by 1799 they were reconciled and reunited. Mrs Fitzherbert was once again mistress of the Marine Pavilion, a position she retained until their final separation in 1811. She resided in her own house facing the Steine and would be seen by visitors and residents sitting, together with the Prince, on the large veranda.

However, by the end of 1794 the Prince had reluctantly committed himself to an arranged marriage with Princess Caroline of Brunswick, which would ensure the allocation of new funds and the payment of his debts. His marriage in April the following year was a disaster. In the months prior to the marriage, plans had been drawn up to

7. His Highness in Fitz. *A graphic illustration of the young Prince of Wales's passion for Mrs Maria Fitzherbert, 1786. On the wall in the background are the Prince of Wales's feathers next to a crucifix, a reference to Mrs Fitzherbert's Catholicism.* © The House of Lords Library.

OUT OF FITS,
OR THE RECOVERY TO THE SATISFACTION OF ALL PARTIES.

8. Out of Fits, or The Recovery to the Satisfaction of All Parties, *1786. A companion to* His Highness in Fitz. *The Prince, his dress adjusted, sits quietly with Mrs Fitzherbert.*

reorganise the Marine Pavilion to accommodate his new wife and her personal needs, but these were never implemented. At the wedding the Prince was drunk and agitated, barely noticing his bride, but perpetually gazing at his current passion, Lady Jersey. Lady Jersey, nine years his senior and mother of nine children, was a charming, elegant, unscrupulous and manipulative woman who had determined to break up the Prince's relationships with both his new wife and Mrs Fitzherbert. Within a year the marriage had collapsed, with the royal couple unable to live under the same roof.

The Prince's new wife stayed only once at the Marine Pavilion, in the summer of 1795, shortly after their marriage. During this period she presumably used the bedchamber and dressing room north of the Saloon, which had no direct access route to the Prince's private apartments (which were located above the Eating Room). George politely wrote about his wife to his mother in June of that year: 'she is extremely delighted with this place which seems to agree with her most perfectly as she is in the best health & spirits possible, excepting at moments a little degree of sickness which is the necessary attendant upon her situation'.[28] Caroline was pregnant with their only child, Princess Charlotte, who was born the following year, exactly nine months after their wedding.

At the Prince's request his mother, Queen Charlotte, concerned about her daughter-in-law's condition, dispatched some young pigs to Brighton. She wrote on 5 August to the Prince, advising him of the pigs' departure that morning on their journey to the coast. She added 'they are to be refreshed upon the road with milk so that they will be fit for killing immediately, & I hope they will prove to the Princess' taste'.[29] The Queen's own black sow was not due to produce a litter for some ten weeks, so piglets of the same breed were procured as the matter was deemed to be of some importance.

The royal couple remained in Brighton to celebrate the Prince's birthday on 12 August. For this occasion, the town burst into festivities with the streets brilliantly illuminated. A magnificent firework display in the nearby public pleasure grounds of Promenade Grove was followed by a concert of popular songs. The Prince attended for the whole evening, which ended with a royal salute from a squadron of ships, commanded by Sir Sydney Smith, which fired rockets and guns to acknowledge the Prince's birthday. Princess Caroline enjoyed various celebrations, including a concert in the illuminated gardens of the Promenade Grove. The Dorset Band played select pieces of military music, interspersed with songs, duets and glees performed by singers.

The young royal couple were joined in Brighton for these festivities by William, Prince of Orange, driven out of Holland and forced to reside at Hampton Court as an exile. According to *The Times*,[30] during a ball held in the Prince's honour, he fell asleep 'whilst he was eating his supper and rather disturbed the harmony of the Band with the loudness of his snoring'. The young Prince honoured the Prince of Orange or 'Old Stadt', as he called him, with a special ball in the Pavilion. He recalled in a letter to his mother that William 'danc'd every dance till four o'clock in the morning but not without a snug napp or two in a little corner, greatly to the diversion of some of the company'.[31]

Regardless of Princess Caroline's disagreeable conversation, physical appearance and indelicate personal habits, the Prince's behaviour towards her was beyond comprehension. He made his current mistress, Lady Jersey, one of the four Ladies of the Bedchamber to his new wife. It was common gossip that Lady Jersey, who was a notorious pursuer of influential married men, had set her bed up in the Prince's dressing room in the Marine Pavilion itself. (fig.9) Lady Jersey's discourteous and indiscreet behaviour rebounded on her. She was spurned both by members of society and by the people. In the summer of 1796, during her stay in Brighton, the locals performed a 'skimmington', a show in which two dummies dressed as Lady Jersey and the Prince were paraded on a donkey through the town as objects of ridicule.[32] Lady Spencer described the event in a letter to her daughter, Georgiana, Duchess of Devonshire:

> The only news I have heard is that the Prince of Wales arrived here last night and heard
> what really happened that a stuffed mawkin with a feather had been carried round about
> two days before with Lady J – written at full length upon it, and it was afterwards burnt.

She went on, 'he is outrageous [*sic*], it is likewise said that she was here but went away very early this morning'.[33] Later that year Lady Jersey was forced to resign her position and Lord Gwydyr replaced Lord Jersey as Master of the Horse.

9. (right) The JERSEY smuggler detected; – or – Good cause for Separation (deleted) Discontent – Marriage vows, are false as Dicers oaths, dated 24 May 1796. The Princess of Wales bursts in on her husband in bed with his mistress, Lady Jersey. To highlight the grossness of the Prince's behaviour, Charlotte, their only child, barely 5 months old, can be seen in a crib in the background.

The JERSEY Smuggler detected; — or — Good cause for Separation Discontent — "Marriage vows, are false as Dicers oaths".

The Prince's birthday each year was always a significant event for the town, and was publicly celebrated with fencing matches, military parades, mock battles, bands and country games. The local newspapers assiduously recorded the festivities to mark the Prince's birthday (and the celebrations for the birthdays of the Dukes of York and Clarence). A typical celebration occurred on 12 August 1789:

> this morning was ushered in by the ringing of bells, bands of music &c. About 9 o'clock pavilions and marquees were pitched about a mile from the town in a valley leading to Lewes close to which place a temporary kitchen was made and an ox roasted whole ... There was also as much strong beer given away as people chose to drink.

The Prince, his brothers, Mrs Fitzherbert (now back in favour) and 'a prodigious number of Nobility and Gentry' seated themselves in a pavilion to watch a display of fencing by master swordsmen. Privileged guests could test their skills against the expert fencers. After the match with the renowned St George, William Windham (a Whig politician, but an infrequent visitor to Brighton) took up a foil with Roland, one of the French fencers, but was shocked to find he had lost not only his youthful skill, but also his strength and vitality. This was followed by foot races, jackass races, jumping in sacks and other country amusements with prizes given by the Duke of York. At 4 o'clock sailing races for local fishermen commenced in three classes, depending on the size of the boat. The Duke of Clarence gave prizes for each class, which comprised a new boat, a set of sails and a set of nets.

Dinner was provided for the Prince and his guests, with music performed by the Duke of York's band. The customary toasts followed. The band, preceded by the Queen's Light Dragoons, then paraded round the town, which was specially illuminated for the occasion. The cricket ground provided the location for the bonfire and firework displays. As the local papers recorded, the day was completed with a magnificent ball 'after which there was a supper, and very few, if any, of the gentlemen, went to bed sober'.

Every year, until 1811 when he became Regent, the Prince spent August to September in Brighton, sometimes extending his stay to Christmas. The Princess of Wales never returned and her role was instantly taken by whichever of George's mistresses was in favour at the time, Lady Jersey, Mrs Fitzherbert or Lady Hertford.

Lady Hertford, wife of Lord Hertford (appointed Master of the Horse in 1804), had progressively supplanted Mrs Fitzherbert in the Prince's affections. Socially correct, she refused to attend the Prince in the Marine Pavilion without the presence of Mrs Fitzherbert for the appearance of propriety. She was a stately woman of good sense, an attractive grandmother and again much older than George. Described as having 'a frigid bearing, a pompous mode of speech' and 'pedantically accurate in her choice of words',[34] she exerted considerable power over the Prince, but wisely declined to intrigue for herself or her family. Her reign of influence endured until 1820, when she was replaced by the ambitious, manipulative and rapacious Lady Conyngham.

Social life in the Marine Pavilion

Lady Bessborough (the sister of Georgiana, Duchess of Devonshire, and the lover for many years of the elegant and attractive diplomat, Lord Granville Leveson-Gower) described the Prince's life in the Marine Pavilion. On one occasion in 1805 she took the place of Mrs Fitzherbert, who was indisposed:

> His way of living is pleasant enough, especially if one might chuse [sic] one's society. In the Morning he gives you horses, Carriages, etc., to go where you please with you; he comes and sits *rather too long*, but only on a visit. Every body meets at dinner, which, *par parenthèse*, is excellent, with the addition of a few invitations in the evening. Three large rooms, very comfortable, are lit up; whist, backgammon, Chess, trace Madame – every sort of game you can think of in two of them, and Musick [sic] in the third.[35]

10. The Pavilion and the Steine, *watercolour by Jacob Spornberg, 1796. The Marine Pavilion is dwarfed by the red-brick Marlborough House; on the Steine in the foreground are military parades and tents. Behind the tents on the right can be seen Marlborough Row.*

Lady Bessborough was impressed by the new Crace interior decorations – to her own surprise: 'I did not think the strange Chinese shapes and columns could have look'd so well. It is like Concetti in Poetry, in outré and false taste, but for the kind of thing as perfect as it can be.' To explain the introduction of the Chinese style, she continued: 'the Prince says he had it so because at the time there was such a cry against French things, &c, that he was afraid of his furniture being accus'd of jacobinism'.[36]

The Prince's day would have necessitated up to four changes of clothing – as prescribed by society and the *élégants*: for breakfast a chintz dressing gown and slippers; day dress or full riding dress with frock coat, boots and so on; formal dress for dinner; and ball dress, as required. The Prince was renowned for his elegance and fashionable appearance, his concern for perfection in all details of his apparel, his extensive wardrobe and his expenditure on articles of personal attire. During the nine years of the Regency (1811–1820) he bought over five hundred shirts. The sale of his wardrobe following his death was a spectacle as he gave nothing away – except his linen, which was distributed annually to his pages. One visitor to this sale, held in early August 1830, described the profusion of knick-knacks and clothes, including coats the King had kept for fifty years: '300 whips, canes without number, every sort of uniform, the costumes of all the orders in Europe, splendid furs, pelisses, hunting coats and breeches, and among other things a dozen pairs of corduroy breeches he had made to hunt in when Don Miguel was here'.[37]

The Prince's lifestyle in Brighton was a constant subject for gossips, satirists and wits, including John Williams (1761–1818) a journalist who wrote under the pseudonym of 'Antony Pasquin'. In September 1796 he published *The Brighton Guide*, a copy of which was dispatched the evening before publication by George's private secretary, Colonel J. McMahon, 'properly sealed up'[38] to the Prince at Carlton House in London. It seems that behind this mischief might have been Lady Willoughby, who replaced Lady Jersey as Lady of the Bedchamber in the Princess of Wales's household. This pamphlet, 'a sentimental epistle from Carlton House to the Pavilion at Brighton', described the Marine Pavilion as 'a nondescript monster … like a mad house or a house run mad … There are four pillars in *scagliola* [imitation marble], in a sort of oven, where the Prince dines; and when the fire is lighted, the room is so hot that the parties are nearly baked and incrusted.'

The interior of the building was notorious for its hot and airless atmosphere. In late November 1805 Mrs Creevey spent another 'horribly dull' evening at one of the Pavilion's many balls in the company of Mrs Fitzherbert, but they soon tired of the amusements, 'sick of the heat and stink'.[39]

Mrs Creevey's husband, Thomas Creevey, a Whig MP and diarist, subsequently wrote his reminiscences of the Prince and Brighton, recalling a time when he still viewed the heir to the throne as the new hope for the Whig party. They first met in 1804, and the following September Creevey and his family went to Brighton, where he was invited to dine at the Marine Pavilion. He became a regular guest, dining with the Prince once or twice a week until they returned to London in January. He described the evenings:

> We used to dine pretty punctually at six, the average number being about sixteen … Mrs Fitzherbert always dined there, and mostly one other lady – Lady Downshire very often, sometimes Lady Clare or Lady Berkeley or Mrs Creevey. Mrs Fitzherbert was a great card-player, and played every night. The Prince never touched a card, but was occupied in talking to his guests, and very much in listening to and giving directions to the band. At 12 o'clock punctually the band stopped, and sandwiches and wine and water handed about, and shortly after the Prince made a bow and we all dispersed.[40]

A late summons to attend on the Prince clearly irritated the Whig MP:

> I suppose the Courts or houses of Princes are all alike in one thing, viz., that in attending them you lose your liberty. After one month was gone by you fell naturally and of course into the ranks, and had to reserve your observations till you were asked for them. These royal invitations are by no means calculated to reconcile one to a Court. To be sent for half an hour before dinner, or perhaps in the middle of one's own, was a little too humiliating to be very agreeable.

Mrs Creevey also complained of being invited late (at 9.00 p.m.) and found the evening somewhat tedious. It was, however, her duty both to attend and to enjoy the frivolous entertainments in order to further the political interests of her husband. She complained of headaches – due, she believed, to the heat in the Pavilion, which was so strong that on one occasion it had almost made Mrs Fitzherbert faint.

11. George IV when Prince of Wales, *by George Stubbs, 1791. During the 1790s the young Prince commissioned Stubbs to paint several pictures of his horses; here he is depicted out riding a favoured chestnut horse. The Royal Collection © 2003 Her Majesty Queen Elizabeth II.*

Apart from cards, conversation and gossip (if not drowned by the band), and dancing (including the fashionable waltz which made the Prince dizzy), special entertainments included 'phantasmagorias' (lantern-slide shows which had the added advantage of providing perfect darkness for the lustful, timorous or drunk) and target practice with the Prince's air gun. Though he was skilful with a gun, a somewhat hazardous performance by his lady guests resulted in a member of his band (in the dining room) being hit, as well as doors and ceilings.[41]

Whilst Mrs Fitzherbert reigned as mistress of the Pavilion, special events were arranged for a child who was the Prince's favourite, Minnie Seymour (orphaned in 1801 and entrusted to Mrs Fitzherbert's care), and other children of the Prince's friends. In 1807 the Irish beauty, Mrs Calvert, who annually brought her family to Brighton, received a last-minute invitation to the Pavilion for a conjuror's show, where apparently all the guests behaved very badly, trying to upset and disrupt the conjuror during his performance.

The Marine Pavilion, even with the later additions, was a modest building in size, not suitable for large social events or entertainments. It was viewed by many as noisy, hot and overfurnished. Miss Berry, visiting in December 1811 to hear a military band, complained: 'Luckily, we only heard two pieces, for the noise of so many loud instruments in a room (the dining room) which could hardly hold them, was not a remedy for my headache.'[42] On visiting the apartments again, her comments were no less favourable:

> All is Chinese, quite overloaded with china of all sorts and of all possible forms, many
> beautiful in themselves, but so overloaded one upon another, that the effect is more like a
> china shop baroquement arranged, than the abode of a Prince. All is gaudy, without
> looking gay; and all is crowded with ornaments, without being magnificent.[43]

Close members of the Prince's family were frequent and regular visitors to the Pavilion, in particular his brothers the Dukes of York, Clarence and Kent, and his sister Augusta. During the winter period of 1815–1816 his mother Queen Charlotte came down, accompanied by several of her children. They were all welcomed with great enthusiasm by the local people.

The visit was the inspiration for a satirical verse called 'Royal Rantipoles' or the 'Humours of Brighton'[44] which illustrated the popular perception of life in the Pavilion. The Prince Regent ('Caesar' in the text) abandons state affairs for the pleasures of Brighton. On arriving, the ungainly Prince is greeted by crowds assembled at the Pavilion:

> Now from his carriage Caesar hopp'd,
> (No second Master Ellar,)[45]
> Just like a butt of porter dropp'd,
> Into an alehouse cellar.

Soon he was followed by members of society; then his mother, brothers and sisters arrived

> And Caesar's glorious sisters came,
> Each like of butter firkin, [46]
> A round, unwieldy, greasy dame,
> With visage gay and smirking.

A gibe at the benefits of being the husband of the favourite mistress could not be missed:

> And H[ertfor]D, too, the Prince of Peers,
> The monarch of the stables,
> Who like a glutton leech, for years,
> Has suck'd the royal tables.

12. The Stables Garden Front, *from Nash's* Views. *To the left was the riding school, to the right a screen to provide symmetry to Porden's new building. It was originally planned to build a tennis court behind the eastern façade.*

The lengthy satire describes the games, frolics and heavy drinking until

Dimly the lights began to burn,
And care appear'd a bubble,
And ev'ry noble, in his turn,
Sour wine and glasses double.

Now Caesar from his cushion popp'd,
And none to help were able,
For, one by one, the whole group dropp'd,
Like logs beneath the table.

Promenade Grove and the new stable complex

Promenade Grove, opposite the Marine Pavilion, was surrounded with large overspreading elms, providing refreshing shade to fashionable promenaders who, by subscription, had use of the gardens. It was the location for concerts, breakfast parties and evening entertainments, attended by the Prince of Wales and his circle. It ceased to be a commercial pleasure garden in 1802, when it was purchased by the Prince to enlarge his own estate. The acquisition of the land provided new opportunities for building.

The Prince considered enlarging and remodelling the Marine Pavilion, directing Henry Holland, Humphry Repton and William Porden to produce designs for his consideration. Having spent much on the additions and redecorations to the Marine Pavilion in 1801–1802, the Prince had to be content with a new stable and riding house complex designed in the Indian style by William Porden. (fig.12)

The existing stabling, attached to the south of the Marine Pavilion, was inadequate in size to satisfy the Prince's passion for horse riding, hunting and carriage driving. In 1784 he had claimed the speed record for the journey from London to Brighton – four-and-a-half hours in a three-horse phaeton. The usual journey took some six hours. The carriage had been specially designed, with three horses, one in front of the other. The postillion rode the first horse; the Prince managed the other two.

The new complex, with the vast cupola above the stables spanning some 80 feet (24 m), took over three years to build. This was partly due to the problems of obtaining timber of sufficient size and partly because the Prince would not pay his creditors and tradesmen. The works had to be completed with support from the infantrymen from the adjacent Church Street Barracks. The Prince took particular interest in the new stables which, as Porden described, was 'of a Circular form in imitation of the famous Corn Market at Paris which was burnt down in 1803'.[47]

The complex, completed in 1808, provided stabling for sixty-two horses (hunters, saddle and coach horses), coach houses, an engine house, a forge and farrier, harness rooms and accommodation for grooms and stable boys (including bedrooms, kitchen, scullery, the grooms' hall and the coachmen's hall). The splendour of the new stables was described in the *Brighton Ambulator*:

> There are two grand entrances to the stables, the one is from Church-street, through a lofty
> archway, which enters into a spacious square court, containing the coach-houses,
> carriage-horse-stables, servants' offices, &c; a similar archway leads to the circular dome,
> opposite to which is a corresponding entrance into the Pavilion lawn. On the east and west
> side of the circle there are similar arches, which have their entrance into the riding-school
> and tennis-court.

13. Interior of the Stables, *from Nash's Views. The spectacular interior, lit by glazed panels in the dome ceiling, gave access to both Church Street and the Pavilion Gardens, as well as to the adjacent indoor riding school.*

Despite the lead and glass-domed roof, 'the whole range of stables receive a proper ventilation and preserve a temperature in the warmest summer days'.[48] The spacious Riding House adjacent was 185 feet long by 85 feet wide and 34 feet high (56.4 x 25.9 x 10.4 m). On the east wall of this building was the Royal Box, furnished with seating, curtains and a stove for heating in the cold winter months.

Horses, riding and driving remained an enduring pleasure as long as the Prince was physically able. In 1815 he wrote to his mother from Brighton, lamenting his lack of exciting news or society gossip, but declaring that 'the air & the constant riding exercise which I take daily, either on the open road or in the Riding House agree with me perhaps more this year than they almost ever have done at any former season'.[49]

To some, these elegant new buildings were excessively opulent premises for horses and dwarfed the Marine Pavilion, the residence of the Prince and his guests. Writing in April 1807, Mrs Calvert, a member of the Prince's circle, described the new stables as 'a most superb edifice, indeed quite unnecessarily so'.[50] Holland's modest building was no longer suitable for the future King. With his new status of Prince Regent, the Prince's thoughts again turned to building a new Pavilion.

3 'Such magnificence and such luxury' – the King and Nash's new Pavilion

Rebuilding the Pavilion (1815–1821)

1. (left) The Saloon, from Nash's Views. *In this room the earlier playful, chinoiserie scheme was replaced with Robert Jones's regal design of crimson, gold and pearl white, more in keeping with the new status of its owner. Jones painted the domed ceiling as a sky with a winged dragon that appears to hold the elaborate cut-glass chandelier.*

On 6 February 1811 George, Prince of Wales, was sworn in as Regent. Finally his father, George III, had been deemed incapable of acting as monarch. George's life was now constrained by burdensome duties and responsibilities, making excursions to the country or Brighton less frequent. However in 1815 he commissioned his architect, John Nash, to transform the Marine Pavilion in Brighton, with much needed new private apartments and grander public rooms.

The Pavilion was constructed over a number of years. It was barely habitable during the phases of work from 1815 to 1821. The Prince Regent involved himself closely in the project, approving designs and personally monitoring the work of his architect and his two interior designers, Frederick Crace and Robert Jones.

Having acquired Marlborough House and Marlborough Row, as well as the Castle Tavern and Promenade Grove, the Prince had established a substantial acreage in which to construct his new palace, with its servants' quarters and pleasure gardens. Progress was slow, hindered by the Regent's precarious financial state and opposition in the House of Commons to his further requests for funding. During 1815–1816 extensive building works were undertaken to construct and fit out the new kitchen and ancillary areas to the south, as well as the new entrance and adjacent areas.

In March 1816 his Prime Minister, the Earl of Liverpool, along with Viscount Castlereagh (Leader of the House of Commons and Foreign Secretary) and Nicholas Vansittart (the Chancellor of the Exchequer), wrote to the Prince Regent firmly suggesting that any further works at Brighton should be abandoned. Parliament would never vote more funds to cover his recent expenditure, particularly bearing in mind 'the distress which is so severely felt by most classes of His Majesty's subjects'.[51] The Whigs, who lost no opportunity to ridicule the Regent for his selfishness and insensitivity, equally condemned the Prince's excesses.

The Prince was forced to accede to their wishes, and all works were discontinued apart from essential items such as completing the roof works to the outbuildings in the kitchen complex. Later that year the Clerk of Works, Mr Nixon, supervised the installation of pipes to conduct water and steam throughout the new kitchens.

In this period the houses in Marlborough Row and Marlborough House were used as accommodation by the Prince, his guests and the Royal Household staff. Early in 1817 the town was honoured by a visit from the Grand Duke Nicholas of Russia. For the ball that followed the banquet the Prince had expressed a wish that all the company should appear in 'costume of British manufacture and taste'. The ball, which was attended by some three hundred members of society, commenced at 10.00 p.m., with a break for supper at 2.00 a.m., and finished at 3.00 a.m. Marlborough House, now structurally linked to the Marine Pavilion, was used to provide suitable grand space for the event.

It was reported that Queen Charlotte liked the Pavilion and newspapers speculated that she might make Brighton one of her residences. In February 1817 the local papers recorded the recommencement of the works at the Pavilion – funded, it was rumoured, by £50,000 from the Queen's private purse. Works progressed through 1817 with the completion of the kitchens and the installation of the tent roofs of the Music Room and Banqueting Room. The *Sussex Weekly Advertiser* regularly watched developments at 'the new Chinese building', observing that the new pagoda roofs gave the whole site 'a grand and cheerful appearance'.[52]

A watercolour executed in October 1817 (fig.2) illustrates the fascinating interim phase: it shows Holland's neo-classical structure still *in situ* with the main kitchen with its lantern roof complete and the Banqueting Room under construction. The tented roofs to the Music and Banqueting Rooms echo the earlier design by Nash for the Rotunda, a temporary building installed in the grounds of Carlton House for the fête of the Duke of Wellington in 1814. Visually this design reinforced the idea of the Pavilion as a temporary garden structure, a folly for pleasure and enjoyment.

2. A Bird's Eye View of the Pavilion, Brighton, Oct. 1817, watercolour, pen and ink documenting the building of Nash's Pavilion around Holland's original building. Marlborough House, on the right, is linked to the Pavilion. The Banqueting and Music Rooms are under construction, whilst the Great Kitchen is already completed. In the foreground can be seen a Brighton 'fly', a small carriage on wheels drawn (and pushed) by two men. © The Art Institute of Chicago (Leonora Hall Gurney Collection).

3. The Saloon, from the cross-section in Nash's Views *(detail), showing the iron structure that held the new dome in place over the Saloon. The Bath stone minarets flanking the dome were supported by an iron core (shown in pale blue). The rooms in the upper section of the dome were accessed by an oval staircase in the south turret and were used as servants' quarters.*

Salon.

Whilst works continued in the spring of 1818, the terraced houses of Marlborough Row were refurbished as short-term accommodation. The Prince's stag-hounds arrived in July and were housed in temporary kennels near the stables. They were given a daily wash and exercise in the sea. Their stay in Brighton was not to be a totally happy one. A report in *John Bull* a few years later gives an account of the destruction of twenty-four pairs of the King's stag-hounds, this action by order of the Master of the Stag-hounds was 'in consequence of hydrophobia',[53] a gruesome symptom associated with rabies.

The improvements to the Palace continued rapidly: 'at present the variety of spire-like ornaments rising from its summit have an appearance not altogether dissimilar to the castles, pawns etc. on the surface of a chess-board'.[54] The extraordinary (and unprecedented) design was observed with amazement as new features such as stone minarets and domes emerged from beneath the scaffolding. Thousands of tons of stone from the quarries in Bath were transported by ship from Bristol to the harbour at Shoreham, a few miles to the west of Brighton. In October 1819 Captain Mitchenore delivered 75 tons of stone by sloop. Bricks were shipped from the Isle of Wight and iron was supplied from a foundry near Lewes, as well as from London. By October 1818 the immense circular iron frame with its ribs to support the new central dome (over Holland's old Saloon) was in place (fig.3), as well as the iron pipes to supply the royal baths with sea water.

In November 1818 the imminent arrival of the Prince gave added urgency to the works: 'The workmen are limited in their times of refreshment; and in all departments there is much activity to complete the work.'[55] During 1818 and 1819, Frederick Crace, with thirty-four assistants, worked in the Music Room, bringing drawings, samples and models for the Prince's approval and changing details of completed works as

4. The Pavilion at Brighton, *Vincent Brooks, Day & Sons, lithograph, c. 1823. View of the completed east front, facing the Steine and enclosed with walls surmounted with railings.*

5. The West Front, *from Nash's* Views. *To achieve a picturesque and harmonious appearance all the exterior rendered surfaces were lined out to imitate blocks of stone and painted to blend with the colour of Bath stone ornaments.*

demanded. The Prince's close involvement is clear from the Crace accounts. For instance in 1820, the year when the Prince Regent succeeded George III, the imitation bamboo-reeded coves in the Music Room were 'tied together' with blue painted ribbons. Following the King's perusal these were all repainted in lilac 'by order of His Majesty'.[56]

The King's impatience was relentless, demanding that the artists and craftsmen worked all hours, including at night. An additional bill in Crace's accounts for 1820 was for a quantity of wax lights 'used in consequence of the great exertion required to complete the works'.[57] It was rumoured that workmen earned the equivalent of sixteen days' wages within one week by working nights and weekends.

Throughout the period of construction, the Prince Regent delighted in showing his guests and friends the progress of his favourite project. John Wilson Croker, the Tory MP and Secretary to the Admiralty, visited the Pavilion in December 1817, following a summons by the Prince. He was given a personal tour of the interior, in particular of the new kitchen lavishly furnished with modern equipment. After dinner the new (but incomplete) Music and Banqueting Rooms were specially lit and dinner guests were shown their emerging splendours. The Prince also entertained his guests by explaining, with Nash's plans in hand, the designs and works yet to be executed.[58]

After some four years of anticipation the overall design of the Pavilion was finally clearly visible in late 1819. The *Monthly Magazine* published an illustration of the exterior, provoking an outburst from a reader.[59] The writer criticised its lack of fitness for purpose and observed, quite correctly, that the complex design, given the English climate, would need expensive maintenance. For an occasional residence it was an extravagant, barbaric structure wanting in good taste. In fifty years' time, he went on, 'it will be an old offensive ruin and it will remain a mouldering monument of tasteless extravagance and wasteful folly'. Fortunately in this observation he was proved wrong.

In the spring of 1819 Marlborough House was finally demolished to make way for the new north-end apartments for the Prince and his personal servants. The building was still in no condition to accommodate the Prince. In January 1820 the main rooms were sufficiently complete to allow local people to inspect the new decorations. The Pavilion was lit up and opened on a Thursday evening; timed tickets were distributed and some 1,500 Brighton residents queued to visit.

The Prince, now King, still could not occupy his new residence and continued to stay in the modest Marlborough Row. With the demolition of Marlborough House he had partially completed public rooms in his new Pavilion and meagre private apartments in a terraced house in Marlborough Row. As a close friend observed, the latter were inadequate for receiving guests as this accommodation was 'no bigger than a parrot's cage'.[60] Finally, in October 1820, it was reported that the King's new apartments were ready, following all-night-long preparation by his servants. However, this proved not to be the case and in late December the King was again forced to make do in Marlborough Row. Finally, in early January 1821 he was able to occupy his new apartments. Many other rooms remained incomplete, to be finished by the artists and craftsmen over the next twelve to eighteen months.

It is ironic that after the interior of the Pavilion was finally finished in 1823, the King only made two further visits, in 1824 and 1827; it was as if he was now bored with his completed, perfect palace.

The King's new private apartments

The King's apartments were located in the new north-end building overlooking the gardens and stable complex. (fig.6) A suite of rooms led to the King's new ground-floor bedroom from the main entrance of the Royal Pavilion in the following sequence: Yellow Ante Room, Library Ante Room and Library. In these rooms the King would receive ministers and undertake state business. The Vice-Chamberlain's bedroom was conveniently located adjacent to the King, in the central west tower, between the main entrance and the King's apartments. With the support of Pages of the Presence (located adjacently, by the wardrobe room), the Vice-Chamberlain could control visitors' access to the King's private apartments.

The Library was amply furnished for visitors, with an ottoman sofa measuring 10 feet (3 m), a second sofa, a chaise longue, nine bamboo-pattern chairs and a large ebony writing cabinet, which served for official business. Imposing double doors 10 feet (3 m) high separated the ante room from the King's Library. In Nash's scheme the King's private apartments were relocated from the first floor to the ground floor, thus providing easy and level access for the King to his private and public rooms when bouts of gout enforced the use of a wheelchair.

6. His Majesty's Private Apartments, West Front *from Nash's* Views. *The King's apartments were sited on the west side in the newly built north end overlooking the gardens. His bathroom was located on the ground floor in the tower to the left (the north-west tower), with pages' rooms above.*

The King's private rooms were all decorated with one of his favourite wallpaper designs, originally produced in a hand-painted version by Robert Jones for the Red Drawing Room. Clearly this complex design of dragons and mythological creatures on a lacquer-red background had pleased the King, and he commanded Jones to reproduce the design for wood-block printing. The intricate pattern required thirty large blocks and a further eight for the dado. For his own apartments the paper was block printed on a pale, blueish green background. This favoured design was also used in the apartments of the Dukes of York and Clarence in the then new and vigorous colour of chrome yellow, which gave the rooms their name of the Yellow Bow Rooms.

His bedroom was furnished with numerous mirrors – a swing dressing glass and a large cheval glass (both fitted with branches for candles), a mahogany framed dressing glass, two large mirrors over the chimneys and a very large mirror fixed to the window pier (standing 8 feet – 2.4 m – tall) facing his bed. In addition, there were two dressing tables, a dressing chair (*en suite* with the bidet chair) and a large elm writing table. The massive mahogany-panelled French bedstead was supplied with five mattresses, a white satin feather bolster, five square pillows of various sizes covered in white satin and two more pillows in cotton cases. Six fine blankets were provided for very cold nights.

The bedroom could be accessed by his pages from the Pages' Room adjacent, from the lobby leading to the back (servants') passage or down the concealed spiral staircase by his water closet. (fig.8) This was one of the two spiral staircases linking the private apartments to the King's personal staff housed above. Usually one of the pages slept close by in the Pages' Room, which was furnished with a couch bed. During the night the page remained dressed and ready to attend to the King's needs.

Given the King's passion for fashionable clothes and his obsession with personal appearance, his new wardrobe was a modest-sized room separated from the bathroom by the Pages' Room. He had no use for a dedicated dressing room, being content to use his bedroom for such a function. The wardrobe room was fitted with three tall wardrobes, about 15 feet (4.6 m) wide in total.

At Brighton the Prince Regent led practically the same life as he did in London. He rose in the morning extremely late, and his toilet was lengthy. According to the Comtesse de Boigne, writing in 1818:

> he was two full hours in his dressing-gown; into his dressing-room he would admit some
> few friends, his ministers, and the foreign Ambassadors when they requested permission to
> enter, and such permission he was always glad to give … His dressing was never finished
> until the last moment when his horses were announced.[61]

After his ride he would visit Lady Hertford at her house, and he remained there until it was time to dress for dinner.

Four years later (in 1822), Croker noted the unchanged daily routine, but a different mistress. Lady Conyngham had supplanted Lady Hertford:

> He never, since he has been at Brighton, has left his own room, except to walk *across* at
> half-past three or four to Lady C.'s house, and at six to walk back, he then dresses and
> comes down to dinner, and that is the whole of his air and exercise.[62]

7. His Majesty's Bedroom*, from Nash's* Views. *A Jib door on the left led to the bathroom; a Jib (or concealed) door to the right in the bed alcove led to his water closet. On the right wall hang the barometer and thermometer.*

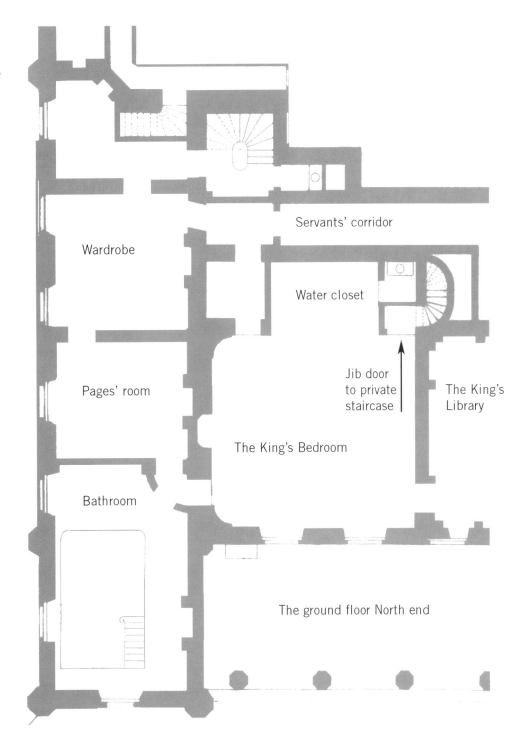

8. Plan of the King's private apartments, *showing his bedroom and the new bathroom, with the large marble plunge bath. Two Jib doors flanking the bed alcove provided private access to members of the Household.*

Servants' corridor

Wardrobe

Water closet

Jib door to private staircase

The King's Library

Pages' room

The King's Bedroom

Bathroom

The ground floor North end

Some mornings the King would engage in public business or meet with his tailor; the only variants to his daily routine were his company and the dishes served at dinner.

Warmth was essential for the King, wherever he stayed. His visit to Buckden Palace, Huntingdon, in January 1814 was recorded in detail by the Bishop of Lincoln's wife, Mrs Tomline, in a letter to her sister.[63] Mrs Tomline noted that the Prince liked his bedroom very warm and that even on that cold January night he slept with only two blankets and no counterpane or quilt. He also brought his own sheets with him, in addition to leather sheets used when travelling. In Brighton, an open fire heated his bedroom; a copper warming pan with a long handle was kept close at hand for chilly nights. A barometer and a thermometer monitored the environment.

The public rooms

Guests approached the Pavilion through the gardens and alighted from their carriages in the shelter of the illuminated *porte cochère*. This entrance was described as the 'temple portico' by Nash as its design derived from an Indian temple (or shrine). Footmen led them into the Entrance Halls, and through to the Long Gallery, which formed a spinal link to all the state rooms arranged along the east front.

The simplicity of the two entrance rooms, the tent-like Octagon Hall (or vestibule) and the cool, green inner Entrance Hall did little to prepare visitors for the splendours to come. Simple hall chairs furnished the Octagon Hall and a roaring fire welcomed guests. The floor was covered with a practical matt-patterned oil cloth, laid in pieces and easy to clean.

The square inner Entrance Hall, lit by day by painted glass clerestory windows and at night by large painted globe lanterns, was furnished with simple chairs and tables on a grey drugget floor covering. This room was the focal point or hub of the Pavilion. Guests who had a private audience with the King would be led to the left into the richly decorated Yellow Ante Room, where under the guidance of the King's pages they would wait until ushered into his presence.

The Yellow Ante Room, sadly demolished in the late nineteenth century, was decorated with large Chinese oil paintings illustrating the processes of manufacturing tea, china and silk, together with landscapes and interiors. These were all pasted onto a rich yellow background and framed with *trompe l'oeil* borders in the style of the Yellow Bow Rooms and the Red Drawing Room (Robert Jones's innovative version of the traditional English print room). Chinese-pattern armchairs and bamboo-pattern ottomans provided seating for the waiting visitors.

To the right of the Entrance Hall lay the Red Drawing Room, available for use by visitors, along with two more modest rooms called the Ladies Red Waiting Room and the Ladies Retiring Room. Here guests could wait and ladies would withdraw after dinner. In the Retiring Room they could adjust their dress and appearance in the dressing glasses provided, as well as availing themselves of the fitted water closet.

Guests invited for dinner, or for a post-dinner concert and supper, would be led into the low-ceilinged Long Gallery and then to the spectacular state rooms, accessed through various doors. All the main public rooms were fully carpeted wall to wall (or 'planned-to-the-room') in either geometric patterned Brussels flat-weave, or deep hand-knotted Axminster wool carpet, depending on the room's function. Only the three grandest, and most dramatic, rooms had hand-knotted Axminsters – the Banqueting

9. (right) The Yellow Ante Room, (artist's impression) provided a waiting room for guests or ministers awaiting an audience with the King. The walls were painted by Robert Jones in Chinese Imperial yellow and decorated with Chinese pictures illustrating the processes of making silk, china and tea, together with landscapes and domestic interiors. This room and the adjacent oval staircase were demolished in the post-1850 period.

Room, the Saloon and the Music Room. Each was of spectacular design, reflecting the individual architecture and design of each room.

The differing room heights, colour schemes and lighting were designed to create a sense of amazement and awe in the visitor. Close friends of the King enjoyed observing the reactions of new visitors, overwhelmed by the rich colours, gilding and decorations so different from the tasteful, neo-classical interiors found in many country houses. The Duke of Wellington, experiencing Nash's Pavilion for the first time in January 1822, was clearly quite astonished by both the decorations and the atmosphere, much to the amusement of Princess Lieven.

Guests at the new Pavilion

As a host the Prince was genuinely concerned that his guests should be comfortable and enjoy their stay. The Comtesse de Boigne, the daughter of the French Ambassador to London, recalled that when her parents first visited Brighton, the Prince's butler had made advance enquiries as to their tastes and customs to ensure they felt at ease in the Pavilion. She continued:

> No householder could be more careful than the Prince Regent or more prodigal in small attentions when he wished to please. No detail was too insignificant for his care. As soon as any one had dined with him three times he knew his tastes and took much trouble to satisfy them.[64]

The Comtesse described the three styles of invitation issued by the Royal Household on behalf of the Prince. Most formal was a large invitation card issued by the Lord Chamberlain: formal dress was essential for these events. Alternatively, as she recorded in 1818:

> His private secretary, Sir Benjamin Bloomfield, would send out a private note in his own writing that the Prince desired one's company for such and such a day. Ordinary dress clothes and the usual formalities of society were then enjoined. These notes were sent to ladies as to men. The dinners were never attended by more than twenty; usually by twelve or fifteen people.[65]

The third manner of invitation was reserved for intimate friends. The Prince would send a footman in the morning with a verbal message to the effect that if Mr So-and-so was not engaged and had nothing better to do, the Prince would be glad if he would come and dine, but begged him not to put himself to inconvenience. At the same time it was understood that people never had anything else to do and refusal was not an option.

Guests invited to stay at the Pavilion generally stayed only a few days, rarely exceeding a week. They usually arrived in time to dress for dinner, always served at 6.00 p.m. 'The inmates of the palace' were joined by guests staying or resident in Brighton, a town 'frequented by brilliant society during the winter months'.[66]

After dinner more guests arrived, and at about 11.00 p.m. a cold supper was served in a drawing room where the Prince presided with his chosen few for intimate conversation and gossip. 'Upon the whole', continued the Comtesse:

> these evening parties which went on until two or three o'clock in the morning, would have seemed desperately wearisome had they been given by a private individual. But the enchantment of the crown kept the whole company awake, and sent the guests away delighted with the condescension of the Prince.[67]

10. The Banqueting Room *from Nash's* Views. *In this magnificent room the King entertained foreign royalty, his ministers, his friends and family.*

Her one complaint, echoed by other guests, was about the Prince's band, which included horns and other noisy instruments, and gave a maddening performance in the vestibule during the dinner and throughout the evening. 'Distance rendered the music bearable, but by no means agreeable in my opinion. The Prince, however, delighted in it, and often joined in, beating time on the dinner gong.'[68]

Supper, a light meal which was served in the late evening as dinner commenced at 6.00 p.m., might be a plate of sandwiches or an elaborate compilation of cold meats, lobster, fish and game. Supper would be served in the Pavilion in one of the more relaxing rooms, for example the Music Room or the Banqueting Room Galleries.

In the morning, guests had the option of breakfasting in their own rooms or sharing a meal hosted by the Prince's Private Secretary, Sir Benjamin Bloomfield, and his wife. The Prince would not appear in public before 3.00 p.m. Breakfast was served in the South Gallery on the first or Chamber Floor, much to the delight and astonishment of the Comtesse:

> but what a landing and what a staircase! The carpets, the tables, the chairs, the porcelain, the china there displayed were as exquisite as luxury and good taste could possibly find. The Prince attached more importance to the perfection of this meal for the reason that he never appeared to share it.[69]

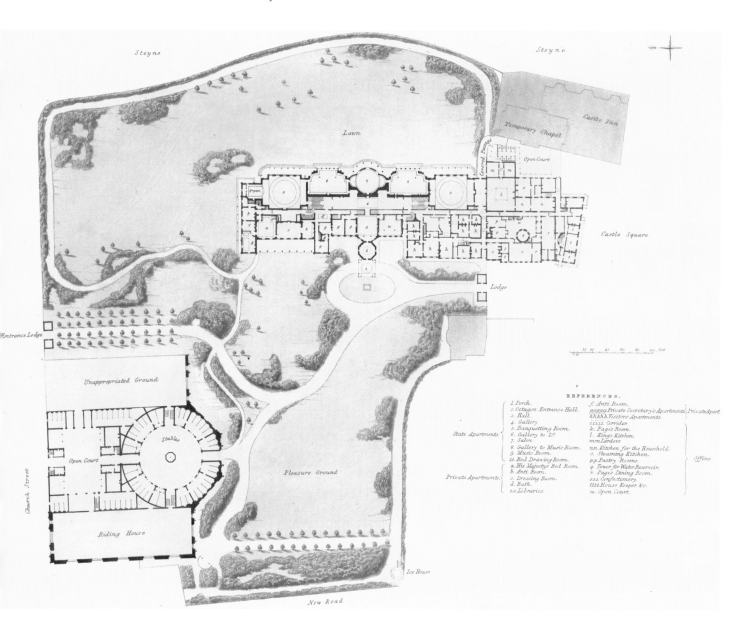

She also noted that some guests declined to join the company for breakfast: 'some of the older lady friends of the Prince, who were attempting to hide the irreparable outrages of time, never appeared, except by artificial light, a very superficial precaution and a very ineffectual sacrifice. The Marchioness of Hertford set the example.'[70] Certainly the brilliant morning sunlight afforded by the large laylight in the South Gallery would do little to flatter the looks of the more elderly guests.(fig.17)

Breakfast was a substantial repast in the 1820s. Thomas Creevey, whilst staying with the Earl of Sefton, could not help but comment on the lavish breakfasts of four silver dishes of hot foods. Once the covers were raised, revealed were 'kidneys at top, mashed potatoes at bottom, 3 partridges at one side with bread sauce, crums &c. &c., Pattys at the other.'[71] The following day breakfast included mutton and mashed potatoes, omelette and pheasant. The King's breakfast, served in his own private apartments, consisted generally of fish, game and poultry.

11. (left) Ground plan
of the Royal Pavilion
Estate, from Nash's
Views, c. 1821. This
plan shows the extent
of the land acquired
and is indicative of
Nash's proposals,
some at this time as
yet unrealised. The
area marked
'Unappropriated
Ground' was intended
as a tennis court, but
later used for Queen
Adelaide's stables.
The ice house (see
p. 148) is indicated on
the south-west corner,
off New Road, and
near the avenue of
elms – some of which
remain today.

Those members of fashionable society who were not invited to stay in the Pavilion itself (or in properties owned by the King) would stay in hotels such as the Royal York (patronised by the Count and Countess Lieven and the Duke of Devonshire), the Old Ship or the Norfolk. Others would rent houses in fashionable squares and terraces near the Steine, or on the seafront. In general, only the King's family and his close friends were privileged to reside in the Pavilion itself.

Some acquired their own properties. The prominent politician George Canning (briefly the King's Prime Minister) bought a seafront house at 100 Marine Parade, and following his sudden death in 1827 it was put up for sale. It was 'fitted up with more attention to comfort than to show' and the furniture throughout was 'remarkably plain'.[72] Canning apparently built an arch under the road, with a passage to the sea accessed by a tunnel from his house. Here in a thickly padded room, lined with green baize, he received guests such as the King who wished to consult him in secret.[73]

The 'Vice-Queen' and Brighton society

During the rebuilding of the Pavilion, the King's current companion, Lady Conyngham, lived in one of the houses in Marlborough Row, purchased by the Prince Regent in 1815–1816. Numbers 1–7 were demolished during 1820–1821, so it is probable that Lady Conyngham resided in number 8, which still remains (now known as Northgate House). She is recorded in 1822–1823 as staying in a house in East Street, adjacent to the Pavilion. This allowed, as one guest noted, the King to be seen by all the world as he made his way out of the south gate of the estate and walked 'a few yards of the common street'[74] to reach his mistress's house.

Lady Conyngham was an avaricious, interfering nepotist who ensured that her family, as well as herself, were well placed and provided for. She had a passion for jewellery, assembling an extensive collection of gifts from the King. She scandalised society by publicly wearing her 'gifts', which were considered to be the property of the Crown. The witty, intelligent and attractive Princess Lieven could not understand the King's attraction to such a woman, who had 'not an idea in her head; not a word to say for herself; nothing but a hand to accept presents and diamonds with and an enormous balcony to wear them on'.[75]

The prolific diarist Charles Greville recorded that she had accumulated enormous wealth from the King and that she (as well as her family) lived at his expense. Even Lord Conyngham's *valet de chambre* was not his own servant, but part of the Royal Household.[76] Lady Conyngham was both disliked and despised by society. She was an object of jealousy as she wielded considerable influence over the King during the last decade of his life. The King was, however, extremely fond of her children, and no doubt she provided him with motherly support and a substitute family environment. Her

A·SKETCH at BRIGHTON   Pub 9ʰ May 1822 by SW Fores Picadilly

arrogance and self-interest, however, caused much indignation amongst the inhabitants of Brighton, to the point where she felt uneasy in the town. It was said this may have been one of the reasons why the King withdrew his patronage in the late 1820s, moving to the privacy and seclusion of Windsor.

The Conyngham family were supplied with carriages and horses from the Royal Stables, and Lady Conyngham behaved as if she were the mistress of the Pavilion, the 'Vice-Queen', as some newspapers and diarists described her. Greville recalled an incident when she asked Sir William Keppel (a member of the King's Household) to have the Saloon lit up, in honour of Lady Bath's visit. When the King arrived he was delighted and 'seized her arm and said with the greatest tenderness, "Thank you, thank you, my dear; you always do what is right; you cannot please me so much as by doing everything you please, everything to show that you are mistress here."'[77]

Visiting Brighton to attend a Council meeting in December 1821, Greville stayed on for dinner with the King. He was not impressed:

> the gaudy splendour of the place amused me for a little and then bored me. The dinner was cold and the evening dull beyond all dullness … The rooms are not furnished for society, and, in fact, society cannot flourish without ease; and who can feel at ease who is under the eternal constraint which etiquette and respect impose?[78]

12. A Sketch at Brighton, by William Heath, 1822. Lord and Lady Conyngham are walking with their daughter, Lady Elizabeth, on the Steine. A comical couple in appearance, the Conynghams were much disliked in Brighton (and elsewhere) for their influence over the King.

13. The Riding House, from Nash's Views. *In this magnificent space the King, with his guests or the Hussars, could exercise in bad weather. Here competitions would be held and young horses trained. A box, high up on the left, draped as if in an opera house, provided an excellent view for spectators.*

Nash's new palace, like Holland's former building, was renowned for its excessive heating and brilliant lighting which did little to relieve the inflamed eye of Princess Lieven whilst visiting in January 1822. However, she delighted in the overwhelming opulence of the Pavilion and was never intimidated by court etiquette:

> I do not believe that, since the days of Heliogabalus, there have been such magnificence
> and such luxury. There is something effeminate in it which is disgusting. One spends the
> evening half-lying on cushions; the lights are dazzling; there are perfumes, music,
> liqueurs … [79]

Such a description of languorous, informal behaviour is no doubt exaggerated, but was observed as characteristic of English society by Prince Pückler-Muskau. He was much taken by the elegance and comfort of modern English furniture with its ingenious mechanical devices for reclining, lounging or reading, and the casual manners in London clubs where 'luxury and convenience … is here to be found in as great perfection as in the best private houses'. He observed:

> the practice of half lying instead of sitting; sometimes of lying at full length on the carpet at
> the feet of ladies; of crossing one leg over the other in such a manner as to hold the foot in
> the hand; of putting the hands in the arm-holes of the waistcoat, and so on – are all things
> which have obtained in the best company and the most exclusive circles.[80]

Nash's *Views* presents very simplified depictions of the interiors of the Pavilion. The 1828 inventory records the profusion of actual furniture and decorative objects used in the rooms. For example, the Music Room Gallery (fig.14) was furnished with four pier tables, two large library tables and four occasional tables. Seating included two 7-foot (2.1 m) oblong ottomans, covered with Persian carpets and decorated with fluted silk and silk tassels. Two square bolsters and four feather pillows, all covered in silk and each embellished with four green and yellow silk tassels, were provided for the comfort of reclining guests. In addition there were four large sofas with cushions, four *têtes à tête*, with four *en suite* elbow chairs and eighteen gilt chairs. Surfaces were covered with fine Chinese and Japanese ceramic jars, vases, bowls, pot-pourris and bottles – over fifty in total.

The King spent Christmas and the New Year in Brighton in 1823, remaining until early February 1824. He returned once more for two weeks or so in the early spring of 1827. According to an exaggerated report in *The Times*, he didn't leave his dressing room for fifteen days, refusing to see a single human being – 'servants, tailors and doctors excepted'.[81] Princess Lieven stayed with him at Brighton, in the company of visiting ministers. In a letter to her brother she describes the King as wonderfully well, enjoying 'his fine bizarre Pavilion, his good table, his very noisy music' as well as 'his fat Marchioness' – of whom, she mused, he was tired.[82]

14. The Music Room Gallery, *from Nash's* Views. *The Gallery was used for playing cards, conversation, musical entertainments and dancing.*

15. Plan showing the layout of the Yellow Bow Rooms on the first floor, the apartments of the Duke of York and the Duke of Clarence (later William IV) and their servants' rooms. As regular and frequent guests, the King's younger brothers had their own designated apartments.

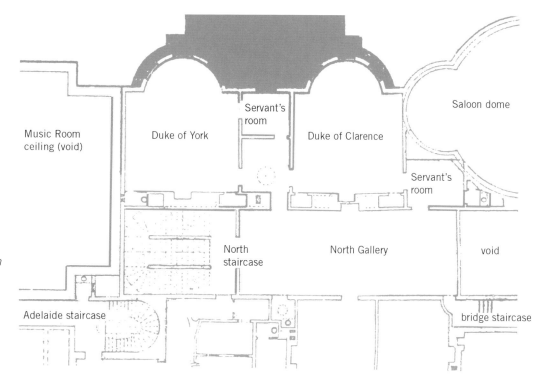

Music Room ceiling (void)

Duke of York

Servant's room

Duke of Clarence

Saloon dome

Servant's room

North staircase

North Gallery

void

Adelaide staircase

bridge staircase

16. The Yellow Bow Rooms, now restored to Robert Jones's original scheme of chrome yellow dragon paper with applied Chinese export oils and watercolours.

The Music Room and entertainments

17. The South Gallery (on the first floor), restored to Frederick Crace's original Regency scheme. This area was used by guests as a breakfast room and for activities much enjoyed in this period such as reading and writing.

Music was always an essential ingredient of the King's life at the Pavilion; guests' accounts invariably record his passion for musical entertainments. In Nash's new design prominence was given to the two new state rooms, which reflected the King's own enthusiasms – music and dining.

After a lengthy dinner, guests would withdraw to the adjacent galleries, the Saloon and the Music Room for conversation, cards, or musical entertainment. When there was dancing the Brussels carpet in the Music Room Gallery, and the Axminster in the Music Room, would be removed and the floor chalked (with elaborate designs) to aid the dancers.

The lighting and richly gilded and lacquered decorations of the Pavilion itself were part of the entertainment. The poet Lord Byron, writing in self-imposed exile, could have been describing the Pavilion in its Regency heyday in his epic adventures of Don Juan in London's society:

… then along the floor

Chalk mimics painting; then festoons are twirl'd.

Then roll the brazen thunders of the door,

Which opens to the thousand happy few

An earthly Paradise of 'Or Molu'.[83]

In designing the structure of the new Music Room, John Nash claimed to have achieved acoustic perfection. During earlier stages of the Music Room's construction it was reported that the Prince perceived that the height of the room adversely affected the sound. To obviate this defect a 'few trifling alterations' were made to create an interior that would attain 'the *achme* [*sic*] of scientific proportions'.[84] Some forty years later, Robert Kerr recommended that the dimensions of a private music room be 40 by 60 feet (12 x 18 m), citing as a good example the Concert Room at Buckingham Palace (40 by 70 feet – 12 x 23 m). Height, breadth and length should be precisely in 'harmonic proportions', such as 2, 3 and 4 – or so recommended the acoustic theorists. Ceilings should not be lofty, and coving would improve the effects of sounds from the performers to the audience. The floor should be covered with a soft and absorbent material such as carpet.[85] The Music Room approximates to these proportions, with convex coving and concave ceiling to reflect sound and reduce echoes. (fig.19) Nash's theory of sound was greeted with scepticism by some guests, who neither understood his theory – nor believed that he did.[86]

The Music Room with its gilded ceiling, carved dragons and serpents and rich wall canvases vied for splendour and approbation with the Banqueting Room. Frederick Crace designed the former in perhaps a more picturesque and feminine style. Guests would compare the two new rooms, each spectacularly lit by chandeliers, and argue about their respective merits. One guest ventured to say that, although they were different, they were equally beautiful in their own way, like 'a handsome man and a handsome woman'.[87]

'The finest in Europe': George IV's private band

Small private bands of wind instruments were a common feature of European aristocratic life, going back at least to the early 1700s. They provided a harmonious backdrop to their patron's life and at the same time tangible evidence for his wealth and cultivation. *Tafelmusik*, for playing during dinner, was the best-known manifestation of this trend. The young leader of fashionable society, with European friends and a taste for harmony, would not have thought his establishment complete without some musical provision.

In creating the Music Room, the Prince Regent provided the perfect setting for his great musical passion, his own private band. Maintained entirely separately from the official state band, at a cost of up to £8,000 annually, it had been formed over twenty years from the cream of Europe's musical talent. The Prince knew all its members by name, chose its programmes and often conducted it himself. It was generally acknowledged to be 'the finest in Europe'.[88]

The Prince of Wales grew up in a family which valued music highly. Queen Charlotte was skilled on the harpsichord and George III kept a band of wind and string performers who played every evening at Windsor. The Prince actively patronised most of London's musical endeavours and famously frequented the capital's theatres. He was also a competent practical musician and in his youth studied the cello under John Crosdill, the most famous virtuoso of his day. On one occasion, when a sprained right arm curtailed that pleasure, George threw himself into vocal amusements. The opinion of John Wilson Croker, though, was that his voice, a bass, was 'not good, and he does not sing so much from the notes as from recollection'.[89]

The 'Prince's Band' had certainly been formed by 24 August 1794, when the *Sun* reported that it played at a public breakfast attended by the Prince and 'near 200 people of rank' in the Promenade Grove, an elm-lined place of fashionable resort.[90] Newspaper

18. The Music Room, from Nash's Views, *the perfect setting for the King's private band. For dancing, the immense Axminster carpet was removed and the floors chalked. On the left is the King, seated between Lady Conyngham and her daughter.*

19. Cross-section of the Music Room roof and ceiling. *The drawing illustrates the curving profile of the ceiling, said to improve the interior's acoustic quality. Thousands of carved and gilt shells, applied to the shallow dome ceiling, decrease in size as they reach the apex, creating an illusion of height. (Plan Registry, Good/17.)*

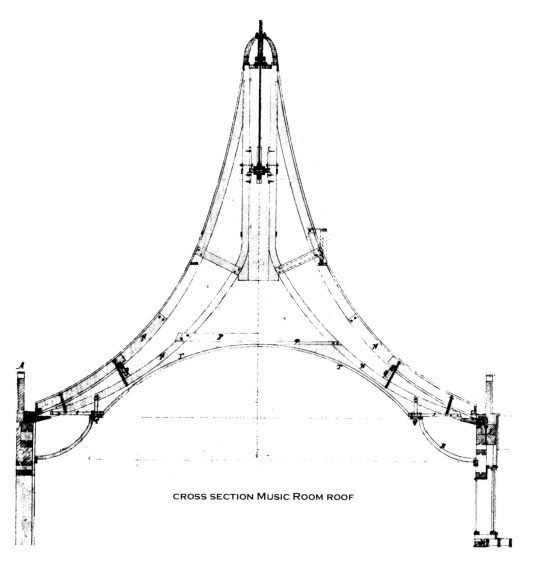

CROSS SECTION MUSIC ROOM ROOF

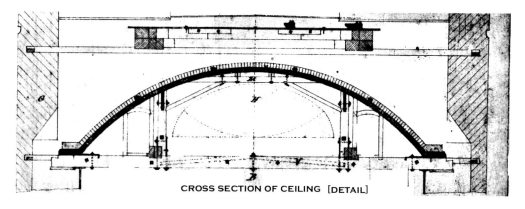

CROSS SECTION OF CEILING [DETAIL]

accounts show that it accompanied the Prince of Wales to balls, promenades, the Brighton Camp and concerts. Its major duty was at the Marine Pavilion where the band played music on the lawn, in front of the Banqueting Room, as well as inside.

By the 1820s the band consisted of up to forty-six wind and percussion instruments, similar to what we think of as a military band today, although it undoubtedly began with many fewer members. In 1818 the *Quarterly Musical Magazine* listed eight clarinets, two oboes, three flutes, four bassoons, four serpents, four trombones, four horns, four trumpets and kettle drums.

The engraving of the Music Room from Nash's *Views* shows the band standing in front of the stupendous Lincoln organ, described as 'the largest instrument in the kingdom … as much distinguished for its peculiar delicacy of tone as for its prodigious powers'.[91] Professional musicians as well as guests used the organ, installed in the Music Room in 1818. Princess Lieven was delighted to try the new organ. She was a talented musician who would play the piano for the Prince and his friends.[92] After a rather inept start, which deafened both herself and the guests, she found her feet and played some sentimental pieces. She was astonished by both the power and beauty of the instrument and amused by her audience, who were moved to respond in delight with 'Ohs' and 'Ahs'.[93]

At either side of the organ, disguised doors led through into the Master of the Band's room. This was crammed full of presses and cupboards for music. The members of the band had their own room in the north end, equipped with deal tables, benches and a range of forty-three small closets. This must have been where the musicians prepared and stored their instruments.

In Nash's Pavilion, the band settled into a regular pattern of life, depending upon whether the Prince was in residence. Daily practice took place in the Entrance Hall, in the presence of visitors calling to leave their names at the Palace. The Old Ship Hotel was an alternative venue. Leonard Shuckard, the innkeeper, was paid over £56 in the first quarter of 1820 for hiring a room for the band's use.[94] By 1821, the band seems to have had its own practice room somewhere in Church Street, probably in the stables complex.

After dinner, which was accompanied by the band playing, guests spread through the drawing rooms. The King often made up musical parties with his more talented friends or professional visitors. In 1822 he took advantage of the presence of the gentlemen of the St James's Chapel Royal to closet himself in the Saloon. One guest recalled that he 'never left the pianoforte: he sang in "Glorious Apollo", "Mighty Conquerer", "Lord Mornington's Waterfall" (encored), "Non nobis, Domine", and several other glees and catches', much to the chagrin of his unmusical favourite, Lady Conyngham.[95]

20. The Music Room, from Nash's Views (detail). The band's elaborate blue and red uniforms, embellished with gold lace, cost £75 each.

The band usually played between 9 o'clock and midnight, with varying formality. It had a wide-ranging repertoire including Mozart, Bach, Haydn, Beethoven and particularly Handel. Every piece was specially arranged by the leader of the band, Christian Kramer, and for an evening's performance their music boxes held up to 300 books of parts.[96] On New Year's Day 1822, the King held a grand concert in the Music Room for the Lord Chancellor and 100 distinguished guests. The programme consisted entirely of extracts from oratorios by Handel including the chorus 'Glory to God' from *Joshua* in which 'the accompaniment of the numerous wind instruments was heard most appropriately to the words as to the falling of the walls of Jericho'. The second act consisted of pieces from Handel's opera *Acis and Galatea*. 'The King frequently conducted the Concert, and kept most excellent time. His Majesty … took particular interest in the whole of the performance.'[97] In 1824, the trio 'Disdainful of Danger' from

Judas Maccabaeus was performed in honour of the presence of the Duke of Wellington.[98]

After the opening of the Royal Chapel in 1821, on the site of the Castle Inn assembly rooms, the band provided music for the two-and-a-half-hour-long services. The full band attended a service in February 1824. Handel's choruses 'Glory to God' and the 'Hallelujah Chorus' from the *Messiah* were played before the sermon. The *Brighton Gazette* asserted that 'it is unquestionable that the accompaniment of his Majesty's band for the great choruses of Handel, are very superior to any stringed instrument whatever'. At the conclusion, 'the crash of the whole band, kettle drums, full organ, and the words of the anthem, "God Save the King" produced an awful and sublime impression'.[99]

Members of the band accompanied both fashionable and servants' balls. The ball held in January 1817 to honour the visit of the Grand Duke Nicholas of Russia was underway by 10 o'clock and opened with the national country-dance 'The Prince Regent'. Several other country-dances were enjoyed, including 'I'll gang nai mair to yon town', 'The Tank', 'Money Musk', 'Sir Roger de Coverley', 'Calder Fair' and 'Bolonja'. These were interspersed with quadrilles and the fashionable waltz.

An undoubted high point for music at the Royal Pavilion was the visit of the Italian composer Giacomo Rossini in December 1823. The King was apparently delighted with Rossini and took him by the arm to the Music Room, where he introduced him to members of the band. In his honour they played the overture to *The Thieving Magpie*, winning the greatest praise from Rossini, who was apparently astonished at the power of wind instruments alone. He then regaled them in turn with Desdemona's 'Assisa al pié d'un salice' from *Othello* (presumably in falsetto) and a comic aria, accompanying himself on the piano. Rossini's relaxed manner with the King rendered the other guests present outraged at this foreigner's familiarity, particularly when he sat himself in an informal manner next to the King. Harriet, Countess Granville, who was a guest at the Pavilion for the Italian composer's visit, described him variously in her subsequent correspondence as a 'fat sallow squab of a man' and 'fat and lazy', though she praised the expressiveness and deliciousness of his singing. Rossini later met the King several times in London, where they sang duets together.

Membership of the band could be the culmination of a variety of careers. Some musicians had risen through military ranks, whilst others had served an apprenticeship in one of the many aristocratic private bands in Europe. A few, such as the Hardy family, came from the local music scene, which was well developed for the benefit of Brighton's fashionable visitors.[100] Recruitment was always subject to the King's sudden enthusiasms. On his official visit to Ireland he expressed his delight in the playing of the Royal Marine Band on board his yacht the *Royal George*. The *Brighton Gazette* reported that he had 'appointed the master one of the Gentlemen of his Band at the Pavilion'.[101]

By 1818, the band was 'very rarely commanded to Carlton House'.[102] This does not seem to reflect any lessening in the Prince's opinion of its merits, but that the Pavilion provided the best possible setting for its style of music. The members of the band took lodgings around the town and remained throughout the year, even when the Prince was not in residence. The members also took part in the musical life of Brighton. For

21. (right) The Regent's Harmonica or – Monopoly a Catch for 21 Voices with a Royal Base, Isaac and George Cruikshank, 1820. A satire on the Royal Harmonic Institution, an offshoot of the Philharmonic Society, formed by twenty-one notable professors of music in London. As its patron the King was associated with the institution's commercial activities, which had created the fear that this new association might put composers and music publishers out of business. The King, renowned for his love of music, is depicted playing a 'cello, in an interior, part concert hall and part music-shop.

example, Mr Gilbert, who was considered by some to be the finest trumpeter in England, had been entrusted with sounding the trumpet solos and the Champion's charge at George IV's Coronation banquet. A month later he was causing much excitement at the Theatre Royal in Brighton by replicating his triumph and presumably earning some much needed money. The *Brighton Gazette* reported that a representation of the Champion proceeded into the auditorium on horseback, passing over a specially constructed bridge to the stage. The whole effect was of 'an immense Hall, and the scenery and decorations brilliantly display to us an epitomised counterpart of that at Westminster'.[103] To complete the spectacle, Mr Gilbert wore the precise dress in which he had originally performed.

Kramer was a well-known figure since he possessed a china emporium on the corner of New Road and North Street, from which he supplied chamber pots and water bottles to the Pavilion. His temper was in the news in 1822 when he forcibly removed a shed belonging to the Chain Pier Company, which was blocking the view of the sea from his house on South Parade.[104] Like the King, Kramer suffered from gout and like him he patronised Mahomed's vapour baths (see chapter 5), even introducing his Hanoverian sister to their merits. Kramer seems to have been well loved by his colleagues in the band, some of whom he had known for over twenty years. In 1824 they presented him, in the practice room at the Pavilion, with a beautiful inscribed gold snuffbox made by Rundell, Bridge & Rundell, the King's silversmiths. It cost 80 guineas – a considerable sum given their average £2 13s. weekly wage.

22. Princess Charlotte's manuscript Music Book (signed by her and dated 1811); numerous fashionable waltzes are notated, including The Brighton Waltz *as well as the young Princess's own compositions.*

In 1826, Kramer wrote a memorandum proposing improvements to the terms and conditions of the band. It listed all the members, their current wages, age, marital status and years of service, with remarks about each individual's skills and personal circumstances.[105] The 'hot tempered' trombonist, Albrecht, was married with five children. One child, aged 10, was employed as a member of the band and paid 14s. 6d. per week. Albrecht's financial circumstances were harsh, as were those of a bassoon player, who was described as 'almost starving'. A 48-year-old drummer and widower with four children was described as wretchedly poor, willing and humble, but drank and was dirty. The most important quality was musical excellence, which overrode occasional laziness, bad temper or poor personal hygiene. Clearly Kramer knew all the band members and their families well, being able to comment that the best trumpeter in England had 'a bad wife' and the band's bugle player 'a vixen for his wife'.

Because of the band's long and close association with the King, his death in 1830 caused the members of the band great sorrow. On the evening of 15 July, they led the funeral procession from St George's Hall, Windsor, in full dress uniform with crepe-trimmed shakos and black cock's-tail feather plumes, playing the 'Dead March' from *Saul* with 'swells of trumpets and drums at intervals'. At St George's Chapel they filed away from the entrance to allow the King's remains to pass. The 'finest in Europe' was soon to be disbanded.

After the death of George IV, the future of the band was uncertain. William IV did not share his brother's enthusiasm for music, particularly when that passion cost nearly £8,000 a year to maintain. Kramer had become Master of the King's Music in 1829 and continued in the role until his death in 1834. Some of the musicians did join Queen Adelaide's private band. Others, such as Gutteridge, Kirchner and Mennich, remained in Brighton and established families whose members became part of the town's thriving music culture.

The Billiard Room

Billiards provided entertainment for gentlemen on a wet day and most country houses in the early nineteenth century had a billiard table located in the main hall or gallery, or in a specially designed room. This was usually on the ground floor on account of the weight of the slate top. In Holland's Marine Pavilion the Billiard Room was combined with the Long Gallery in a prominent position adjacent to the Saloon.

In Nash's reconstruction, the Billiard Room was located south of the main entrance (in the area now occupied by the Pavilion Shop). The room was furnished with a table 12 ft 8 in. by 6 ft 6 in. (3.9 x 2 m), crimson cloth curtains and a 7 ft 6 in. (2.3 m) blue morocco leather-covered ottoman on a platform accessed by two carpeted steps for spectators. There are no references to George IV playing billiards in the Pavilion. Possibly the room was used by guests and by staff of the Royal Household. Its location, adjacent to Mr Brent's office, the Chair Entrance, the Equerries' Breakfast Room and visitors' rooms would seem to confirm this view.

The Pavilion Gardens

The Royal Pavilion's gardens were conceived by John Nash as a picturesque pleasure ground for the King, with sinuous gravel paths and shaped beds planted with a wide variety of seasonal herbaceous plants and clusters of shrubs and trees.

Planting began in 1816 in parallel with the building works and was completed by the early 1820s.[106] The gardens, covering some 7 acres (2.8 hectares), provided a charming location for strolling or riding, and a spectacular setting for the Pavilion itself. Although there was no fashionable orangery, orange trees, all bearing fruit, were imported from France in June 1821 to be 'planted in the Palace grounds, several on a raised border, contained in a frame of stone work, exhibiting a species of oriental coridor [sic], above the colonnade walk to the north of the Grand Entrance Hall'.[107]

A German visitor (and passionate landscape gardener) lamenting the demise of Bath as a fashionable resort in the 1820s, could not comprehend why 'fashion' had fled 'with a sort of feverish rage to the unmeaning, treeless and detestable prosaic Brighton'.[108] The town, as well as the Downs and coast, lacked trees and greenery, but the Pavilion Gardens formed an oasis of mature shrubs, plants and large elm trees – an attractive, shady sanctuary on a hot, sultry summer's day. On one occasion George Canning made a formal request for permission for himself and his wife (who was unwell) to walk in the shade of the gardens' trees as they were the only trees for miles around.[109]

4 Managing the Pavilion: the complexities of the Royal Household

The departments of the Royal Household

As a royal palace, the Royal Pavilion was managed by the Royal Household, which was organised into three departments each headed by a peer, usually of the rank of earl or higher. The heads of department were appointed by the Prime Minister and changed with every change of government.

The Lord Chamberlain's was the largest department of the three, responsible for the ceremonial, social and artistic life of the monarch and the court, the interior decorations and refurbishments. The 'upper' or 'above stairs' servants included housekeepers, housemaids and the King's personal staff.

The Lord Steward's Department was responsible for the kitchens, the gardens, the provision of wine, beer and foodstuffs, fuel, linen and supplies. It employed the corresponding 'under' or 'below stairs' staff, including the Clerk of the Kitchen, cooks and porters.

The third department was that of the Master of the Horse, which managed transport, the Royal Stables, grooms, footmen and under-butlers. In addition to these three departments, the Office of Works, a new separate government department under the Treasury, was responsible for new public building and structural alterations, spending nearly £2.5 million over the last fifteen years of George's life to complete his architectural schemes.

Absurd situations arose in the palaces on a day-to-day basis as a result of the historic divisions of labour between these large departments. For example, the Lord Steward's Office would lay a fire, but the Lord Chamberlain's Office was responsible for lighting it. If the heating was inadequate, no single official was accountable. One department supplied lamps, another cleaned, trimmed and lit them. In 1844 Baron Stockmar, a close friend of Prince Albert (Queen Victoria's consort), wrote a memorandum on this confused management and gave the following example of bureaucratic procedures:

If a pane of glass, or the door of a cupboard in the scullery, requires mending, it cannot now be done without the following process: A requisition is prepared and signed by the chief cook (Lord Steward's department), it is then counter-signed by the clerk of the kitchen, then it is taken to be signed by the Master of the Household, thence it is taken to the Lord Chamberlain's Office, where it is authorised, and then laid before the Clerk of the Works, under the office of Woods and Forests; and consequently many a window and cupboard have remained broken for months.[110]

By the late eighteenth century the monarch's control over the Royal Household (as well as over the government) had been significantly reduced. Burke's Economical Reform Bill of 1782 sought to restrain Royal Household expenditure (which always exceeded its annual budget) by 'down-sizing'. It abolished numerous offices – some 140 in total. Some officers ceased to be part of the royal establishment, losing their regular salary (and benefits). Instead they become purveyors of goods and services and were paid accordingly. Such areas, which were 'outsourced', remained under the responsibility of the relevant head of department.

Despite reforms and Treasury controls, the Royal Household still continued to overspend. The Prince's excessive expenditure during the Regency period further exacerbated the problem, resulting in legislation that gave the Treasury more financial control. The need to manage the Household's budget necessitated the abolition of further posts in 1823, but this was done as vacancies occurred.

Apart from the most senior posts, to which appointment was made by the Prime Minister, all posts fell within the patronage of the monarch or his senior officers. Promotion was limited, though there were opportunities in the lower ranks (e.g. housemaids and kitchen staff), in which staff tended to remain all their life. Children often followed in their parents' footsteps.

Conditions of employment

Salaries and perquisites

It is difficult to establish the equivalent value today of early nineteenth-century salaries, but one can get a sense of the different incomes and levels of expenditure of the upper and working classes. Louis Simond, travelling in England in 1810, made notes of various salaries and wages. A manservant would receive a salary of £35 4s. 0d. per year. Labourers received a weekly wage of 14s. in summer and 12s. in winter. Female labourers were paid 8d. a day, or approximately 5s. a week.[111] In full employment a male agricultural labourer could earn £30 per annum. A skilled town worker (with a specific trade) earned about £100 per annum, which would support a reasonable lifestyle. An unskilled city worker, paid £12 per annum, lived in poverty.

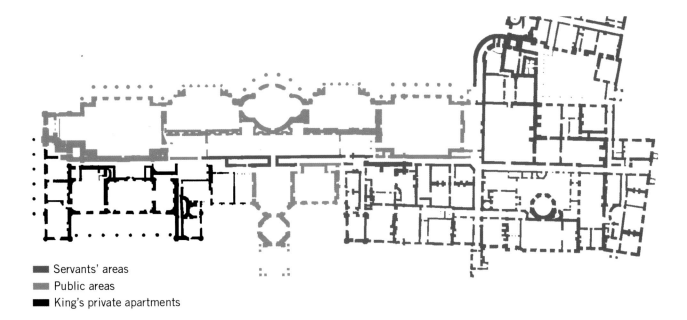

2. Ground-floor plan of the Royal Pavilion, *indicating the broad allocation of space for different functions: the King's private apartments and his personal staff (black), public (or state) rooms (red) and kitchens/ servants' quarters (blue).*

■ Servants' areas
■ Public areas
■ King's private apartments

William Cobbett, travelling through England in the late 1820s, was appalled by the conditions of the agricultural community in the south east. He estimated that a family of five needed some £60 a year for bread, meat and beer alone. In contrast, to run a sizable establishment in London with ten to twelve servants required £4,000 to £6,000 a year.[112]

Records show that members of the King's private band were poorly paid, despite their status. In 1826, in an attempt to ameliorate the conditions of his musicians, Christian Kramer prepared an estimate of the costs of the essential food, drink, candles and fuel for a married man with three children. This came to £2 9s. 6½d. per week, more than the average weekly pay of band members: £2 6s. 0d. (excluding lodging and livery). The annual wage of some members of the band (about £120) was not insubstantial compared to other members of staff, but according to Kramer could not cover costs of clothing, furniture and schooling for the children. His list of necessary food for a family of five for one week included 3½ pounds (1.6 kg) of sugar, 3 pounds (1.4 kg) of butter, 1½ pounds (0.7 kg) of cheese, condiments, tea, table beer for the children, 24½ pints of porter and 14 pounds (6.4 kg) of butcher's meat.[113] Whether this was a realistic list of need or was partly designed to shame his gluttonous master into increasing their weekly pay is uncertain, but clearly in Kramer's view it was inadequate for a family man.

Accounts for 1823 recorded the annual allowances or wages of members of the Lord Chamberlain's Department as, for example: 'Steward and Comptroller of the House Establishment at Brighton' (£300), Housekeeper of the Pavilion (£112), Housemaids (£45), Pages of the Presence £140–£290 (depending on class and rank), Personal Physicians (£214), Personal Apothecary (£229), Master of the Music (£262), Keeper of the Swans (£28), Rat Killer (£80), Messengers (£35), and the Chaplain of Brighton

(£100). The Lord Chamberlain and his Secretary were the highest paid officials, receiving £885 and £750 respectively.[114]

In the same year the Lord Steward (the Marquis of Conyngham) received a sum in excess of £1,000, whilst skilled or manual staff received annual salaries as follows: the baker £50, the coffee room woman £52, the lamplighter £90, and kitchen apprentices £15.[115] The payments to the Lord Chamberlain, Lord Steward and the Master of the Horse were not intended as salaries, but more as honoraria accompanying these prestigious posts.

A memorandum on the household establishment of the Duke of Devonshire, prepared for the 6th Duke after his father's death in 1811, provides a useful comparison with the Royal Household's salaries. Domestic servants residing in unoccupied houses received board wages (i.e. an allowance of money instead of food), but if the Duke was in residence their food and allowances were supplied from the housekeeping budget. Board wages varied from location to location according to the current market price of provisions; in the Duke's London houses upper servants received 21s. a week and under-servants (e.g. housemaids) 15s. At Chatsworth House in Derbyshire, staff were only given 14s. a week, with less at Hardwick Hall (also in Derbyshire) and Londesborough (in Yorkshire), where housemaids received 7s. The allowance made to the servants for wine, 17s. 6d. a week, was abolished: drunkenness seems to have been a problem, at least at Chatsworth.

The housekeeper at Devonshire House in London received an annual wage of £40, compared to the Royal Pavilion's housekeeper who received £112. The Duke's cook was paid £150, whereas the King's Chief Cook, Armand Vilmet, received £240 and the Master Cook, Peter Crepin, £221. The house steward at Chatsworth received £150, compared to the Steward Comptroller of the House Establishment at Brighton, who was paid £300. These figures do not take account of free accommodation, board wages or perquisites, but it would seem that the Royal Household paid staff competitive salaries.[116]

The salaries of Royal Household staff were augmented by a range of additional benefits, such as board wages, lodgings (or an allowance in lieu of them), pensions and medical care, travel allowances, livery (uniforms) or occupational work clothes and perquisites obtained legally or by manipulating the system. Staff had been allowed to claim remains from the table (wine and food), the use of candle ends, and ruined linen. Such 'perks' were clearly open to abuse and could encourage dishonesty and theft. Loyal and favoured servants might also receive substantial gifts of clothes, furniture or plate from the monarch.

Members of the Royal Household also received certain special benefits. Accounts covering the year 5 April 1815 to 6 April 1816 list special allowances for '22 pitcher days' for Royal Household staff. The establishment at Brighton (the housekeeper, housemaids, baker, lamplighter, grooms etc.) all received two bottles of port each on these twenty-two days. Such allowances were perks for members of the Royal Household commemorating royal birthdays and anniversaries of royal events such as dates of accession and marriages. Extra 'pitcher days' were added to commemorate notable military events – '4 September Madrid', '10 September Cadiz' and '6 October

3. Linen shirt, formerly the property of George IV and marked with a crown, GR and 1830 in fine red cross-stitching. The descendants of the King's apothecary, John Nussey, gave a number of linen shirts belonging to the King to the Royal Pavilion. All are individually marked with the King's (or Prince's) insignia and a date.

Detroit' are listed as 'extra' days in the Lord Steward's papers. In total 798 bottles of port were issued at Brighton and 6,762 at Carlton House, with 84 bottles of claret (a much finer quality and more expensive wine) for Jean-Baptiste Watier, the Prince's Clerk Comptroller of the Kitchen at Carlton House.[117] Foreign wines, particularly French, were extremely costly. The cheapest foreign wine was port, which became the patriotic beverage during the period of war with France.

The drink of the ordinary Englishman was beer, which was brewed in varying degrees of quality and alcoholic strength. The poorest quality was 'small beer' used as part payment to casual labourers – as, for example, to the Pavilion's garden labourers. Beer was drunk at any time of the day in lieu of spring or bottled water. Water in large towns and cities was polluted and not safe for general consumption.

The Lord Steward's accounts for the Royal Pavilion also list 'platters' served to members of the Royal Household during 1815 over twenty days. Samuel Wharton, Clerk of the Kitchen, received '20 Platters, 4 Chickens, each equalling 80 birds at 6/- each'. Frederick Badua, Master Cook, received twenty loins of veal and 10 pounds (4.5 kg) of butter; the silver scullery staff received twenty legs of mutton each, as did the gardener and six pages. In addition, vegetables were supplied from the royal gardens, which are noted in the accounts with a notional value. The eight housemaids at Brighton were provided with '2 legs of mutton each Platter day at 10/6 each leg making 560lbs of mutton'.[118]

Staff received board wages in addition to their salaries as well as an allowance for wine or table beer. For example, housemaids and porters received 4d. a day for table beer. In 1822 E. Whittle was employed as an extra servant during the Christmas period to care for the linen and provide water at table for guests to wash their hands. She worked as part of the kitchen section under the Clerk Comptroller, Samuel Wharton, and received board wages of 4s. a day. Mrs Sarah Whittle, the housekeeper, received 4s. 6d., reflecting their relative status in the household. This compared favourably with a housemaid working for the Duke of Devonshire, who received a little over 2s. day.

The personal staff of the monarch, such as the pages (or *valets de chambre*) would receive perquisites from the King's wardrobe. George IV, however, never gave away any of his clothes except his linen. (fig.3) Favoured senior members of the King's Household might receive gifts from the King, which might explain how some inventory-branded pieces of furniture (i.e. original to the Pavilion) have appeared on the market in Europe and the United States over the last century.

Welfare and pensions

Such a stable and hierarchical institution as the Royal Household offered secure employment for life for many servants. When Samuel Wharton died on 14 October 1823 his death merited a notice in the *Brighton Gazette*. Wharton, who died aged 66 after a short illness, had served both George III and George IV. From the 1780s he progressed from Fourth Under Clerk to First Clerk, but lived to serve as Clerk Comptroller for little

4. (right) The new MASTER of the CROWN INN, discharging BETTY – the head chambermaid. *H. Heath 1830. Here the new King, William IV, is shown dismissing Betty (Elizabeth, Lady Conyngham) and her husband Lord Conyngham. They leave laden with perquisites, pensions, gifts, appointments and so on for the family. In the public mind the Conynghams epitomised greed and the abuse of power and influence that might be found within the Royal Household.*

The new MASTER of the CROWN INN discharging BETTY the head Chambermaid.

more than a year. George Moorfield achieved promotion in April 1823 from Second to First Clerk. George Wharton, probably Samuel's son, succeeded Moorfield. George's sister, Miss E. Wharton, was the King's housekeeper at Carlton House.

Staff were cared for throughout their years of active service, in retirement and at death. A physician, a surgeon and an apothecary served the Household. On the advice of the physician, a variety of pills, lotions, powders, embrocations and draughts were provided for staff by the apothecary. The Surgeon to the Household also undertook physical interventions such as bleeding and tooth extraction.

Treatments were in the form of purgatives, diuretics or stimulants with – for more serious complaints – the application of leeches and direct bleeding. Tincture of benzoin (balsamic resin dissolved in rectified spirit) was used as a stimulant and antiseptic for skin conditions. Magnesium oxide served as an antacid and laxative and tincture of myrrh (dissolved resin) was used for mouthwashes and as a mild general disinfectant. Castor oil proved an excellent mild purgative; rhubarb root, valerian, red cinchona bark, lavender, orange, senna and, of course, opium were used in various forms to soothe ailments mostly related to the digestive system.

Pensions during the reign of George IV were generous and in proportion to the years of service. A servant who had worked for between ten and fifteen years received a pension equivalent to a third of his salary and emoluments. Service of between thirty and thirty-five years brought a pension of three-quarters of the value of the salary, and over fifty years a sum equivalent to the full salary. Only staff in the Royal Household who were 'warranted' servants – those who had an official document confirming their appointment – were entitled to claim pensions. Retirement due to ill-health also brought pensionable benefits. A list of proposed pensions submitted to the Treasury in 1837 suggested an annual pension of £50 for a housemaid who, after twenty-five years service, could no longer undertake her duties due to ill-health.

Under William IV a new Act was passed reducing the pensionable benefits, affecting all staff employed after August 1829. For service of forty-five years or more, a maximum of two-thirds of the salary could be paid as a pension. Staff, or their relatives, might also be rewarded for loyalty or long service. On the death of George IV's loyal servant and confidant Claudius du Pasquier in 1824, his widow, Catherine, a lowly seamstress, was appointed to the vacant and more remunerative position of housekeeper at Kew.

Towards the end of 1823, William Collins, an errand man in the kitchen on a salary of £50 per annum, died. Thomas and John Saunders undertook his funeral arrangements at a cost of £12 1s. 11d. These included the coffin, pillow and so on; the hire of cloaks, hoods and scarves for attendants; the minister's fees and the wages of thirteen coffin bearers (at a cost of £3 10s.).[119] Funeral arrangements were made by the Lord Steward's Department on behalf of the entire Royal Household.

Accommodation

Key members of the Royal Household, and friends and advisers, always accompanied the King on his visits to Brighton. The quality of accommodation allocated to members of the Royal Household naturally depended on their rank. Space in the Pavilion was at a premium. The small servant's room adjoining the Duke of York's bedroom was fitted with a high mahogany press (or fold-up) bed measuring 6 ft 9 in. high by 3 ft (2.1 by 0.9 m) wide. With the additional pieces of furniture listed in the Pavilion's inventory (a chest of drawers, a dressing glass, a corner wash-hand stand and a table and two chairs) there can have been very little room to move when the press bed was in use. These type of beds, sometimes called 'turned-up' bedsteads (enclosed in furniture to resemble chests of drawers or bookcases), were commonly used by servants or in lodging houses – a necessity arising from the need to accommodate many people in a space designed for few. (fig.5b) Footmen who accompanied the King to Brighton shared a room in the south-end servants' quarters. Nine to a room, each footman was supplied with a chest of drawers, a press bed and a mirror.

More spacious servants' rooms, for example those used by the King's Pages of the Backstairs, were equipped with a tent bedstead (fig.5a) furnished with dimity (a white patterned and woven cotton), a straw palliasse, one hair and one feather mattress (called a 'feather bed'), a bolster, pillows and three blankets. The feather mattress, similar to a modern duvet, was covered with a blanket and placed under the sheet. The

5a. Tent or camp beds were provided in the Pavilion for the King's personal servants, such as Pages of the Backstairs. Designed by Thomas Sheraton, illustrated in The Cabinet Dictionary, *1803.*

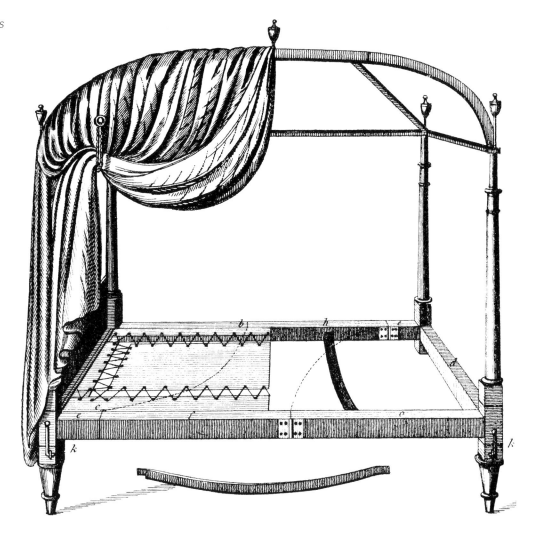

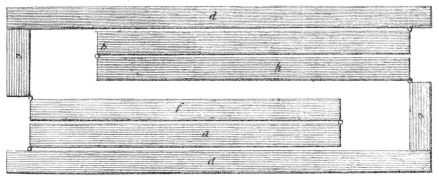

The plan of the bed folded in.

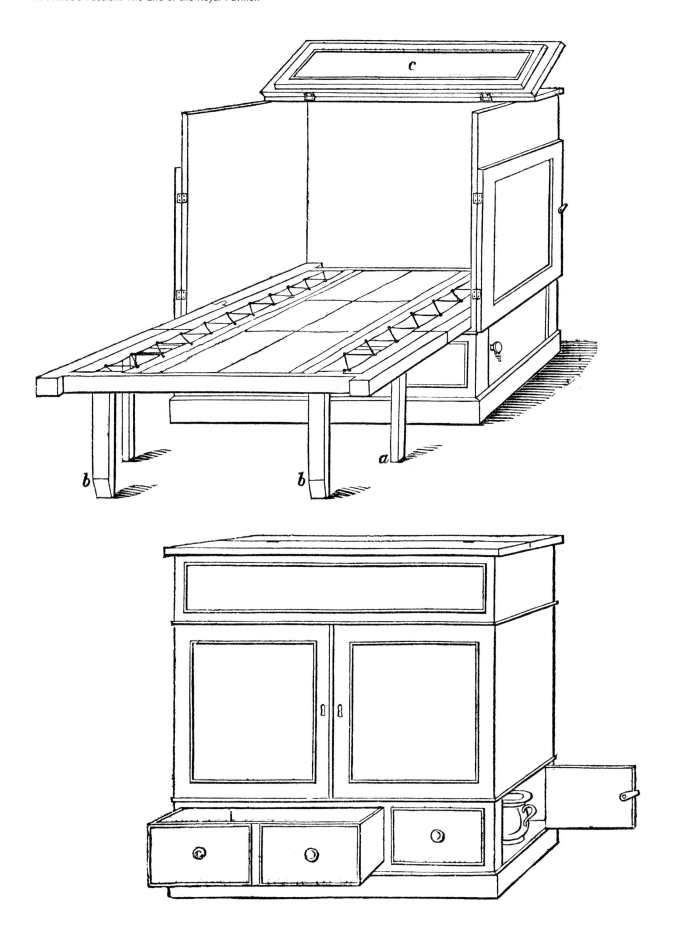

5b. (left) A press bed
of the kind used by
servants when space
was constrained, as
for example in the
Yellow Bow Rooms.
From J. C. Loudon's
Encyclopaedia of
Cottage, Farm and
Villa Architecture and
Furniture*, 1846.*

feather bed, forming the final layer over several mattresses, gave a distinctive domed profile. It was such a familiar shape that George IV's sister, the Duchess of Gloucester, described her poor brother – bloated with water and swollen in the final months of his illness – as 'enormous like a feather bed'.[120]

The small size of the Pavilion limited the number of guest bedrooms available. These were mostly located on the first floor, in the main body of the building, and were usually reserved for members of the Royal Family and Royal Household. An 1824 inventory of beds in the Pavilion (and its ancillary buildings) lists the distribution as the King (1), visitors including the Royal Family and senior members of the Household (27), upper servants, pages and so on (50) and under-servants (56). Servants and grooms were also housed in the complex of the Royal Stables; others took lodgings in the town. A second inventory, made during William IV's reign in 1832, includes the new buildings on the estate, constructed to meet his needs and those of Queen Adelaide. Guest facilities were increased by only 7 beds but upper servants by 31 beds, and under-servants' beds almost doubled in number to 111.

Though many Royal Household staff accompanied George when he came to the Pavilion, only a small establishment remained in Brighton on a permanent basis. In 1823 accounts list the following staff from the Lord Chamberlain's Department at the Brighton establishment: Steward and Comptroller of the House Establishment, housekeeper, ten housemaids, Chaplain, Surgeon, Copyist of Music and Keeper of Musical Instruments and Books, *Tapassier* [sic], who cared for the furniture and furnishings. From the Lord Steward's Department are listed: Yeoman of the Cellar, Coffee Room Woman, Baker, Watchman, Porters, Errand Man, Gardener and Under Gardener.

Sir William Knighton, former physician to the King, held a very powerful position in the royal inner circle as Keeper of the Privy Purse, having also absorbed the duties of the post of Private Secretary. He occupied apartments on the first floor of the Pavilion (over the King's private apartments) within the new north end which housed the King's personal servants and advisers. From here he had direct access to the King without venturing into public areas, and use of a private drawing room adjacent to his bedroom. Broadly speaking, the Lord Chamberlain's staff had their accommodation allocated at the north end, above or near the King's apartments. The personnel from the Lord Steward's section were located to the south of the Entrance Hall in the area of the kitchens, offices and courtyard. The Lord Steward inhabited premises in an adjacent building known as Shergold's House.

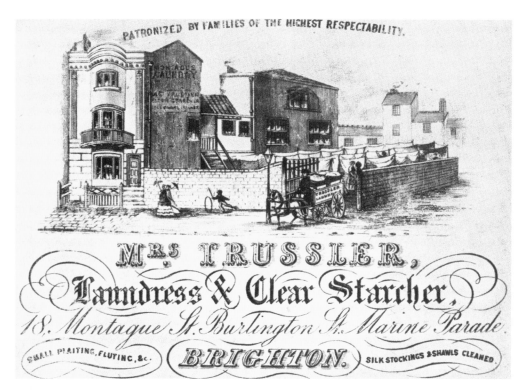

PATRONIZED BY FAMILIES OF THE HIGHEST RESPECTABILITY.

MRS TRUSSLER,

Laundress & Clear Starcher,

18. Montague St. Burlington St. Marine Parade.

SMALL PLAITING, FLUTING, &c.   BRIGHTON.   SILK STOCKINGS & SHAWLS CLEANED.

6. A trade card for Mrs Trussler, laundress and clear starcher, 1870s. The illustration shows her extensive premises in Brighton, for washing, drying, starching and ironing. In 1824 there were ninety-two laundry establishments in Brighton.

The Lord Chamberlain's Department

The Lord Chamberlain's Department was responsible for the public life of the King, for example ceremonies, both religious and secular; entertainments, music and the arts; hunting and so on; as well as the King's bedchamber and personal needs. It was the largest department, with 'above stairs' staff of some 450 which included housekeepers, housemaids, footmen, pages, ushers, the apothecaries, physicians and surgeons to the Household.[121]

Most important to the day-to-day functioning of the Royal Pavilion were the staff who cared for the palace itself and those who cared for the King on his visits and his guests.

The housekeeper

Each royal palace had its own housekeeper, resident in the building (or in the town, depending on accommodation available), who was responsible for the housemaids. In 1817 Sarah Whittle was appointed housekeeper at the Pavilion, succeeding Miss White, who moved to the Prince Regent's cottage at Windsor.

It was the housekeeper's responsibility to manage day-to-day cleaning and oversee repairs to the interior and its furnishings. Whilst the Prince was in residence, she would engage additional staff to manage the cleaning. From October 1818 to April 1819 the Prince spent long periods in Brighton and consequently Mrs Whittle engaged ten extra

7. A section from Mrs Lovatt's notebook, Memorandoms.

Mrs Lovatt was the Pavilion's permanent housekeeper during Queen Victoria's period of residency. These notes record tasks undertaken prior to the Queen's first visit in October 1837: carpets sent to be cleaned and sheared, wallpapers, lamps and gilding cleaned and cabinet panels resilked.

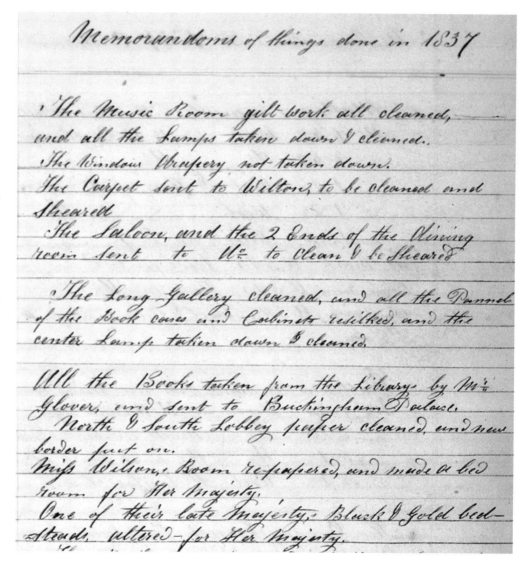

charwomen,[122] each paid 2 shillings per day. She would also be responsible for the laundry, which, given the inadequate facilities for washing and outdoor drying on site, was sent out to laundresses in the town. No provision had been made in Nash's layout of the servants' areas for laundry facilities for the King, his guests or the Household.

The range of the housekeeper's duties is indicated in the *Memorandoms* [*sic*] book, the notebook of Mrs Whittle's successor, Mrs Lovatt, who kept records of the preparations made in the Pavilion for the young Queen Victoria's visits. Mrs Lovatt's *Memorandoms* book spans the years from 1837 to 1845. (fig.7) Queen Victoria's visits were infrequent and of short duration; consequently for a large part of the year the Pavilion remained unused. If the monarch was not in residence, the housekeeper's duties included showing authorised visitors around the Pavilion. Permission had to be sought from the Lord Steward or the Lord Chamberlain, who would then authorise the housekeeper to admit the guests to the public rooms on the ground and first floor. A tip

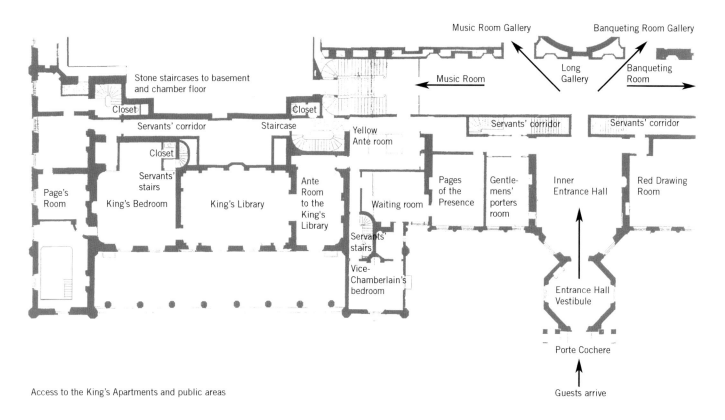

Access to the King's Apartments and public areas

was in order. No less than one gold piece (25 francs) was appropriate in the view of the Comte de la Garde, visiting in the Pavilion in 1834.[123]

Reflecting the directive of financial stringency during Queen Victoria's period of residency, Mrs Lovatt noted the furniture and linens that were cut down and remade to meet the needs of the new Queen. Beds were altered, mattresses remade and old carpets cut down and relaid. Two press beds, formerly used by the King's footmen, were converted into wardrobes, and furniture was moved around. As in earlier decades, the interior was cleaned and prepared in anticipation of a royal visit, and lists were drawn up indicating who would occupy which rooms on the estate.[124]

8. Serving the King, ground plan of the area from the Entrance Hall to the King's private apartments showing how guests, arriving at the porte cochère, *accessed both public and private rooms.*

Pages of the Backstairs

The Pages of the Backstairs provided personal and intimate services to the monarch, and consequently were party to many private and personal conversations. Thomas Batchelor (page to George IV in 1828) revealed intimate details of the King's last months of illness to Charles Greville (Clerk to the Privy Council and a prolific diarist), as well as gossip about Lady Conyngham and her greedy nature. Batchelor, a trusted servant, was privy to the King's indiscretions and outbursts, and clearly enjoyed this privilege, passing on all the latest court rumours and scandal.

Greville also describes the influence and greed of William Robinson Holmes, First Page of the Backstairs (and the most senior), who occupied a bedroom in the north end of the Royal Pavilion, above the King's apartments:

9. The north end of the Pavilion, *from the cross-section in Nash's* Views *(detail), showing the area behind the Lincoln organ in the Music Room. On the ground floor, above the Band Room (to the left of the organ and furnished with shelves for music) and in the attic, were rooms used by the King's personal servants.*

Organ.

> The first of his pages, William Holmes, had for some time been prevented by ill health from attending him. Holmes had been with him from a boy, and was also a great favourite; by appointments and perquisites he had as much as £12,000 or £14,000 a year, but he had spent so much in all sorts of debauchery and living like a gentleman that he was nearly ruined. There seems to have been no end to the *tracasseries* between these men [the Pages of the Backstairs]; their anxiety to get what they could out of the King's wardrobe in the last weeks, and their dishonesty in the matter, were excessive, all which he told me in great detail.[125]

In 1814 two pages accompanied the Prince Regent on a visit to Belvoir Castle and Buckden Palace, the residence of the Bishop of Lincoln. One, Claudius du Pasquier, the Prince's confidant, slept close by in the Prince's dressing room, and a press bed was made available for this purpose. A brace of pistols was placed on a table near the Prince's bed for protection. The two pages also served the Prince at dinner at Buckden Palace. They stood behind his chair, served and cleared, acting as intermediaries between the Prince and the Bishop's servants.

In October 1824 the King's six pages were William Robinson Holmes, Benjamin Lucas, Thomas Stevens, John Whiting, Hugh Kinnaird and Augustus Gerding. The six pages were graded 'first' to 'sixth', reflecting status and salary, the 'first' being paid £290 per annum, the 'sixth' £240. Kinnaird, Holmes and Whiting occupied the three pages' bedrooms over the King's apartments, and the attic bedrooms (in the small domes) were probably used by the other pages. (fig.9) Each of the pages' bedrooms was amply furnished with tent bed, dressing table, chests of drawers, stove, bidet, table and chairs.[126]

Baths were provided for the pages (and other household staff) at the Royal Baths at 38 Old Steine. In the quarter ending 5 April 1825 Kinnaird received five warm baths (at a cost of 17s. 6d.); Whiting had only two.

Running north–south on the ground floor was a partially concealed servants' corridor which linked the kitchens and domestic offices to the south with the King's new apartments at the north end, and his guest apartments on the first floor. (fig.11) An extensive system of bells linked the King's apartments to his pages (located adjacent to him in the north end) and to his Private Secretary. In turn bells linked the pages' rooms with the servants' hall and apartments in the south end. All the new buildings to the south were linked, as well as the new public rooms.

Pages of the Presence

Pages of the Presence (eight in all) were ordered into two classes, and within each class categorised as 'first' to 'fourth'. For example, the First Page of the Presence received £260 per annum, whereas the Fourth Page of the Presence of the Second Class received £140. The pages were invariably young men of good birth, who joined the

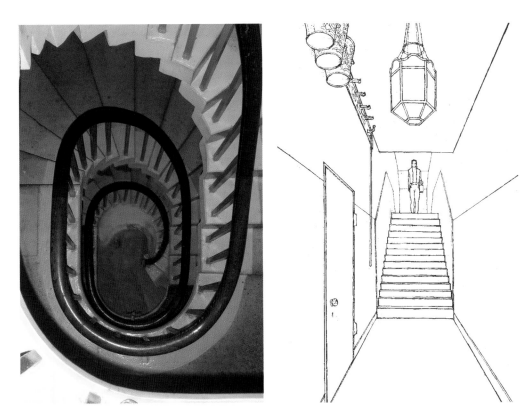

10. (right) Spiral servants' staircase at the north end, linking the pages' rooms to the King's apartments and the basement.

11. (far right) The servants' ground-floor corridor. Drawing reconstructing the original concealed north–south servants' corridor where the stairs ascended over the visitors' entrance to the Long Gallery from the Entrance Hall. The stairs descended on the far side (north) providing the servants with direct access to the basement and the north end of the Pavilion. This allowed servants to move through the building without being seen by the King and his guests.

Royal Household to learn the duties of court life and to seek promotion through the ranks of this exclusive hierarchy.

Duties of the Pages of the Presence included attending to guests and liaising with the Pages of the Backstairs regarding the King's wishes or movements. They worked in rotation, one month on, one month off; when on duty they dined in the Steward's Room. When off duty they received compensation for lodgings and board wages.

To these posts were attached certain perquisites, sometimes supplemented by gifts. A Page of the Presence in the 1780s received £220 per annum, as well as supplies of linen for the home, coal, wood, leftover meals and two tallow candles a night, plus two bottles of wine on every royal birthday, and the anniversary of the Accession, the Coronation and New Year's Day. Mrs Papendiek, the daughter of one of Queen Charlotte's German pages, was herself part of the Royal Household and married to a page. She recalled that in 1783:

> two of our rooms were furnished by her Majesty, and a case of plate was also sent by her, which contained cruets, salt-cellars, candlesticks, and spoons of different sizes, silver forks not being then used. From the Queen came also six large and six small knives and forks, to which mamma added six more of each, and a carving knife and fork.[127]

In addition to the gifts and regular perquisites of candles, tablecloths, napkins, fuel and pitcher wine, relevant members of the Lord Chamberlain's Department were allowed to purchase any redundant furniture or furnishings following the refurbishment of royal apartments. When the Princess Royal decided upon a refurbishment of her rooms and closet at the Upper Lodge, Windsor, the Papendieks sent a man to measure a sofa, twelve chairs, tables, curtains and so on and purchased them (cleaned and in good order) for £25 – as Mrs Papendiek noted, 'a very fair-priced bargain'.[128] The Princess also sent them a worktable as a gift for their new home.

Mrs Papendiek recalled that in the late 1780s the appointment of bedchamber woman to the Queen was worth £300 per annum and the perquisites – including a share of the court clothes – amounted to an additional £200 per annum. In times of war, when there was an embargo on importing foreign lace, the loss would be made up by an extra allowance of £100 per annum, given to the six bedchamber women.[129]

Chairmen and sedan chairs

Though transport was the responsibility of the Master of the Horse, the chairmen formed part of the Lord Chamberlain's Department. The Chair Entrance in the Pavilion was suitably sited near the main entrance. Here guests or members of the Royal Family could arrive or depart in a sedan chair, similar to the one described in the Pavilion 1828 inventory: 'A sedan chair in black leather, lined with drab cloth, squab seat and silk curtains'. The sedan, a more common means of transport in the late eighteenth century than in the Regency period, provided an opportunity for a display of wealth and rank. When the Duchess of Devonshire or the Duchess of Northumberland went out in a sedan chair, they were preceded by eight footmen in the most splendid liveries, who at night would light the way through the dimly illuminated streets.

William Squire and Samuel Bedford were employed as chairmen by the Prince Regent in 1818 for thirty-five days during January and early February, whilst the Regent was resident in Brighton. Each chairman was paid 10 shillings a day, plus 5 shillings per day board wages, and 1s. 6d. per night for lodgings. The bill for both men, including transport to London for five weeks' work, was £56 9s. The chairmen do not appear on lists of the Lord Chamberlain's permanent establishment, so presumably they were hired as needed over the period 1815–1827.

Though the sedan chair was an old-fashioned means of transport, a curious variant with wheels was developed in Brighton and launched in 1816. It was apparently the creation of John Butcher, a carpenter who was injured whilst working on the construction of the Royal Stables and could not continue with that physically demanding trade. Fixed on four wheels, the chair was drawn by hand in the same manner as Bath chairs, while an assistant (when the person being conveyed was heavy) pushed from behind. It became a favourite form of transport amongst visiting nobility, and a second was soon constructed. These vehicles were extensively patronised by the Prince of Wales and his companions. It is said that as a result of being used by them on special occasions on a midnight 'lark', they received the name of 'fly-by-nights' (or flys), and soon superseded sedan chairs (see p. 42, fig.2). The rates for flys (and sedan chairs) were strictly regulated by the Town Commissioners; a two-hour journey cost 2s. 6d.

The Lord Steward's Department

12. Castle Square,
(The south end of the
Pavilion), from Album
de Brighton, *1838,*
showing the servants'
quarters, the Clock
Tower, and the South
Gate House added by
William IV. All were
demolished in the
latter part of the
nineteenth century.

In the 1820s the Lord Steward's Department was headed by the Marquis of Conyngham, the husband of the King's last mistress. In addition to overseeing the kitchen and garden staff, this department was responsible for the provision of foodstuffs and household materials (for example oil, wax and tallow candles, charcoal, ironmongery and earthenware) as well as incidentals such as funeral expenses and Christmas boxes for the staff. It dealt with minor joinery and craft labour as relevant to the department's role in the Household.

The most important officer below the Lord Steward was the Secretary to the Board of Green Cloth, a post created in 1813 and occupied by Timothy Brent until 1830. Brent dealt with all the day-to-day issues and needs of the Lord Steward's Department. His office was strategically located near the kitchens and ancillary rooms, to the south of the Pavilion entrance. (fig.14)

Management of the kitchens

Brent had overall responsibility for the accounts and expenditure, staff, tradesmen and operational issues. Reporting to him were a series of small departments, the largest of which was the Kitchen Offices, managed by the Clerk Comptroller. This officer was responsible for checking menus, ordering provisions and managing the Clerk of the Kitchen, the cooks, yeomen and more menial staff such as scourers and porters. The menus were drawn up by the chief or master cooks, who were responsible for the care and maintenance of all the kitchen equipment and for the provision of ingredients to the other cooks. The ordering of foodstuffs, and their verification and consumption, were carefully recorded in ledgers. The Clerk Comptroller was supported by three clerks and an under-clerk, who could be promoted through the ranks from a lowly messenger through the clerk on £15 2s. 6d. per annum to the Clerk Comptroller on £380 25s. per annum.

13. Servants' corridor. The corridors linking servants' areas to the King's apartments or public rooms were lined with Dutch glazed tiles.

In 1823 Armand Vilmet was Master Cook. He prepared menus and managed the staff of cooks, roasting cooks, apprentices, bakers, pastry chefs and so on. When the King was resident the skeleton staff permanently housed at Brighton were augmented by other members of the kitchen staff – master cooks, yeomen of the confectionery, pastry cooks and so on – who moved with the court as required and received appropriate reimbursement whilst resident at Brighton.

There were many opportunities for staff in the Lord Steward's Department to defraud their employer and increase their incomes with unscrupulous and dishonest practices. In regulations drawn up for the Board of Green Cloth in 1822, rules governing the purchase of goods were clearly defined to avoid any abuse or theft by staff or tradesmen. The Clerk of the Coalyard, responsible for the accounts for coals, charcoal, billets (small logs), faggots (bundles of sticks) and brushes, required the yeoman in that office to attend the delivery of coal at the dock and check the weight of deliveries for the Royal Household.

The Clerk of the Kitchen daily recorded all foodstuff consumed and was instructed to ensure that no staff (or himself) received presents or gratuities. No outsiders, friends or relatives could, without authorisation, attend meals in the servants' hall. Very careful records were kept of wine and beer served to the King and to the Household.

The Ewry, the section responsible for all table linen in royal palaces, was managed by the Principal Table Decker. He had to keep an accurate account of linen used by the monarch and given out to members of the Royal Household (where entitled to this privilege). He was instructed to 'be very careful that the same number of Cloths and Napkins is returned to the Ewry when foul, as was delivered out when Clean'.[130] Each section – whether the Wine and Beer Cellar, Coalyard, Ewry, Confectionery, Silver Pantry or Pastry – had a clerk responsible for checking and certifying orders and ensuring there was little opportunity for misappropriation or abuse of the system.

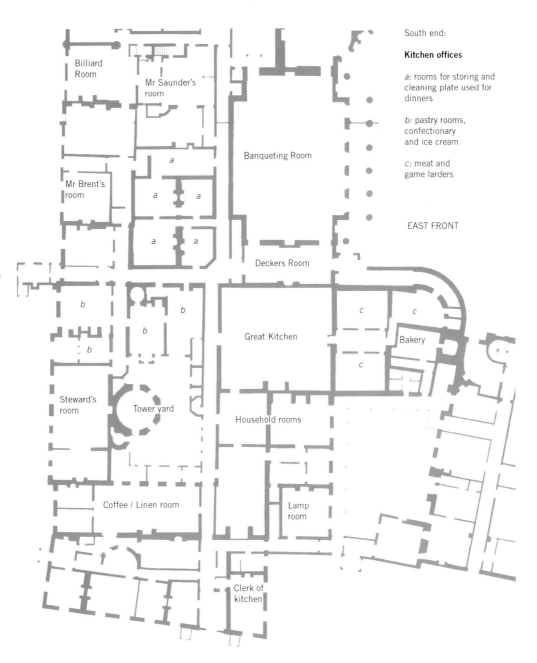

14. Plan of the kitchens and ancillary rooms. *Originally all access to the Table Deckers' Room and Banqueting Room was via the north–south spinal servants' corridor, which led to food-preparation areas as well as the plate rooms. The two existing doors from the Great Kitchen to the Table Deckers' Room were post-1850 alterations, inserted to facilitate public flow.*

South end:

Kitchen offices

a: rooms for storing and cleaning plate used for dinners

b: pastry rooms, confectionary and ice cream

c: meat and game larders

EAST FRONT

Billiard Room

Mr Saunder's room

Mr Brent's room

Banqueting Room

Deckers Room

Great Kitchen

Bakery

Steward's room

Tower yard

Household rooms

Coffee / Linen room

Lamp room

Clerk of kitchen

John Redifer, Yeoman of the Cellar, who was resident in Brighton, cared for the quantities of wine and ale stored in the cellars beneath the Banqueting Room. He attended at dinners and luncheons. He reported to James Christie, Gentleman of the Wine and Beer Cellar, who accompanied the King during his residency in Brighton, where he had a permanent office close to the housekeeper's apartments. Christie's duties included selecting and purchasing wines for the royal establishment and attending at dinner to answer any questions regarding the wines. It was essential for him to be an expert judge of foreign wines, and to be well acquainted with the best markets and vendors.

The Lord Steward's Department was also responsible for the care and maintenance of the gardens and greenhouses. John Furner, the gardener, and Robert Furner, the under-gardener (possibly John's son), were part of the Household permanently resident in Brighton, and received annual wages of £100 and £46 per annum respectively. In the busy periods extra labourers were hired on a weekly basis to manage the gardens, paths, greenhouses, ice houses and stables.

Vegetables and herbs were cultivated in the grounds of the Pavilion, but given the acreage, the provision would have been woefully inadequate. The Pavilion was regularly provided with fruit and vegetables from the gardens of the London palaces, notably Hampton Court, Kew and Kensington, whose produce was designated primarily for the King's table. The purpose of all the royal gardens was both to serve as pleasure grounds and to produce fruit and vegetables for royal consumption. There were, according to the accounts, some greenhouses in the Pavilion Gardens, and tobacco was supplied to fumigate and kill the pests.

Security

Given the lack of any municipal police force at this period and the vulnerable position of the Royal Pavilion in the centre of Brighton, it was the responsibility of the resident infantry regiment to protect the perimeter of the estate when the King was in residence. (fig.16) Night porters and night watchmen protected the interior of the palace at night. The night porters remained within the building to prevent theft and ensure tranquillity; the watchmen undertook similar roles and patrolled by the entrances. Both groups worked from nine at night until eight in the morning, receiving substantial victuals before going on duty, which they were allowed to take home after work. Joshua Townsend was the resident watchman at the Royal Pavilion, receiving an annual salary of £76.

15. (right) The Prince of Wales's Phaeton, by George Stubbs, 1793. On the left, stands Samuel Thomas, the Prince's State coachman, dressed in full livery of a scarlet coat with gold trim and a black cocked hat with gold tassels. He holds one of the magnificent dark bays, bred and trained as carriage horses. The blinkers on the bridles are decorated with the Prince of Wales's feathers. The Prince, a connoisseur of horses as well as of art, assembled an exceptional collection of Stubbs's pictures. The Royal Collection © 2003 Her Majesty Queen Elizabeth II.

The Master of the Horse's Department

As the third senior officer at court, the Master of the Horse gave place only to the Lord Chamberlain and Lord Steward. In 1823 the Duke of Dorset was Master and presided over all matters pertaining to the Royal Stables, whether wagons or coaches for transport or racehorses, hunters and saddle horses used for pleasure. He commanded the equerries, footmen, Pages of Honour, grooms, coachmen, farriers, smiths and all other related tradesmen employed by the King, for example coach makers and repairers. He alone had the right to make use of the King's horses (and staff) and always accompanied the King in ceremonial processions.

Equerries

The post of Chief Equerry and Clerk-Marshall, second in importance to the Master of the Horse, received a salary of £1,000 per annum. The Chief Equerry, in conjunction with four equerries (receiving £750 each per annum), waited on the King in rotation, remaining in attendance for twenty-eight days. The equerries passed all orders from the King to the Clerk of the Stables, and when on duty dined at the monarch's table.

One of the duties of the equerries was to train the young pages in horsemanship. The Pages of Honour were young boys of noble birth who served in the Household as pages until they reached the age of sixteen-and-a-half, when they had to resign. Pages of Honour could be appointed as young as nine, as was the case with Lord Kilmarnock, page to William IV, although usually they seem to have been aged about twelve to thirteen.

These appointments, of which there were four, were anxiously sought after by members of the aristocracy as they would invariably lead to a commission in one of the Household regiments or a more senior post in the Household itself. Although patronage for the pages was vested in the Master of the Horse, it was not uncommon for the sovereign to select his own. For example, Lord Francis Nathaniel Conyngham (the son of Lady Conyngham, the King's mistress) was a page to the Prince Regent until 1814. He progressed in 1820 to the post of First Groom of the Chamber and Master of Robes, finally achieving the status of Lord Chamberlain under William IV and Queen Victoria.

Footmen

In the sixteenth century (and earlier) footmen attended their aristocratic or royal employers when on horseback or travelling by sedan chair or carriage. They would run by the side of the carriage, bearing lamps at night. By the eighteenth century their duties had been transformed into those primarily of indoor servants, though in the Royal Household structure they still remained under the department of the Master of the Horse.

During George IV's reign there were eighteen footmen in total, led by the First Footman who received a salary of £132 per annum. Although no longer fashionable in society, powdered wigs remained *de rigueur* for liveried footmen, who received a special allowance of £6 15s. 6d. for 'hair-powder, bag and silk stockings'[131] per year, as well as 'bread and beer money' amounting to £13 6s. 8d. per annum. The Marquis of Conyngham tried to abolish this last perquisite in 1826, but after protests by all the royal footmen he was forced to capitulate, compromising by reducing the annual sum to £12, though footmen in the future would not receive this 'perk'.

One duty of the footmen was to accompany the Prince in his travels. When he stayed a night at Buckden Palace he was accompanied by four footmen and two pages. Whilst travelling, a footman was allowed 6 shillings a day for refreshments, whether it was a long or short journey. For more senior and experienced footmen, duties included attending at court, waiting on members of the Royal Family, directing guests and attending at meals and social events.

The footmen received new liveries twice a year, at Midsummer and at Christmas; old livery became their property once replaced. State liveries cost £120 each to make and were the footmen's perquisites once new ones were provided. The gold alone in the suits (when melted down) was worth more than £10. Although the footmen's livery (dress suits for their various different duties) was provided by the Royal Household, the cleaning and maintenance of the uniforms was their responsibility, as was the purchase of polish and brushes for cleaning their boots.

In his own establishment the Master of the Horse had the privilege of using four footmen paid for from the Civil List. This provided a training ground for new entrants, and once experienced they could be transferred to more significant duties in a royal residence. Here duties included attending to the ladies and gentlemen of the court, as well as the King. An additional benefit of these posts was the possibility of promotion to Page of the Presence in the Lord Chamberlain's Department, an appointment that received twice the salary of a footman.

The stables

16. The Stables Front towards Church Street, *from Nash's* Views (detail). *The entire perimeter of the Royal Pavilion Estate was protected by the military, seen here on duty flanking the north entrance to the stables complex. Sentry boxes were provided on the eastern front, facing the Steine.*

The more menial staff – the coachmen, grooms, stable boys and 'helpers' – mostly lived in modest lodgings in the stable complex, which also housed the riding and carriage horses. They were provided with old half-tester or iron bedsteads and bedding (redundant from the Pavilion and remade for their use), common chamber pots and strong ash chairs. The grooms had a hall, separate from the coachmen's hall (which would have been used by coachmen bringing guests to the Pavilion as well as George's own staff). The coachmen and regular grooms were provided with liveries and, subject to good behaviour, there were opportunities for promotion from helper to groom and to coachman.

The care of the Riding House, however, fell to the gardeners (part of the Lord Steward's Department), who were responsible for providing sawdust for the extensive floor measuring 185 ft by 85 ft (56 x 30 m). Bagged in sacks, the sawdust was transported in wagons from a supplier east of Chichester in West Sussex. After much use, the sawdust became compacted and extra labourers were employed to fork up the floor covering. The annual bill for caring for the Riding House was £10. It was also the responsibility of the gardener John Furner to provide straw for the ice house, and supply, repair and sharpen ice hooks and necessary equipment.

The Royal Household at work

The winter season in the Pavilion

The King spent the winter season, including Christmas and the New Year, in Brighton in both 1822 and 1823. On these occasions he spent several months in the Pavilion, broken by short trips to London for government business.[132]

During his stay at the Pavilion in 1822 members of his family, friends and guests came to Brighton to enjoy the winter season of dinners, balls and concerts. The King arrived on a wet, windy and unpleasant day in late October and was greeted by the regiments of the 7th Fusiliers and the 1st Life Guards, lining the approach road to the Pavilion. Two military bands played to welcome him.

The King was suffering from gout but this did not prevent the regular annual balls from taking place. Nor did his ill-health stop his guests from enjoying his hospitality. In early February he held a Privy Council in the Pavilion, followed by a splendid banquet with the King's band in attendance. The Lord Steward presided at the dinner as the King was unwell and confined to his private apartments.

Preparations for a royal visit

A key duty of the Lord Chamberlain's Department was the preparation and cleaning of the Pavilion's interior prior to, and following, the King's visits. In the weeks before the King's return to Brighton in October 1822, the *Brighton Gazette* noted activity in the Pavilion and the arrival of the Life Guards to attend on the monarch. Workmen were employed on the gasometer 'in making preparations for the supply of the Palace with gas'.[133] The previous week the same paper commented 'that the greatest bustle prevailed amongst the domestics generally in preparing for His Majesty's arrival'.[134]

When not in use, the main rooms were always 'put to bed' by staff under the guidance of the housekeeper. Henry Saunders, *tapissier*, was responsible for the care, arrangement and movement of furniture within the Pavilion, organising activities (and tradesmen) from a small office south of the Entrance Hall. When not in use all the furniture, chandeliers, curtains, lamps and so on were covered and protected by specially made brown Holland cloth covers. Carpets, druggets and curtains were removed for cleaning and furniture and fittings repaired as needed.[135] Bed linen, mattresses, pillows and blankets were checked, repaired and cleaned. Skylights were cleaned and broken glass replaced. Ceilings, wallpapers and woodwork were carefully cleaned to remove the effects of smoke from the oil lamps, chandeliers and candelabra.

The highly decorative painted, carved and gilt surfaces, extensive canvases and hand-painted or block-printed wallpapers needed regular maintenance and repair. Wallpapers – such as the 'India' papers (eighteenth-century Chinese hand-painted papers) and Robert Jones's block-printed 'dragon' papers – were cleaned by first clearing the surface of dust and then wiping it with pieces of stale bread in light, downward movements.

All linen and blankets, as well as muslin roller blinds, were marked to ensure that they were not mislaid and were reinstated correctly following cleaning. This was essential given the vast quantity of washing and cleaning done during and after the King's visits. For example, one quarterly account for washing linen listed 1,548 muslin blinds and 740 dozen and 11 towels. Even when the towels (some 8,891) were one short of 741 dozen, this discrepancy was noted – every single item was counted and recorded in the accounts.[136]

How such a quantity of linen was washed and dried with the rudimentary facilities of the early nineteenth century is hard to conceive. Prince Pückler-Muskau, whilst on his visit to Brighton in 1827, made a comment on a particular local method of drying linen which he considered worth imitating: 'It is laid in a sort of Wardrobe lined with tin, and kept at an equal heat by means of Steam.'[137] This is reminiscent of both the hot closets in the Great Kitchen, which were heated by steam from the kitchen boiler, and a 'very large Strong Drying Closet' supplied to the Pavilion in 1817.[138] William IV, in extending the servants' premises in the early 1830s, made some provision for linen sorting and drying areas in the new South Gate.

The annual servants' balls held in January required elaborate preparations. In 1824 a supper and a ball, with music provided by the King's own private band, was held in the Pavilion at the invitation of the Lord Steward, Lord Conyngham. The jobbing account of Thomas Saunders for the quarter ended April 1824 records the various preparations (and reparations) undertaken for Christmas and New Year festivities: 'Taking up Music Room Carpet, moving all the furniture of Do [ditto] and preparing for a Ball, uncovering the whole of the furniture in the Apts dusting cleaning and putting up clean curtains and recovering the same up again twice.' It also details 'preparing the rooms for 2 Balls for the Servants and putting the rooms in Order again'.

The account continues:

> taking down and putting up Beds … sorting and examining moving and replacing the
> Furniture again, examining cleaning and putting the Books away, Dusting and cleaning
> Draperies Lamps China Ornaments Chimney Ornaments furniture &c &c taking down and
> covering the same up taking up the Carpets Druggets Oil Cloths &c and taking down
> Beds window Curtain &c &c throughout the whole of the Pavilion … Beating the Music
> Room carpet.[139]

The King stayed only for December and January, leaving on 12 February 1824. A six-week period of residency generated considerable employment (some 437 days) for local labourers.

The Axminster hand-knotted carpets were beaten, cleaned or sheared, presumably depending on their condition. Despite the use of a drugget (a felt covering for protection) in the Banqueting Room, wax from candelabra, grease, oil, food and wine stains would inflict regular damage on the thick wool-pile carpets. Carpets were cleaned with tea leaves or, in the case of bad oil or grease stains, with a mixture of eggs, Fuller's Earth (a highly absorbent soft clay) and paste. The mixture was applied by hand and dried with a hot iron, causing the oils to be drawn out and absorbed.

Alternatively, as recorded in the Pavilion housekeeper's *Memorandoms* book, the Axminster carpets might be sent to Wilton to be cleaned and sheared. The process of shearing by hand, undertaken at the factory, refreshed the colour and general appearance of the tufted carpet by removing the dirty, matted top layer. A fragment of the original Music Room carpet has survived, having been cut up to fit the Chinese Luncheon Room in Buckingham Palace in the early 1850s. This fragment has no pile, presumably having been sheared several times in its long lifetime.

Stone or marble floors were cleaned with Fuller's Earth mixed with fine pipe clay and a soapy fluid. Oil (floor) cloths, laid in the Entrance Hall, corridors and servants' areas, were swept and wiped with a damp cloth, then wet with milk and polished with a dry cloth until bright.

The numerous clocks throughout the Pavilion had to be regularly serviced and wound up before a royal visit. This was the responsibility of Edward Buckwell, clock repairer and winder, and the royal clock maker, Benjamin Vulliamy.

The provision of food and materials

To cope with the busy Christmas and New Year period of 1822/3, the Lord Steward employed, in additional to the permanent establishment, extra staff including lamplighters, kitchen and linen staff, coal porters and an extra watchman. These were retained through to April 1823 when the King returned to London.

The King spent the first three-and-a-half months of 1823 at the Pavilion, returning in early December that year and remaining until 12 February 1824. The Lord Steward's accounts for 1823 reflect the pattern of the King's residence during the first and final quarters. During the last three weeks of December 1823 numerous members of court and society converged on Brighton to attend His Majesty, including the Duke of York, the Duke and Duchess of Clarence, the Duke of Wellington and Count Lieven, all of whom dined with the King at the Pavilion. In a three-and-a-half-week period of residence, some £300 was expended on butter, eggs and cheese; £500 on meat, sausages and bacon; £300 on poultry; £180 on fish and oysters; and over £700 on groceries, hams and tongue. Brown bread was specially imported from Hanover and delivered into the personal care of the King's Page of the Backstairs, Augustus Gerding, at Brighton.[140]

To quench the thirst of the King and his guests during this same short period, some 3,456 gallons of stout, 234 gallons of mild, 2,565 gallons of ales and 981 gallons of table ale were delivered to Brighton, as well as boxes of teas (mixed, Souchong, Hysan) and raw mocha coffee. The most expensive tea was 'Finest Hysan at 14/- a pound'.[141]

Milk and cream were supplied by Charles Root, who also provided a cow for fresh milk at a weekly rental of £2 12s. 6d. A cow could also be rented at a daily rate of

17. The Great Kitchen, *from Nash's Views (detail). Roasting cooks stoke the fire and prepare the meat and poultry for the spit.*

7s. 6d. as needed to allow for extra regular supplies, and to make it possible to prepare syllabub in the recommended way, with fresh, warm milk direct from the cow.

Quality wines were only consumed by the wealthy, while the middle classes drank port, sherry, Madeira and gin, as well as ale. Punches were popular and were generally made of alcohol (brandy or rum) combined with fruit juice and green tea or milk. Connoisseurs (including the Prince Regent) were happy to pay a considerable price for a rare wine. At the sale of the Duke of Queensbury's effects in 1811, bottles of Tokay were sold for £7 each. When in 1817 the cellars of Alexander Davison were sold to the highest bidders, the prices were unusually high. Three dozen bottles of red Madeira, bottled in 1801, were knocked down at 18 guineas per dozen – sold, it was supposed, to a distinguished member of the Royal Family.[142]

Lighting the main rooms of the Royal Pavilion incurred significant costs in terms of fuel and labour as George tended to stay in Brighton during the dark winter months. In 1823 the annual bill (covering approximately four months of residency) for oil for lamps was £940, and for wax and tallow candles approximately £1,100, making a total well in excess of £2,000. The Pavilion was renowned for being overheated through open fires and its under-floor hot-air system. The total bill for coals and wood exceeded £1,000. Expenditure on fuels for heating, lighting and cooking over a period of four-and-a-half months of royal occupancy totalled some £3,300.

5 Ill-health and remedies

'My old enemy … the gout'[143]

1. (left) Taking an Emetic, *c. 1804. Many of the remedies available in the Regency period reflected the ancient belief that expelling bad humours and restoring the balance of the four humours would reinstate good health. Clearing the system with induced vomiting was a popular remedy. Here the cat seems to be retching in sympathy*

It is possible that the Prince's fluctuating health was one reason for his decision to construct a private home in Brighton in 1787. Certainly, in later years, it determined the new layout of the north end of Nash's Pavilion, which housed the King's new apartments and elaborate therapeutic bathing facilities. Since the early 1780s the Prince had been advised by his physicians to avail himself of these sea treatments and Brighton's good climate. From a young age he had suffered from a range of maladies including glandular inflammations, rheumatism, abdominal colic, bowel inflammations, chest problems, constipation, fevers and the gout.

Brighton's health-giving sea-water remedies were made famous by Dr Richard Russell, a physician from nearby Lewes. Since 1750 Dr Russell had successfully promoted the beneficial effects of sea water as a cure for a variety of complaints including glandular disorders, deafness, ulcers and bowel inflammations. He prescribed doses of sea water, drunk in combination with other potions such as crushed woodlice, viper's flesh, milk and crabs' eyes, or applied topically to areas of the body. An essential part of his treatment was sea bathing, which involved total body immersion – dipping, not swimming in the modern sense. He observed that the place should be clean and neat with the water 'as highly loaded with sea salt, and other riches of the ocean as possible'.[144] The sea shore should be sandy and flat, 'for the convenience of going into the sea in a bathing chariot'. The shore should also be bound by cliffs and downs providing the opportunity for healthy horseback riding after the therapeutic dip. The location for the treatments was crucial, and Brighton met most of his requirements, though the sea shore was not sandy and flat.

Dr Russell was not alone in advocating the benefits of the healthy environment and climate of Brighton. Dr Relhan, in 1761, asserted that Brighton's chalky ground 'has little or no perspiration' and that the town was 'free from the insalutary vapour of stagnant water, distant from the noxious steams of perspiring trees, and every other cause aiding to produce a damp, putrid atmosphere'.[145]

In a letter from Brighton to his mother in December 1817 the Prince described the 'pot-pourri' of complaints that had incapacitated him for several weeks:

> I do not know under what denomination to class the attack, or by what name regularly to define it & call it, for it seems to me to have been a sort of mishmash, Solomongrundy, Olla podrida kind of a business in itself that is quite anomalous; a good deal of rheumatism, as much of cold, with a little touch of bile to boot, not a very pleasant mixture on the whole, & compos'd of as unpleasant ingredients, as can be well thought of or imagin'd.[146]

2. A VOLUPTUARY under the horrors of Digestion, *by James Gillray, 1792. The Prince of Wales, barely 30, slumps in a chair, drunk, obese and picking his teeth. Debris of his profligate lifestyle and the consequent effects on his health surround him.*

At this period the causes of gout, a common affliction of the wealthy, were not well understood. An attack would come on very suddenly, preceded by a feeling of listlessness or fever, flatulence or irregular bowels and cramps. The pain in the joints, usually feet or hands, was extreme, and could last a few days or several weeks or months. Invariably severe attacks would affect the digestive system and the heart.

Though it was acknowledged that gout was in part hereditary, the principal causes were considered to be an indolent, sedentary and luxurious lifestyle, poor diet, anxiety and stress and 'immoderate indulgence in acid or vinous liquors'.[147] Claret and port were considered more harmful than Madeira and sherry, being stronger and more acidic.

The Prince's bouts of gout caused extreme pain, affecting his ankles, feet, hands and wrists. His limbs sometimes swelled to twice their normal size, severely affecting his

3. Merlin's Mechanical Chair, *from a design by Morgan and Saunders; illustration from Ackermann's* Repository of Arts ... , *1811, vol.6. Two invalid or 'gouty' chairs were kept in the Pavilion for the Prince's use.*

mobility. A Merlin mechanical or 'gouty' chair was kept close at hand in the Pavilion for his personal use. On a visit in 1816 his daughter, Princess Charlotte, remarked on his high spirits despite his ill-health: 'He wheels himself perfectly in a Merlin Chair & in that sits the whole e.g. [*sic*, evening] with his legs down.'[148]

An illustration of a Merlin chair was published in 1811, in Ackermann's *Repository*, a periodical of fashionable designs.[149] (fig.3) This chair worked with winches and gears and could go forwards or backwards, left or right, by turning the handles on the arms. It was fitted with an adjustable back and footboard. The ground floor of the Pavilion was designed with no changes in floor levels or steps so he could move easily between private and public areas.

BY ROYAL AUTHORITY.

A New way of mounting your Horse in spite of the GOUT!! *Dedicated to all fashionable Equestrians afflicted with that Malady!*

The Prince's ill-health was a frequent subject of gossip and speculation amongst society, both in conversation and correspondence. Lady Sarah Spencer, writing from Althorp to her brother Robert in 1812, conveys the latest news from London about the Prince's gout. On this occasion it was in his right hand and arm: 'his hand swells so that his rings were sawed off t'other day, and the torture is dreadful'.[150] Such was the severity of the attack that he had recourse to a stamp for his signature, being incapable of signing with his hand.

His incapacitating gout and his propensity for being overweight, combined with his passion for horse riding, fired the imagination of caricaturists and satirists. (fig.4) The following satirical (and certainly untrue) description of his special mounting equipment appeared in *The Times* on 25 March 1816 and became the subject of the caricaturist's wit:

> An inclined plane was constructed, rising to about the height of two feet and a half, at the
> upper end of which was a platform. His Royal Highness was placed in a chair on rollers,
> and so moved up the ascent, and placed on the platform, which was then raised by
> screws, high enough to pass the horse under: and finally, his Royal Highness was let gently
> down into the saddle.

4. BY ROYAL AUTHORITY A New way of mounting your Horse in spite of the GOUT!! *An anonymous cartoon based on the* Times *report (25 March 1816). The Prince's gouty feet are heavily bandaged and the saddle is fitted with huge boot-shaped stirrups.*

As a youth, the Prince had been somewhat fleshy and inclined to put on weight. Corsets applied with vigour could reduce his waist by some 6 inches (15 cm). A pair of George's breeches in the Royal Pavilion's collections have a waist measurement of 54 inches (137 cm), suggesting a natural waist of some 60 inches (152 cm). Remarks about his corpulent frame were common. 'Prinny has let loose his belly which now reaches his knees,' gossiped Lord Folkestone to his fellow MP Thomas Creevey.[151] And Sylvester Douglas, Lord Glenbervie, concluded his diary of twenty-five years by musing on the idea of the Prince Regent and Lady Hertford sitting on opposite sofas at some distance from each other. With delight he imagined that if their stays and girdles were cut, 'the elastic protuberance of their confined stomachs set loose would immediately make contact across the room'.[152]

In the 1820s his daily exercise was limited to walks in the enclosed Pavilion Gardens and occasional rides in the covered riding school. In 1821 an underground tunnel, illuminated by day by six glass circular laylights in the lawn, was built directly linking the King's new private apartments with the riding school and stables, providing both much desired privacy and protection from inclement weather. (fig.5,6,7) This tunnel, though not constructed until George was nearly 60, was probably the source of apocryphal stories of various secret tunnels in Brighton, used by the Prince for his nightly trysts. For only a very short period did the tunnel provide concealed access to Marlborough Row, via the stables. It was also used by members of the King's band to reach the Pavilion's Band Room (and Music Room). Additional watchmen were employed to guard the tunnel entrance at the stable end and to allow the members of the band access.

The King's new bathroom

During the late eighteenth century, bath houses, whether for health or hygiene, tended to be located in the grounds of stately homes or, occasionally – as designed in the early 1790s by John Soane for Wimpole Hall in Cambridgeshire – on the ground floor.

Baths or bath houses were undoubtedly a luxury and George IV's new facilities incorporated every piece of fashionable bathing equipment. Sadly, the King's bathroom, which was adjacent to his bedroom with access through a jib door, was demolished in the mid-nineteenth century following the sale of the building to Brighton. The Pavilion inventory,[153] however, records the extensive bathing equipment that had been installed for the King's health and pleasure:

> A plunging bath lined with veined marble 16ft by 10ft and 5ft 6 deep with jointed floor over, 8 veined marble steps, mahogany hand rail, and the tank, pipes, cisterns, boilers, pumps, engines etc. thereto belonging

> A vapour bath in a mahogany frame with brass caps, collars, screws, hoops, sockets, tubes and other fittings – cane bottom and seat – 2 white cloth covers …

5. View of the tunnel, which led from the King's apartments to the stables. Sketched in 1946 by Bryan de Grineau for the Illustrated London News.

6. *The underground tunnel from the Pavilion, opening at basement level, into the area proposed as a tennis court (later built as more stables by William IV). The photograph was taken during the refurbishment of the Dome and Museum complex when the floor of the new Museum Entrance had been completely removed.*

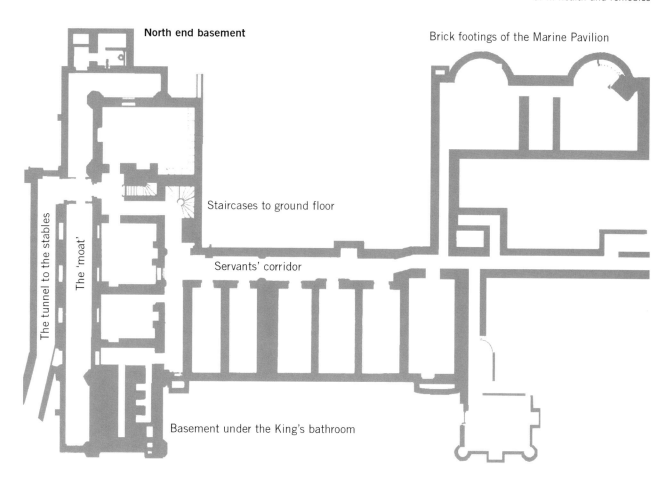

North end basement

Brick footings of the Marine Pavilion

The tunnel to the stables

The 'moat'

Staircases to ground floor

Servants' corridor

Basement under the King's bathroom

7. Plan of the basement beneath the new north end, showing two staircases to access the tunnel to the stables, the cellars and the brick double bow-shaped footing of the original Marine Pavilion.

A large warm bath with mahogany pannelled case and cover, brass pillar standards and rods with 5 linen curtains 7ft 4 by 4ft 1 …

The shower bath with its various fittings …
The douch bath with various falls, cistern, platform, oilskin frame and other fittings

An oval Japanned foot tub with brass side and top handles …

By 1820 the King had long since abandoned his practice of total immersion in the sea. The plunge bath, accessed by eight marble steps, was supplied not only with fresh water, but also with salt water pumped from the sea. Accounts record the building of a room and a chimney stack to house the large boiler that heated the salt water for the King's bath. The sea water was pumped from an engine house by the Fish Market on the beach to the reservoir in the Pavilion Gardens. Another boiler, probably located in the basement beneath the bathroom, heated the fresh water pumped from the well. The plunge bath, which held over 6,000 gallons of water, was covered with a jointed wood floor when not in use. Probably the oval plunge bath at Wimpole Hall which fortunately still survives (fig.11) gives the best approximation of the Pavilion's original plunge bath, even though it is a different shape and smaller.

8. Portrait of Sake Deen Mahomed, *in court dress, from J. Erredge,* History of Brighthelmston, *1862.*

Vapour baths, 'shampooing' and Sake Deen Mahomed

Sake Deen (or Dean) Mahomed[154] was an author, entrepreneur and businessman. (fig.8) At the age of 25 he left India for Ireland, and finally settled in England in London in 1809. Here, in the area around Portman Square fashionable with wealthy British 'nabobs', he settled with his Anglo-Irish wife Jane. Within a year, he had established the 'Hindostanee Coffee House', which, like many other establishments called 'Coffee House', was in fact a restaurant. Aimed at a European clientele who had worked or ruled in India, it served authentic Indian cuisine in an authentic ambience; it was the first

9. Mahomed's Baths, at 39 East Cliff, Brighton by Joseph Cordwell, 1823. These new premises were conveniently located near the Pavilion and the Steine, on the sea front. In the street is a 'fly', presumably awaiting a client from the baths. Women tend the fishing nets and on the beach fishermen care for their boats. Out to sea can be seen a steamer. In the summer nine cross-Channel steam-packets were used for the ten-hour trip from Brighton to France.

Indian restaurant in London. Sadly it was not a financial success and, bankrupt, Mahomed and his wife moved to Brighton in 1814 to work in the more familiar business of vapour baths and bath houses. Here he attained the ultimate accolade of being appointed 'Shampooing Surgeon to His Majesty King George IV'.

The use of vapour baths for medical and pleasurable purposes was not new in England, though it was vigorously promoted as such by Sake Deen Mahomed. The novel element, added by him, was the extensive application of therapeutic body massage, called in the late eighteenth century 'shampooing' from the Hindi word for massage. Vapour baths, followed by massage with Indian oils (not dissimilar to aromatherapy), were used to treat a range of ailments including asthma, paralysis, gout, sprains and nervous complaints. His treatments, undoubtedly more relaxing (or stimulating) and agreeable than warm or cold sea baths, were eagerly sought by fashionable invalids. (fig.9)

The Pavilion's vapour bath had a mahogany frame with flannel curtains and a mahogany cane chair, on which the King sat. Le Comte de la Garde (a connoisseur of vapour baths in both Moscow and Constantinople) described the decorum of his visit to Mahomed's Baths in Brighton. He was 'enclosed under a tent of flannel which promptly fills with a cloud of perfumed steam; then two arms belonging to an invisible body penetrate the tent, subjecting each limb in turn to a pressure, sometimes hard and sometimes gentle, which is called *shampouer* (to shampoo), and which gives rise to as much vigour as elasticity'.[155] Such modesty did not prevail in Moscow. There the bather was covered in thick soap and, lying naked on a marble bed, was pleasurably massaged by scantily clad young slave girls.

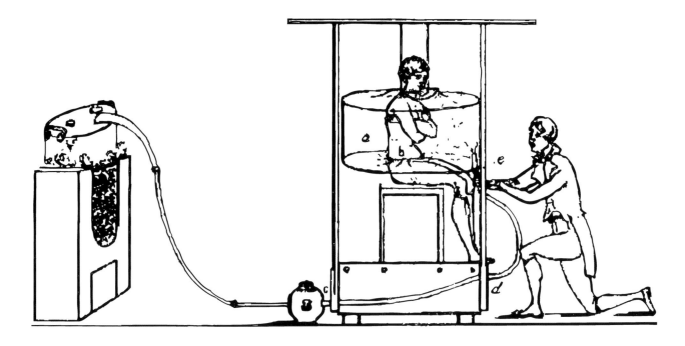

In 1822 Mahomed published *Shampooing; Or, Benefits resulting from the Use of the Indian Medicated Bath*, a volume replete with testimonials to the supremacy of his treatments and dedicated to the 'King's most excellent majesty'. Not lacking in modesty, he included in his book an 'Ode to Mahomed' (published in the *New London Magazine* in 1822), where the author attributes the expansion of Brighton to Mahomed's reputation and vapour treatments:

> While thus beneath the flannel shades,
> Fat dowagers and wrinkled maids
> Rebloom in adolescence,
> I marvel not that friends tell friends,
> And Brighton every day extends
> Its circuses and crescents.

Indeed, he claims the architectural style of the Pavilion itself pays homage to this talented eastern gentleman:

> While Turkish dome and minaret
> In compliment to Mahomed
> O'ertop the King's Pavilion.

Vapour baths seem to have been a favoured indulgence of the King. In addition to those *in situ* at Brighton and Carlton House, he ordered a further two portable vapour baths in 1825 from Captain Edward Jekyll of the Royal Navy, who had apparently

10. Vapour baths.
a. Steam from the boiler on the left passed through (c) a vapour receiver; the pipe directs the vapour to the desired part of the patient. Figs. 10.a and 10.b from Basil Cochrane's An Improvement on the Mode of Administering the Vapour Bath, *London, 1809.*

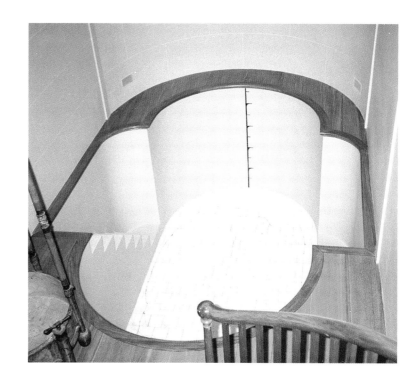

10. Vapour baths.
b. (above) The patient sits on a cane seat with a foot rest, beneath a flannel tent which retains the vapour.

11. (above right) The plunge bath designed by John Soane for Wimpole Hall in Cambridgeshire. When in use it held nearly 3,000 gallons of water, having half the capacity of the Pavilion's bath. Reproduced by courtesy of The National Trust

invented a portable bath apparatus far more convenient than the fixed baths used by Deen Mahomed. The portable version came complete with a tent frame with swan's down covering, seats, foot stool, flexible tubes and nozzles to direct the steam as desired, and 'oiled silk and calico dresses of extra size and quality'.[156]

Remedies: laudanum and leeches

To counteract the pain of gout the King took large doses of laudanum, which in itself induced constipation and painful motions. Laudanum was a liquid form of opium, a narcotic drug freely available in the early nineteenth century. Opium had been extensively used as a pain killer for centuries. The opium poppy is also the source of heroin, prepared from the unripe poppy seeds. The repertoire of remedies available at this period – such as blood-letting, sweating, purging and vomiting – still reflected the long-held belief that expelling the bad humours and restoring the balance of the four humours or bodily fluids (blood, phlegm, yellow bile and black bile) would restore good health.

In this context, opium was seen as a medicine of great value, stimulating the nervous system and allaying pain as well as invigorating all the mental and bodily functions. It was used for conditions ranging from typhus fever and smallpox to 'checking morbidly increased evacuations as in *dysentry, diarrhoea, haemorrage* after delivering, *cough* and etc'.[157]

A popular treatise on modern domestic medicine published in 1840 suggested 'twenty drops to a drachm' (60 grains or one-eighth of an ounce) of laudanum for continuous pain, although in violent cases much larger doses were necessary. The author of this treatise preferred the use of 'Battley's Solution' or 'Black Drop' to laudanum, as this preparation of opium in vinegar or some other vegetable acid did not 'affect the head or confine the bowels so much'.[158]

The Prince's dependency was acute; whilst suffering from an attack in 1811 he wrote to his mistress, Lady Hertford:

> The greatest blessing is that the laudanum has not in the least lost its effect, notwithstanding the immense quantities I have taken & must still for a time be under the unavoidable necessity of taking; nothing but the steady perseverance in these frequently repeated dozes [sic] can or does afford me the smallest relief.[159]

In subsequent years, as he did become accustomed to the drug, the laudanum had less and less effect. In the last year of his life he was able to take over 250 drops in a thirty-six-hour period and still remain capable of rational conversation.

During the King's period of illness in Brighton in the spring of 1827, the Royal Apothecaries, Walker & Nussey, supplied over a six-week period some twenty-eight bottles of Battley's Sedative (or Solution) and twelve bottles of laudanum. The total bill for the quarter ending 5 April was £212 14s. 6d.; a bill for medicines supplied by the Brighton-based apothecaries Barratt & Blaker totalled £22 8s. 6d. and a second bill for medical and surgical services (potions, pills and bleeding) for the same quarter came to £20 0s. 6d.[160] Barratt & Blaker were paid £6,000 over fifteen years, receiving from 1825 onwards a quarterly allowance of £75 for attendance and medicines.

In Nash's new building His Majesty's bedroom was amply furnished with two toilet facilities: a mahogany night convenience and a separate, private water closet. In addition, in line with French custom, the King had the use of a bidet. His former apartments on the first floor (known as the Prince of Wales's apartments) housed a simple mahogany bidet on square taper legs. His new apartments were furnished with a more decorative appliance, a bamboo-pattern bidet chair with a cane cover and back, with the edge of the seat and top rail upholstered in blue leather. In England the bidet still carried a certain aura of Continental impropriety; Samuel Johnson's massive three-volume dictionary (revised in 1827) made no reference at all to its function, describing only the believed etymology of the word – as coming from the French word for 'a little horse'.

The same dictionary defines closet as 'a small room of privacy' with no mention of its function. There is no entry for water closets. Such matters were not for polite conversation. Mrs Arbuthnot, in describing the 'odious' and 'vulgar' Lady Stranach and her (at least verbal) intimate relations with the gouty and apparently decrepit Lord Hertford (son of George's former mistress Lady Hertford), remarked in her diary 'he appears to tell her things that a woman never speaks of but to her husband, & not always that (such as the building [of] water closets in the house)'.[161]

12. (right) Breathing a Vein, *by the Rev. John Sneyd, published by H. Humphrey, 1804. Following an incision the surgeon catches the blood of his patient, who turns away in pain.*

13. (far right) Colchicum Autumnale or meadow saffron, used in the treatment of gout; from Medical Botany, *by John Stephenson and James Morss Churchill, 1829*

These facilities were essential. One treatment recommended for gout (and the constipation caused by taking laudanum) was to clear the stomach and bowels by the administration of powerful laxatives and diuretics. The effect could be dramatic: an intimate lady friend confided, 'he continues very ill … having had 60 motions after a stoppage of 4 days'.[162]

Pain and attacks of breathlessness rendered sleep almost impossible. His French bedstead in his new apartments was furnished with a white satin bedstead bolster and seven pillows of various sizes, as some relief was attained by being propped up in bed. For his last visit to the Pavilion in January 1827 'a very large mechanical invalid bedstead'[163] was brought down from London for his use, along with other 'gouty' appliances borrowed from the stores at Carlton House. The day after the King's arrival in Brighton a mahogany night stool with earthenware pan and stuffed leather seat cushion was sent down from St James's Palace. The following week two more earthenware pans for the King's night stool were delivered to Brighton to be kept in store, as replacements in case of an accident.[164] All were returned to London once the King left Brighton for the last time on 7 March of that year.

George demanded that his private apartments were kept very warm. He slept only in sheets of white satin, with a few fine wool blankets for warmth, even in the depths of winter. This may have been to avoid further discomfort, which the weight of a counterpane or quilt might have imposed on his tender frame and aching joints.

The King's personal physicians Sir Henry Halford and Sir Matthew Tierney tried to ease the effects of his illness, advising the avoidance of any anxiety and restraint with regard to exercise: 'we are decidedly of the opinion that His Majesty's frame must not be exposed to any great exertion in the way of exercise'[165] they wrote in 1822. A two-hour carriage ride to take the air, weather permitting, was recommended, but no horse-riding. The delicate subject of his diet was raised; provided care was taken not to excite or heat the circulation of the blood, abstinence was not necessary, though indulgence would be dangerous.

In subsequent years, Sir Henry Halford – delivering a lecture on the subject of gout at the Royal College of Physicians – recommended another preparation, 'Colchicum', which the King had used as well as laudanum. Colchicum derives from the bulb of meadow saffron, an indigenous crocus-like plant poisonous to animals. It had sedative, and dramatic diuretic and purgative, effects. Sir Henry believed its use prevented the painful, inflammatory stages of gout.

In Sir Henry's view the best approach was prevention: a sensible diet, gentle exercise, no anxiety or excitement, and chastity. It had been noted in ancient medical treatises that gout was not common amongst women or pre-pubescent boys or *castrati*. Sir Henry suggested that sexual activity was best avoided 'for nothing enervates the system so much as this indulgence, especially in excess: and an enervated state of the body is that which renders it most assailable by Gout'.[166]

A further contemporary remedy for many ills was blood-letting by incision or by the application of leeches to the body to draw off blood. Patients could be bled until they fell unconscious, and some French medical practitioners recommended the removal of up to 3 litres (over 5 pints) of blood. Blood removal could be more easily controlled by using leeches. The leech used in medicinal practise (*Hirundo Medicinalis*) was common in English ponds and damp places. Indeed, the popularity of leeches for blood removal almost resulted in the species becoming extinct – such was the demand for them, particularly in Europe.

Leeches inject an anti-blood clotting agent into their victim (or patient) which stops the blood thickening and allows it to flow freely. A leech before feeding is about 1.5 inches (3.8 cm) long and has ten stomachs on either side of its body. After being applied to a patient the leech might expand to some 6 inches (15.2 cm) in length. It was a common practice in the nineteenth century for families to keep special ceramic jars of leeches, available for use at home.It is not clear if George preferred bleeding by incision or the use of leeches. Given his fastidious nature, one would imagine he preferred the former. During a bad bout of illness in late 1817 the Prince was reported as being bled some 60 ounces (about 3 pints) by his physicians. This figure, which may be exaggerated, was quoted in a letter from Lady Holland to Mrs Creevey.[167] To remove such quantities of blood without the benefit of the anti-coagulant effect of the leech must

A peep into the Punch room at the Pavilion, or the Gouty Adonis!

14. A peep into the Punch room at the Pavilion, or the Gouty Adonis! *George, with bandaged feet and propped up in bed on pillows, is fed with punch that 'cures the gout' by his physician.*

have been both exhausting and painful. Some accounts of the quantities of blood taken from the King are beyond belief or simply misquoted in ignorance. The MP Henry Brougham wrote to Thomas Creevey in February 1820 claiming that the new King's life had been saved following blood letting of 150 ounces (over 7 pints).[168]

In a letter to Sir William Knighton in 1822[169] the King described how, having been bled again, he managed to pass a night of tranquillity though he slept little. His younger brother Ernest, the Duke of Cumberland, felt most of the King's complaints could be ascribed to that common English malady, piles, which he considered affected 99 per cent of the population.[170] The prevalence of piles, he claimed, exacerbated by the King's sedentary life, was the problem, and could be relieved by the judicious application of leeches to the arms. Indeed Ernest appears to have had little sympathy with his elder brother's discomfort. Ernest recalled spending four months with the King during which he enjoyed good health apart from one bout of illness, which he considered his brother had 'in great part drawn upon himself by inaction'.[171]

The King employed four personal physicians and two personal surgeons. Association with the King brought both honours and prestige. Sir Henry Halford, his personal physician, attended four successive monarchs during his career. Astley Cooper, a debonair, socially adroit and talented surgeon, received a knighthood after removing, in a difficult operation, a wen (a fleshy excrescence or protuberance) from George's head. On George's accession to the throne, Richard Walker was appointed Apothecary to the Person, and his partner, John Nussey, Apothecary to the Royal Household. Walker constantly attended the King and accompanied him on his travels to Ireland, Scotland and Hanover.

6 French chefs, dining and social etiquette

In the year in which the Pavilion's spectacular interior was finally completed, Lord Byron published the following lines in *Don Juan*:

> Gaunt famine never shall approach the throne,
> Though Ireland starve, great George weighs twenty stone.[172]

George's reign, both as Regent and King, was marked by the highest recorded level of expenditure on poor relief in England and Wales, only to be exceeded in 1871, by which time the population had doubled. The cost of the war with France (1803–1815) resulted in higher taxation. This, combined with a serious reduction in exports, a consequence of Napoleon's policy of blockades, caused unemployment and price increases. By 1812 wheat had nearly tripled in price. The end of the war brought more unemployment, economic depression and poverty. In this context the Prince's extravagant lifestyle caused anger and bitterness amongst radical writers and poets, such as Byron, as well as amongst his own subjects and ministers.

The fashion for French cuisine, French chefs and Antonin Carême

Since his youth the Prince had admired French culture, whether *objets d'art* or *l'art de la cuisine*. However, in the decade after the French Revolution he was publicly criticised for retaining French staff in his employ. On 28 February 1797 his pastry cook, C. Taurade, was arrested under a Home Secretary's warrant. A warrant was also issued for the arrest of J. Gody, one of the Prince's cooks, on a charge of sedition. *The Times* said that they were both to be sent out of the country immediately, but a few days later it declared that Taurade (a German by birth) had been pressed into the Navy and was on board the *Sandwich*. *The Times* expressed its satisfaction at the news that the Prince intended to dismiss all the Frenchmen employed in his service, and hoped that every English nobleman would do the same.

The Prince's continued obsession with employing the best French chefs moved Lady Bessborough to write in December 1810 to her lover, Lord Granville Leveson-Gower, who was staying with the Prince of Wales in Brighton. She warned him about the Prince's habit of stealing friends' chefs, particularly as he had just lost one of his own. 'Have you heard of poor Simon, the Prince's Cook, being burnt? I knew him, and was quite shock'd at hearing it.' She continued:

> take care of Le Clerc – I do not mean of his burning, but of the P.'s teazing [sic] to get him, which I do not think unlikely; and it is not only que les Princes marchent vite en amour, mais en Cuisiniers – du moins, sont ils peu scrupuleux en tout ce qui regarde leurs plaisirs. Witness a cook of my Father's, who was kidnapp'd away from him when one of the P.'s had died.[173]

It was not just the Prince who wanted to impress. It was essential for those aspiring to be part of fashionable society to acquire the services of a French, and preferably well-known, chef. The anonymous author of *Almack's A Novel* mocked the pathetic attempts of the wealthy, but vulgar, to achieve acceptance with lavish entertainments, displays of immense wealth, innumerable servants, extravagant interiors furnished in the latest styles – and, of course, a French chef. The author's dreary and odious Lady Birmingham eagerly acquired the services of 'Monsieur Rissole', the most expensive *chef de cuisine* in London. This did much for her status amongst the *ton*, 'for people were beginning to tire of the wealth and dullness of the Birminghams, but a first-rate French cook no one can tire of'.[174]

2. Pièces montées *designed by Antonin Carême. From left to right: Turkish Pavilion, Rotunda in Ruins, Grand Modern Fountain. From* French Cookery, *translated by William Hall, 1836, pl. 36.*

In 1816 the Prince enticed the renowned French chef Marie Antoine (or Antonin as he preferred) Carême to work for him at Carlton House and in Brighton. He received the generous annual sum of £500, half of which was paid as a life annuity in the event of his patron's untimely demise. With George's own blessing, he made money on the side by selling leftover pastries filled with *foie gras* and pheasant to local aldermen. He was only engaged to superintend the Regent's kitchens (whether at Carlton House or at the Royal Pavilion) for one week in two, leaving him free to devote himself to his ambitious but seminal work *L'Art de la cuisine française*.

In Carême's eyes, English cooking amounted merely to meats cooked in salt water, fruit preserves, puddings of all kinds, chicken and turkey with cauliflower, salt beef, country ham and several similar *ragoûts*. But not everything about English food met with his disapproval. He was particularly impressed by the quality of British meat – in particular beef, which he considered to be superior to the French. This was because the animals were slaughtered at a younger age. Carême also preferred the cleaner Anglo-Saxon method of suffocating poultry in contrast with the butchery that took place in Parisian kitchens, although he did find fault with the London poultry sellers who had fallen into the bad habit of dusting chickens to make them appear whiter.

Carême could not be induced to remain for long with the Prince Regent, and in 1817 he returned to his native land.

The importance of food and dining to the Prince was acknowledged in the allocation of space in Nash's design. More than a quarter of the ground floor of the Pavilion was devoted to the kitchens, household kitchens and ancillary offices. These included the meat larders, a steam kitchen, baking ovens, an ice room and five pastry and confectionery rooms. The last-named areas perhaps reflect the influence of Carême, who was working in Brighton whilst the kitchens were being built and furnished. Famed for his confections, Carême created eight *grosses pièces de pâtisserie* for the banquet held in the Pavilion to honour Grand Duke Nicholas of Russia in January 1817. The same menu also included thirty-six *entrées* (main dishes) and thirty-two *entremets* (side dishes).

Carême's love of architecture and design expressed itself in his elaborate *pièces montées*, (fig.2) creations inspired by his own studies and made primarily of almond paste and sugar, coloured and decorated with fruits, nuts, sweets, biscuits and icings. Columns and entablatures were formed of almond paste, with puff-pastry rocks and icing-sugar snow. In his view such pieces required knowledge of the classical orders, combined with the design skills of an architect. These confections stood 30 to 48 inches (80–120 cm) high and up to 24 inches (60 cm) wide. *Ermitage Chinois* and *Syrien*, for example, were presented in the Pavilion as part of eight *grosses pièces de patisserie* for the banquet on 15 January 1817 along with *Ruine de la Mosquée turque*, flanked by almond brioche, nougat and pastries. These were essentially display pieces, designed to amuse the guests and stimulate conversation.

The fashion for extravagant and ostentatious dinners prepared in the French manner was satirised by the anonymous author of *Almack's A Novel*. Here the dinner prepared by Monglas, Lord and Lady Norbury's *chef de cuisine*, was a triumph of invention and elaboration. It provided opportunities for conversation and witticisms, allowing the guests to shine with humour and erudition. After numerous dishes, the centre of the table groaned with 'the Temple of Paestum, formed of macaroons; the Greater Pyramids of Egypt graced either side, in spun sugar; while Chartreuses, Macedoines, and other compositions of equal merit, filled up the other spaces'. To Lord Dorville's request for some spun sugar from the base of the Pyramid, the blue-stockinged Miss Bevil quipped (and to no effect), 'Is not your Lordship afraid of disturbing the mummies?'[175]

In France the roles of cook and pastry cook were separate professions. In England one cook usually undertook both roles. William Hall noted in his introduction to *French Cookery* (a compilation of Carême's publications) in 1836:

> it is obligatory on the Cook in England to be conversant with every branch of his profession,
> as few of the establishments of our nobility or gentry, even of the most wealthy or highest
> in rank, include an assistant under the denomination of a Pastrycook.

George, however, not only ensured that the Pavilion's kitchens included areas dedicated to the art of the *pâtissier*, but also employed two pastry cooks: Henry Brand, who received £140 per annum, and Mary Morton, who was paid only £50 per annum.

The gracious customs and table settings of the Prince Regent's court inspired Carême to perfect his own art 'for this truly royal table was served always in the French manner, and the service of silver so superb and elegant, that I was struck with wonder'.[176] He was concerned that the 'larger pieces of cookery of the first course never corresponded with the elegance of the bronzes, the glass, and the plate',[177] and determined upon reforms, enabled by the Prince Regent's practice of serving dinner in the French manner.

The practice of *service à la Russe* adopted by many of Carême's European patrons meant that all dishes were carved before being served to guests or placed on the table. With *service à la Française* all the dishes, including the *grosses pièces* (large, elaborate dishes), were carried to table and presented to the guests intact. This gave Carême the opportunity to create culinary works of art to impress his patron. They were shown to the guests, then carved and served. To ensure perfection Carême even designed (and had made at his own expense) silver skewers (*hâtelets*) to garnish his *entrées* and *grosses pièces*. (fig.3)

The actual arrangement of, and relationship between, the dishes on the table was of equal importance. Carême gives an example for a table layout for 80 to 100 covers (or place settings):

> sixteen *grosses pièces* as follows: four large fishes, two in the centre and two at the ends;
> next, in the four *contre flancs*, large pieces of meat; the eight large dishes in the extreme
> flanks are composed of poultry or game, or from the oven, as casseroles of rice, timballes,
> pies, or croustades of bread, as the designs represent; eight of those *grosses pièces* should

3. Two grosses pièces
by Carême: Saumon à
la Régence *(fig.1) and*
Saumon à la Dupperé
(fig.2). The skewers,
also designed by
Carême, hold
(in fig.1) truffles
dressed in
champagne wine with
pieces of sole. From
French Cookery, *translated by William*
Hall, 1836, pl. 4.

be garnished with the *hâtelets*, also eight *entrées*; by this division of the *entrées* more effect is produced, and the whole service displays the highest elegance.[178]

One of the *grosses pièces* was visually related to four or five *entrées*, repeated along the table. As a guide, every five covers required one *grosse pièce* and four or five *entrées* (multiplied according to the number of guests).

The elaborate concoctions of French chefs such as Carême fed the Prince's desire for novelty, as well as display. For some *La cuisine française* and the endless French names of dishes bore little relation to the food itself. The science and art of cooking had become pure affectation. In *Don Juan* Byron mocked such dinners and their pretentiousness, once all too familiar to him:

Then there was God knows what 'à l'Allemande,'
'A L'Espagnole,' 'timballe,' and 'salpicon' –
With things I can't withstand or understand,
Though swallow'd with much zest upon the whole;
And 'entremets' to piddle with at hand,
Gently to lull down the subsiding soul; …[179]

As the courses and drinking progressed, Byron continues:

> And fruits, and ice, and all that art refines
> From nature for the service of the goût –
> *Taste* or the *gout*, – pronounce it as inclines
> Your stomach? Ere you dine, the French will do;
> But *after*, there are sometimes certain signs
> Which prove plain English truer of the two.
> Hast ever *had* the *gout?* I have not had it –
> But I may have, and you too, reader, dread it.[180]

4. The Banqueting Room and Great Kitchen, *from Nash's* Views *(detail). The cross-section shows the proximity of the Great Kitchen to the Banqueting Room separated only by the Table Deckers' (or Pages') Room. Beneath are cellars to store spirits, wines and beer.*

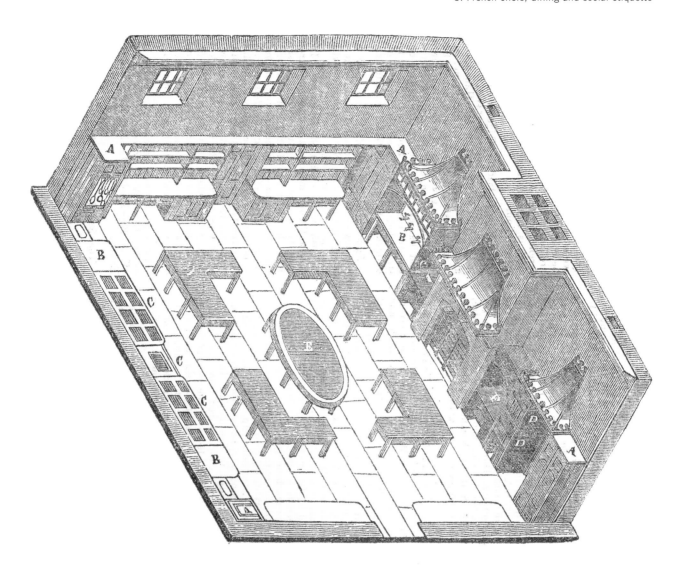

The Great Kitchen: equipment and the steam table

5. The Great Kitchen. *Isometric drawing from the* Mechanics' Magazine *(11 October 1834). Hot closets are marked (A), stewing stores (C), steam kettles (B) and, in the centre, the steam table is (E).*

The extensive new kitchens and ancillary areas were one of the first elements of Nash's reconstruction to be completed in 1816/17. Designed to a high standard of modernity and efficiency, they complemented the decorative grandeur and splendour of the proposed new Banqueting Room. The Comtesse de Boigne observed in 1817 that the Prince took great delight in showing visitors the new developments, 'a special point being his kitchens, which were entirely steam heated by a system at that time new, with which he was charmed'.[181]

In Holland's first manifestation of the Pavilion (1787), the kitchens were situated to the north, at an angle to Marlborough House. When Nash's reconstruction of the building began in 1815, the stables area, made redundant by the construction of

Porden's stables in the grounds, provided a suitable location for the kitchens, adjacent to the proposed Banqueting Room. The new location was determined by the land available for development, by Nash's symmetrical ground plan and by the desire to provide conveniently placed domestic offices to service the elaborate banquets desired by the Prince Regent.

The proximity of the new kitchens to the Banqueting (or dining) Room is unusual in this period. (fig.4) In the Pavilion these two areas were separated only by the Table Deckers' Room, a small room used by footmen for final adjustments to the presentation of dishes and as a serving and clearing area. Usually kitchens were sited at a distance from the dining room to obviate the risks of fire and the inevitable smells and heat of cooking.

The Great Kitchen was completed by 1816 and finally furnished in 1817–1818 by the ironmongers William Stark & Son. Illustrated in Nash's *Views of the Royal Pavilion*, published in 1826, it was a source of wonder to contemporary observers. C. Wright remarked:

6. Hot closet, one of four in the Great Kitchen and heated by steam.

> in the furnishing of the kitchen and other offices every modern improvement to facilitate the process of the culinary art has been introduced in all its boasted perfection. It is not exceeding the faithful observation of a narrator, in stating that the recency of the above alterations forms one part of the most useful and convenient appendages to a mansion that is to be seen in the British Empire.[182]

The Great Kitchen measured 45 feet by 36 feet (13.7 x 11 m); a high lantern in the ceiling, fitted with twelve sash windows for ventilation and illumination, gave the interior a light and airy feel. Four cast-iron columns, ornamented with painted copper palm leaves, support the ceiling. Copper tent-like awnings, decorated with cast-copper ornaments, form the canopies over the ovens, stewing stoves and kitchen range, drawing away excess heat, smells and steam. Through such decorative features as the columns and canopies the oriental theme was extended into the kitchen. For the Prince, the Great Kitchen, or the King's Kitchen as it was also known, was a continuation of the palace's main rooms.

Ancillary kitchens and household offices were located around a courtyard to the south, with an octagonal water tower built in 1816. A pumping engine drew water from the nearby well; another small forcing engine pumped water to the lead-lined reservoir at the top of the tower which supplied water through iron mains and leaded pipes to all parts of the Pavilion. The kitchen offices provided facilities to service the King and his guests, as well as the staff of the Royal Household. Beyond the Great Kitchen in the area to the south were sited service rooms for cleaning and storing plate, coffee and linen rooms, sculleries and store rooms, confectionery and pastry preparation rooms (including an office for the confectioners), a range of larders for meats, poultry and game, a dedicated steam room, a bakehouse and a range of kitchens and sculleries for

the household staff. Wines and ales were stored in the extensive cellars beneath the Banqueting Room.

Nash's *Views*, together with the Pavilion inventory, bills and contemporary descriptions, provide valuable information on the interior of the Great Kitchen itself, and on its use and equipment.[183] One of the aquatints vividly portrays the activities of the Great Kitchen: a chef directs his staff, who are chopping, preparing meats and sauces and stoking the fire for the spit. A footman carries a tray of prepared dishes towards the west door. In the centre, flanked by four large L-shaped beech preparation tables, there is a 13-foot (4 m) long oval steam table.

The large steam table, installed by Stark in 1817, was fitted with a cast-iron top and bound in brass. (fig.7) It was supplied with steam from 'a very large strong copper steam boiler' located behind the kitchen range and cisterns were provided to receive the condensed water. By the mid-Victorian period such equipment, called a hot table, was recommended for 'good kitchens', though the suggested size was somewhat smaller at 4 feet (1.2 m) long.[184]

The steam table was a remarkable innovation, designed to keep large numbers of *entrées* warm whilst awaiting carriage to the Banqueting Room by footmen and reducing some of the problems created by the King's preference for *service à la Française*. When in use, the table was covered with a cloth, presumably to prevent condensation on the silver dishes. If required, only half of the table could be activated, allowing for the assembly of both hot and cold dishes. Dinner was served promptly at 6 o'clock. Indeed Nash's aquatint of the interior of the kitchen records 5.45 p.m. on the wall clock, with over thirty *entrées* prepared for dinner and laid out on the steam table. The Great Kitchen was also equipped with a 23-foot (7 m) range of stewing stoves and steam kettles, hot closets and a smoke jack, fitted with five 7-foot (2.1 m) spits. As all five spits could be operated simultaneously the chef could prepare a number of different roast dishes at any one time.

The rituals of dining and social etiquette

The Pavilion is undoubtedly one of the most ostentatious buildings of its period. Display was an essential part of English society, whether through a profusion of plate, fantastic culinary creations, exotic foods or extensive (and expensive) French wines. Prince Pückler-Muskau reflected that this practice in English aristocratic houses did not represent true hospitality, but rather a show of the host's possessions, designed to dazzle and impress the guests.

The splendour of the Banqueting Room more than matched the modernity and design of the kitchens. Nash's illustration shows some twenty-four or so guests seated for dinner, the main gastronomic event of the day (fig.1). They are attended by eighteen footmen serving drinks and bringing dessert dishes through from the Great Kitchen. George IV is clearly visible to the right, centrally placed with six guests either side, and with his architect, John Nash, seated in the foreground. As was customary, the centre of the table is furnished with a spectacular display of ormolu candelabra and biscuit porcelain ornaments.

Gentlemen, in order of rank, led the ladies into the Banqueting Room by the arm, not by the hand, as was the French custom. Normally guests for dinner did not exceed forty in number. The furniture makers Bailey & Saunders supplied thirty-six plain chairs with two armchairs in 1817, in ebonised wood with brass and satinwood decoration. The service of plate used at Brighton was one ordered by George III for Kensington Palace 'with such additions as was judged necessary to make it complete for forty persons'.[185]

In the eighteenth century social etiquette determined that seating arrangements should be made strictly in accordance with rank, with no regard to female/male balance. By 1788 this protocol was being amended, as noted by the author of *The Honours of the Table, or Rules for Behaviour during Meals*:

BEAUTIES of GREASE or Luxuries of the Kremlin. vide Brighton Vagaries. a Kitchen Frolic.

8. BEAUTIES of GREASE (altered to) GREECE or Luxuries of the Kremlin. Published March 1819. One of at least five caricatures satirising the occasion when the Prince dined in the Great Kitchen with friends in the company of his kitchen staff. His Private Secretary, Sir Benjamin Bloomfield, offers one of the kitchen maids a glass of claret. A French chef looks on in horror at the scene.

Custom, however, has lately introduced a new mode of seating. A gentleman and a lady sitting alternately round the table, and this, for the better convenience of a lady's being attended to, and served by the gentleman next her. But notwithstanding this promiscuous seating, the ladies, whether above or below, are to be served in order, according to their rank or age, and after them the gentlemen, in the same manner.[186]

It was said that the Prince of Wales was instrumental in introducing this new fashion of 'promiscuous seating', which enabled him to sit next to the ladies of his choice.

Given the delicacy of his relationship with Mrs Fitzherbert (both before and after his marriage to Princess Caroline), it was customary in Brighton to avoid normal social etiquette, and guests sat at table without regard to rank. However, when the Prince, obsessed with Lady Hertford, wished to signal a final break with Mrs Fitzherbert, he did this by publicly resorting to formal court etiquette at a dinner in the Pavilion given for Louis XVIII. Discovering that guests at table were to be seated according to rank, and that consequently she would, as a commoner, be seated far from the Prince, she declined the invitation. The Prince's objective was achieved.[187]

The *Brighton Menu Book* for 1819 in the Royal Archives at Windsor Castle lists the dishes served at the Pavilion during that year. Between forty and seventy dishes would be prepared for a dinner, depending on the importance of the occasion and the number of guests. A two-course dinner for eighteen guests held on Thursday, 7 January 1819 comprised, for the first course: '3 Soups, 3 Fish, 4 Removes, 12 Entrées, Assiette Volante. Side Board'; and for the second course: '4 Roasts, 4 Removes, 12 Entremets'.[188]

For the first course elaborate soups were followed by a choice of fish, which might be salt cod, carp, salmon and haddock. Next came the four *removes* – pâtés and meats, followed by twelve e*ntrées*, elaborate main dishes of meat and game. An a*ssiette volante* was a dish of pâtés. A side table, or sideboard, laden with beef, venison, mutton, game, cold meats and pies was available for the pleasure of the guests.

The second course began with four roasts, which might include chicken, partridge, wild duck, rabbit, grouse and veal, followed by four different *removes* such as trifle or brioches. The *entremets* (side dishes) were both savoury and sweet dishes, the latter including a range of jellies flavoured with fruits, flowers or wines; fruit tarts; ice creams; meringues; rice dishes and 'poudings' as Carême described them – crème puddings of traditional English origin. *Crème à l'Anglaise* and *Crème à la Caramel* frequently featured on the Prince's menus, as did *blancemanger* (blancmange), commended by Carême as a most nutritious dish and made from the milk of pounded almonds – the progenitor of the unappealing white milk pudding many experienced at school in the 1950s.

Several ice houses[189] in Brighton, in the service of the King, ensured supplies for making sorbets and creams, as well as for keeping wines cool. Ice, collected from frozen ponds and streams in winter, was impure in its content. It was, however, used not only to chill bottles but also in drinks. Lord Glenbervie recalled the alcoholic preferences of the Prince at a dinner in 1811 where the Prince drank 'at least three bottles of wine, besides punch made with maraschino with lumps of solid ice in it, and a sort of spicy *liqueur* which he takes in great quantity'.[190]

The side table of meats and game had to be laid out in a suitably elegant manner. Thomas Cosnett, instructing future footmen on the etiquette of waiting at table, advised his pupils to consider both convenience and grandeur in setting the sideboard. He reminded them that 'you cannot think that ladies and gentlemen have splendid and costly things without wishing them to be seen or set out to the best advantage'.[191] Equally, the entire table had to be set with great precision. Firstly the dining table was covered with damask, velvet or green cloth and, depending on the grandeur of the occasion, two fine white tablecloths, one of which would be removed prior to the third, and final, dessert course. In the grandest houses this revealed the second, even finer cloth. In less wealthy households the dessert course was placed on the bare polished wood table. It is clear in the depiction of the dessert course being served in Nash's *Views* that there is a second white cloth. (fig.1) Superb tablecloths of linen damask, with elaborate designs and borders, were supplied to the King by J. W. Coulson of Lisburn in Ireland. Clean glasses, plates and dessert knives and forks were laid with fresh linen napkins. Cheese was generally eaten with porter or ale, not wine, and finger glasses or

I think your Comforters are bigger than my Johns.

Won't you take another Comforter? we must make haste, I expect Noodle here presently.

DARBY and JOHN

Comforter

Brandy

A BRIGHTON BREAKFAST or *Morning Comforts* Fashionable Follies. Plate 1st

9. A BRIGHTON BREAKFAST or Morning Comforts, 1802. Breakfast was a substantial meal in the Regency period. Here an overweight Mrs Fitzherbert and her friend Lady Lade are satirised indulging in a hearty breakfast of meats washed down with brandy and gin.

bowls, once used, were removed along with the debris from the second course. Wine glasses, cooled in wine-glass coolers, were prepared and brought to the table on silver-gilt trays.

The comportment of footmen serving at dinner was subject to many rules. Cosnett also felt the need to specify behaviour considered unacceptable, such as picking one's nose, snuffing up mucus, or scratching the head (or any part of the body) in the dining room. The most heinous crime was hawking or spitting. Prince Pückler-Muskau, describing manners of the English aristocracy at dinner, observed that putting one's knife in the mouth instead of a fork, picking up asparagus or sugar with one's fingers or, worst of all, spitting on the floor, were considered to be the most appalling lapses of good taste.

Another English custom was the use of finger bowls filled with water, placed in front of each guest at the end of dinner. At this point the ladies had not yet retired. A French visitor, horrified by this practice, described in his journal the dinner guests stooping over their glass bowls, sucking up the water, spitting it out, sucking again, rinsing and cleaning the mouth with the aid of a finger. Then they washed their hands in the same bowl, and dried them (along with their mouths) on napkins or the tablecloth.[192]

L'APRÈS-DINÉE DES ANGLAIS

Scènes Anglaises dessinées à Londres.

Carême, from his particular professional perspective, clearly appreciated the sophistication of English court life as dictated by the Prince Regent. In general the French were rather dismayed by both English food and dining etiquette – in particular the formality of dinners. François de la Rochefoucauld, relating his experience as a guest of the Duke of Grafton in the 1780s, considered dinner to be 'one of the most wearisome of English experiences, lasting, as it does for four or five hours'.[193] Guests must be 'well-washed' and well groomed. The standard of politeness was uncomfortable and etiquette was rigidly adhered to.

However, as the evening progressed, formality, and notions of social grace and comportment, vanished. Once the ladies had retired 'one proceeds to drink – sometimes in an alarming measure. Everyone has to drink in his turn, for the bottles make a continuous circuit of the table and the host takes note that everyone is drinking in his turn.'[194]

George enjoyed the custom of continuously proposing toasts, urging his guests to fill their glass. 'A bumper!' he commanded – it was simply a glass filled to the brim for a toast. After dinner, in jocular mood, he would join his guests and burst into song with one of his favourites such as 'Life's a Bumper', a glee for three voices, as sung in *The Review or the Wags of Windsor*. Toasts followed toasts (as an excuse for more drink)

10. L'Après-dinée des Anglais, a French print, c. 1814, satirising the unseemly behaviour of English gentlemen after dinner. On the left a guest grasps (too late) a chamber pot. As if to emphasise the point the picture on the wall shows a landscape under heavy rain. Reproduced by courtesy of the Trustees of the British Museum.

and, in La Rochefoucauld's view, conversation – even in the best society – descended to indecent topics in poor taste.

La Rochefoucauld also noted the following and, to his mind, indelicate English practice. 'The sideboard too is furnished with a number of chamber pots and it is a common practice to relieve oneself whilst the rest are drinking; one has no kind of concealment and the practice strikes me as most indecent.'[195] Not only was urination a public activity, but it did not stop the flow of conversation from the guest using these facilities. The Comte de la Garde in *Brighton scènes détachées d'un voyage en Angleterre* (Paris, 1834) described with amazement the English custom of relieving oneself in public during dinner. It seemed even odder to him that toasts continued to be made to the temporarily absent diner, who then delivered a carefully prepared reply without interrupting his delicate activity. (fig.10)

The Prince, fastidious by nature, would not have sanctioned the practice of using chamber pots publicly during a meal. There is no evidence in the Pavilion inventory of commodes or sideboards specifically designed to conceal chamber pots. Nor are there concealed cupboards of the kind designed for Holkham Hall, where a false pedimented and panelled door in the South Dining Room opens to reveal two small domed alcoves to hold chamber pots.[196] Flushing water closets were, however, located within easy reach of male guests, as well as being provided for the women in the Ladies Retiring Room. The Pavilion (a small building by country house or palace standards) was served with over thirty water closets.

The Banqueting Room

The Prince's lengthy and elaborate feasts were much enhanced by the spectacular interior of the Banqueting Room. The drama and grandeur of this room were further emphasised by the modesty of the approaches, which were via the Long Gallery or the very low-ceilinged Banqueting Room Gallery.

The design of the Banqueting Room was the responsibility of Robert Jones, who first became involved with the Pavilion in 1815. In 1817 the decoration of the rooms, as remodelled by Nash, was divided between Jones and Frederick Crace, Jones undertaking most of the final schemes including the Banqueting Room, the Saloon, the Red Drawing Room, the King's apartments and part of the Chamber Floor.

The late flowering of chinoiserie in the Banqueting Room is pure decoration and highly theatrical in style. The painted canopy decorations, resembling sagging gilt-leather and decorated with complex designs of fantastic beasts, were embellished with Masonic symbols. The emblems of Freemasonry, widespread in the eighteenth century, evoked the world of noble craftsmen, the dignity of labour and the creation of a noble architecture. High on the canopy, amongst symbols of the moon and planets, is the All-Seeing Eye; in a triangle within a circle, it is the Masonic symbol for 'knowing and seeing all'. The inclusion of these symbols reflects the Prince of Wales's involvement with

Freemasonry. He was the Grand Master of the Prince of Wales Lodge, constituted in 1787 (the year of the completion of the Marine Pavilion), until 1828. From 1790 to 1813 he was also Grand Master of the Grand Lodge of England, established in 1717. The Prince of Wales Lodge comprised mostly his friends, who would have appreciated the significance of the symbols woven into Jones's design.

The walls were hung with eleven large canvases of Chinese domestic scenes. Though reminiscent of rococo chinoiserie paintings, Jones's figure groups float on a silvered background of dragons, waves and stars, in a style with no contemporary parallel. The silvered backgrounds echo the gilding and silver-gilt decorations displayed within the room, shimmering with light from the numerous chandeliers.

From the centre of the shallow dome hangs the immense 'dragon' chandelier, 30 feet (9.1 m) long, a ton in weight, held in the claws of the dragon in the apex of the dome. From a fountain of cut glass, six silvered dragons exhale light through lotus shades. Fantastic birds hold four flanking lustres, one in each corner. The room was lit by five substantial lustres, eight large torchères and numerous candelabra standing on the dining table and sideboards. The high-level painted-glass windows were lit by gas[197] from the exterior at night, suffusing the room in subtle coloured tints.

The torchères (or lampstands), made of Spode blue jars, were embellished with ormolu dragon mounts. Carved and gilt wood bases supported the four on the window side and the four on the west wall. Those on the window wall were free standing and had additional carved dolphin decorations on their bases. They flanked three portable mahogany sideboards, covered with white damask. These sideboards, 6 ft 2 in. by 3 ft 6 in. (1.9 x 1.1 m), had folding legs and were installed only for dinners; like all the furniture they were supplied with green cloth covers. Two more portable tables, slightly smaller in size, were available if needed for large dinner parties. The torchères on the west wall had plain bases as they pierced the long dragon sideboards, which were a permanent feature in the room.

The Banqueting Room was also furnished with seven rosewood sideboards of various lengths, decorated with satinwood and carved and gilt dragons, made by Bailey & Saunders to Jones's design. Each was supplied with painted crimson baize covers to match the broad striped crimson silk of the continuous drapery to the windows. The central mahogany table consisted of nine bedded leaves with four shifting leaves, the whole measuring 47 feet by 7 ft 6 in. (14.3 x 2.3 m). The table would be adjusted in size depending on the number of guests.

No contemporary views show the complete design of the magnificent Axminster carpet, hand-knotted and 'planned to the room'. Its formal design echoed the interior architecture. In the centre, visible when the table was removed, was a large dragon and lotus motif with sunflowers, echoing the Chinese inspiration of Jones's scheme.

11. The Banqueting Room today.

The Royal Pavilion, though modest in size, contains one of the most spectacular dining rooms in Britain. One guest, on seeing Nash's reconstruction in an early stage, was overwhelmed by the grandeur and splendour of the Banqueting Room (and the Music Room). He considered them:

> too handsome for Brighton and in an excessive degree too fine for the extent of His Royal Highness's premises. It is a great pity that the whole of this suite of rooms was not solidly built in or near London … It is, I think, an absurd waste of money, and will be in a ruin in half a century or sooner.[198]

He was to be proved wrong.

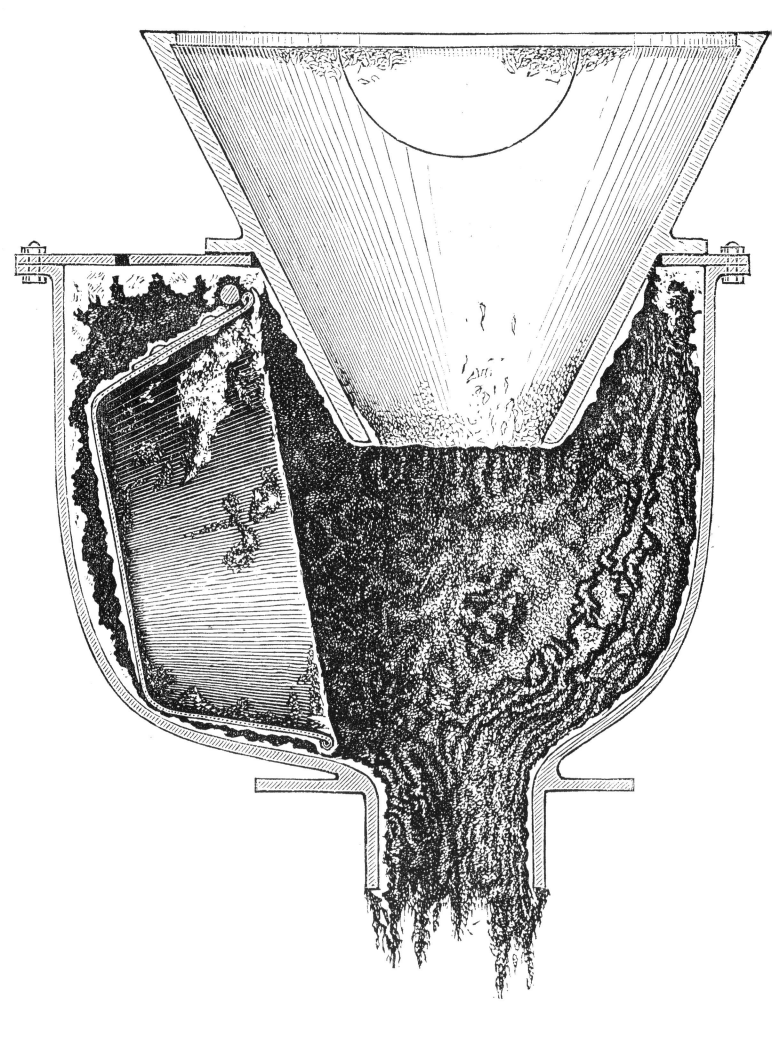

7 Technology in the new Palace

1. (left) An old, used pan closet from an illustration in The Plumber and Sanitary Houses *by S. Stevens Hellyer, 1882. This kind of closet, both smelly and unhygienic, was fitted in servants' area in the Pavilion, and remained popular in England throughout the nineteenth century. (See fig.9)*

Nash's new building was designed to incorporate the latest technology and equipment to meet the King's demands for warmth, comfort and convenience. New gadgets were supplied for the kitchens and gas lighting was introduced for the first time to illuminate the interior of a royal palace.

Lighting the Pavilion

For many contemporary observers the interior of the Royal Pavilion was excessively opulent and theatrical. Lighting played a key role in the overall effect: 'the lights are dazzling', noted Princess Lieven in 1822, whilst also commenting on the luxurious and 'effeminate' atmosphere of the Pavilion. Lighting by day and by night was crucial in creating the dramatic atmosphere.[199]

2. (right) The Long Gallery, from Nash's Views. *The Long Gallery was top-lit by painted laylights by day, and at night by a chandelier, lanterns, candelabra and oil lamps.*

The form of lighting was determined by the size, location and function of the different rooms, providing in each area a particular and individual atmosphere. Nash introduced dramatic light sources from above to illuminate both the Chamber Floor and the ground floor. By day the Long Gallery, for example, resembling a bamboo grove of pink and blue, was lit by three tall windows of painted glass at each end. A large central painted skylight (flanked by two vertical painted windows, which pierced the first-floor galleries) allowed muted natural light to illuminate the central area of the Gallery, where visitors entered. (fig.2) All the galleries and stairwells on the Chamber Floor were also lit by painted skylights. The main rooms on the east front (Saloon, Music and Banqueting Rooms) had full-length arched French windows; painted-glass elliptical windows at clerestory level also illuminated the latter two rooms. The overall effect was of a colourful, light interior, reminiscent of a garden pavilion and full of sunlight softened by the hues of the painted glass.

Wax and tallow candles and oil lamps

At night the interior of the Pavilion was lit by a combination of candles, oil lamps and gas. Wax candles were still a luxury in the early nineteenth century, costing five times as much as the more common tallow candles.

Tallow candles could be bought or were made by the housekeeper and her staff. They came in three types: rush lights made of tapers of rush dipped in tallow; store candles with wicks repeatedly dipped in melted tallow until they reached the desired size; and mould candles, whose cotton wicks were put with melted tallow in a tin, lead or glass mould. Tallow, made from animal fat, preferably a mixture of beef and mutton, burnt quickly with a feeble light and was extremely smelly.

Wax or beeswax was expensive. It burnt more slowly and with a less unpleasant odour. Beeswax candles came in various sizes described as three to the pound (in weight; 450 g) or four or six to the pound, which were smaller. A 'four to the pound' candle burnt for some eleven hours, whereas a six to the pound lasted only six to seven hours.

The use of wax candles indicated status and wealth. A German visitor staying at an English inn noted in the late 1820s: 'if you ask for them, you are treated with redoubled civility, but your bills are also doubled throughout'.[200] In *Emma* the snobbish Mrs Elton, bent on ensuring that Jane Fairfax should find employment as a governess in the best circles, had only to comment that the object of her approval, Mrs Bragge, actually used wax candles in the schoolroom. This was indeed a sign of class and financial well-being.[201] An example of extravagance in more elevated circles was the character Lord Glenthorn, who 'suffered nothing but wax to be burned in his stables'.[202]

The responsibility for lighting the lamps fell to the Lord Steward's Department. Lighting the high chandeliers must have been a considerable task for the lamplighters, who were supplied with robustly built pairs of very high steps with platforms for use in the Banqueting Room. Each room was furnished with numerous chandeliers, lanterns,

3. (above) The sets of painted-glass windows at each end of the Long Gallery were illuminated at night from the exterior by gas.

4. (above right) The Octagonal Hall, from Nash's Views. *A roaring fire welcomed guests; an easily portable Argand oil lamp is conveniently placed on the chimneypiece, for use by the footmen waiting to receive guests.*

oil table lamps, *torchères* or candelabra, inspiring one guest to describe the Pavilion as being 'as full of lamps as Hancock's shop'.[203]

Whilst the King was in residence for a three-month period in 1823 four different suppliers delivered candles to the Pavilion. Edward Baker provided tallow candles: 264 pounds (120 kg) for moulds, 756 pounds (343 kg) for store candles and 24 pounds (11 kg) for rush lights. These would probably have been used by the servants and to provide light in the numerous kitchens and passageways.

In the same period, John Field, J.Toussaint and William Barclay delivered 54 pounds (25 kg) of mortars (thick wax nightlights), 6,320 candles of the 'four to the pound' size, 2,376 candles of the 'six to the pound' size, and 1,944 candles of the 'three to the pound' size. This provided over 10,000 wax candles with burning capacities each varying from six to fourteen hours. Literally hundreds of candles would be burning nightly to illuminate the Pavilion (alongside the Argand[204] lamps and oil lamps), adding, despite the lofty ceilings, to the intense heat.

Four large bronze and brass hexagonal lanterns, on rise and fall mechanisms, artificially lit the Great Kitchen, which was top-lit by day by twelve high-level sash windows. The twin-branched Argand fitting in each lantern is clearly visible in contemporary illustrations of the interior. Copper wall sconces with tinned reflectors supplied supplementary lighting for the staff.

The Lamp Room, located at the south end near the kitchen and household offices, was fitted with floor-to-ceiling closets and presses, a dresser, shelves and a lead sink. Lamp stools, with carpeted tops, and mahogany lamp steps were stored here for use by the lamplighters. The Pavilion inventory, describing the contents of the adjacent Oil Cellar, lists nine large oil vats, two tin oil pumps, five large oil cans, 26-gallon tin measures and funnels. Another lamp room was located in the north-end basement, as a store and for trimming lamps.

The smoke from the numerous chandeliers, lanterns and lamps caused considerable damage to the paintwork and ceilings, necessitating regular cleaning. The Crace accounts, for example, include bills for the Saloon for 'cleaning and repairing the whole of the ornamental painting, being very much injured by smoke of lamps'[205] and for cleaning paintwork and skylights in the Long Gallery, 'much damaged by the smoke of lanthorns [sic]'.[206]

The introduction of gas lighting

Coal gas was little used in England to light private houses in the first decades of the nineteenth century. It had been successfully pioneered in 1807, in a cotton mill in Manchester. The Prince had used gas lighting to illuminate the exterior of Carlton House in London, but whether this included the interior is unclear. In the early years of the development of gas lighting arguments raged about the relative benefits of gas made from coal and gas made from oil and 'animal substances'. Damaged copper gas pipes, observed in Carlton House in 1815–1816,[207] were cited as evidence of the corrosive effect of sulphur, found in gas produced from coal but not to be found in gas made from oil.

In the Pavilion gas lighting was not installed in a conventional manner – for example to replace the oil or candles in lamps and chandeliers – but rather to illuminate, from the exterior, the painted-glass windows.[208] This may have been a deliberate choice on the part of the Pavilion's architect and decorators, or simply the result of the impracticality of gas lighting such complex chandeliers as those designed by Crace and Jones for the Music Room, Saloon and Banqueting Room.

Innovations proposed by Humphry Repton for Uppark – the home of Sir Harry Fetherstonhaugh, a friend of the Prince of Wales – might have been a source of inspiration. In 1813 a painted-glass window was installed in the north wall of the Serving Room. Repton, most concerned with the decorative impact of the coloured glass both by day and night, decided to illuminate the panel from behind at night. He wrote 'the effect will be magic as all the light may proceed from this window from Argand Lamps properly adjusted from behind'.[209]

The possibility of using gas lighting in Brighton was first mentioned in May 1816, when Sir Benjamin Bloomfield (Private Secretary to the Prince Regent) informed the Town Commissioners that, if they decided to light the town with gas, the Prince Regent would contribute to the lighting of the exterior of the Royal Pavilion and its outbuildings. Two years later the Brighton Gas Light & Coke Company was established and undertook to light the Pavilion Gardens with gas. In a letter dated September 1818, their agent Jonathan Taylor refers to the laying of necessary pipes to supply the Pavilion.[210] It would seem that at this time gas lighting was restricted to the gardens of the Royal Pavilion, as the building itself was undergoing extensive remodelling by Nash. In December 1820, the Governor of the Brighton Gas Light & Coke Company anxiously wrote to Sir Benjamin Bloomfield on the subject of lighting the Royal Pavilion.[211] He was concerned that, although George IV had signified his interest in having the Pavilion lit by gas, no further action had been taken, even though a gas works had been erected for the Pavilion, at some cost to the company.

However, by the following December local newspapers could enthusiastically report the lighting of the Pavilion by gas. That same month members of the Committee of the Brighton Gas Light & Coke Company visited the Pavilion to inspect the installation of piping. The Governor reported that he went on to the roof of the Pavilion 'for the purpose of inspecting the state of the lights in the Music Room', and that 'notwithstanding a high wind and very heavy rain they gave a brilliant and steady light'.[212]

Misunderstandings about the nature of the gas lighting abounded, provoking a somewhat irritated report in a local paper, which stated 'it is still said, in many quarters, that the interior of the Pavilion is lighted with gas, but it is erroneous – in no single instant has gas been used within the walls of the palace'. The report clarified the extent of the use of gas:

> exteriorly it is so illuminated, and most brilliantly, when needed, and the stained glass of
> the Music and Banqueting Rooms, together with that of the hall etc are made to display
> their rich variety of tints inwards by the blaze of gas without – no further is it used at the
> palace, nor is it intended that it ever should.[213]

The visitors' entrance to the Pavilion was the *porte cochère*, illuminated by a superb lacquered-metal glass globe suspended on eight metal ropes with eight flying dragons, each supporting on lotus branches a glass globe lit by gas. For reasons unknown, this dramatic feature was removed and put in store. From other references, it appears that the sets of three painted-glass windows above the North and South Staircase, which illuminate the stairs, the Chamber Floor Galleries and the Long Gallery, were also lit from behind at night. (fig.3) As the newspaper report above suggests, the painted clerestory windows in the Entrance Hall may also have been gas lit.

Heating systems, flues and chimneys

Open fires and an under-floor hot-air heating system kept Nash's Pavilion extremely warm.[214] The 1821 accounts for ironmongers Cutler & Sons list works to install the hot-air system for the Music Room and the supply of brass floor ventilation grills: 'Taking up the pavement in passage to Cellars, North Wing, digging out the Ground, cutting through the brick & stone making a cold Air drain, making a double hot Air Flue building a powerful hot Air Stove.'[215]

The accounts for the following quarter record the erection of scaffolding in the Music Room and Banqueting Room 'to increase the size of ventilation in the ceilings', presumably to rectify the impact of the powerful hot-air stove. A further account in the same quarter supplied by James Watts reads: 'taking up and making good floors in

Yellow Room, Saloon and Blue Room, to form hot air flues'.[216] The 'Yellow' and 'Blue' rooms refer to the Banqueting Room and Music Room Galleries, names still used which recalled the earlier chinoiserie decorative schemes based predominantly on yellow and blue. The hot-air system would have extended throughout the ground floor, probably in both public and private rooms.

The King's obsession with warmth throughout his palace extended to the new chapel, located at the south end of the building. Though incomplete in January 1822, the chapel was furnished for temporary use and heated with two large fireplaces and a stove. The chief concern was to keep it warm by any means and, as a guest observed, somewhat scornfully, 'they had no idea of what temperature they were aspiring to, and no thermometer'.[217]

Nash picturesquely clustered the chimneystacks on the Pavilion's roof in groups of up to eight stacks, as well as single stacks. They appear to the viewer as miniature minarets with onion-shaped finials, key elements in the rhythm of the skyline. (fig.5) Practicalities were subjugated to style by the architect, and many of the chimney flues extended a considerable length (horizontally and vertically) to link chimneystack and fireplace. Over two hundred open fires, stoves and kitchen ranges on the estate required regular flue cleaning, a task undertaken by William Noble. Noble received a regular quarterly payment to keep all the chimneys clean. A bill for the first quarter of 1831, following a two-month period of residency by William IV, records that a total of 528 chimneys were cleaned. Presumably heavy use required some flues to be cleaned more than once.[218]

The convoluted route of some of the flues would have presented problems for chimney sweep apprentices, young children forced to climb into 9-inch (23 cm) square flues to clean the soot from the sides and sharp angles. The aperture above the fireplace was usually a 14-inch by 9-inch (36 x 22 cm) parallelogram. Mechanical sweeping systems made of linked tubes and brushes were available, but were only effective for straightforward, single-directional flues.

John William Hiort, an officer with some thirty-six years' experience as Chief Examining Clerk in the King's Office of Works department, was appalled by the absurd complexity of some of the flues in the royal palaces. (fig.6) He devised a new system with a circular flue made of shaped bricks, vitrified on the inside to prevent the adhesion of soot.[219] This system improved the draw air and, most importantly, could be easily cleaned with mechanical devices as the circular section flue created no awkward angles. Hiort had unsuccessfully proposed the use of his new design at Buckingham Palace though it was installed in Clarence House in London as well as in certain new public buildings. Having worked closely with Nash at Carlton House in the early years of the Regency it would seem logical, given the King's interest in innovation, for his new patent system to have been used in the Pavilion. However, Hiort's system would have imposed constraints on Nash's freedom of design and perhaps for this reason the traditional square-section flue was used.

The roaring fire in the Octagonal Entrance Hall (fig.4) that welcomed guests on their arrival does not have a simple vertical chimney flue, as there was no place in Nash's

5. (right) The west front of the Royal Pavilion. Picturesque clusters of five and seven chimneystacks arranged amongst the turrets, domes and minarets enliven Nash's roofscape.

6. (far right) Drying Room Chimney at Buckingham Palace. This drawing was presented as evidence in the House of Lords by campaigners trying to abolish the use of child labour to clean chimneys. The circuitous route of the flue in this example prevented the use of mechanical sweeping machines, ensuring the continued employment of children. House of Lords Sessional Papers, vol. 23 (Part I), 1834. © The British Library.

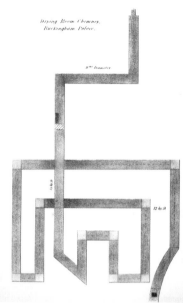

design of the exterior for a chimneystack or pot. Instead the flue descends behind the grate, down under the floor and horizontally across the building, to meet up with another flue in the main part of the building.

The warm atmosphere of the Pavilion was further enhanced by the English custom, noted by Prince Pückler-Muskau, of using rugs as draught-excluders: 'rugs (sheep-skins with the wool nicely prepared and dyed of bright colours) are laid before the doors to prevent drafts'.[220] For the King's apartments Thomas Saunders supplied in 1821 '12 wool Skins for the window'. The Music Room and the Banqueting Room were each furnished with 'five brown Sheep Skin rugs' and the Saloon with '3 white Sheep skin rugs for the windows'.[221] These rugs, used only in winter, would have reduced draughts from the tall French windows in the main public rooms and retained the stifling atmosphere.

Clearly the new hot-air system was problematic and its intense heat continued to cause much discomfort to guests. Princess Lieven complained after two days in Brighton: 'I have an inflamed eye – the heat of the Pavilion and the lamps do not improve it.'[222] However, this malaise did not deter her from attending a ball in the Pavilion and dancing, nor from a dinner with The Duke of Wellington, who was invited by the King for her benefit.

Following her visit in 1842, Queen Victoria also complained about the heating and ventilation of the Pavilion. Dr David Boswell Reid (1805–1863), renowned for his ventilation works at the Houses of Parliament, provided plans for improvements. Clearly the installation of new ventilation shafts in the Pavilion's unusual and complex structure proved difficult. When criticised for exceeding his budgets, Reid replied 'the arrangements at the Pavilion may have been attended with considerable expense', but that 'the extreme peculiarity of structure, and the total absence of an adequate supply of air, rendered it impossible to attempt any amelioration of the state of the atmosphere in the apartments to which my attention was directed without considerable alterations'.[223]

7. (left) The Water Tower, from Nash's Views (detail). The Water or Clock Tower can be seen on the right. It was demolished after the town bought the Pavilion in 1850.

8. (right) Cross-section of the upper part of the Water or Clock Tower. Below the support stand for the Vulliamy clock sits the large lead water tank; a forcing engine beneath pumped water throughout the Pavilion. (Drawing from the Plan Registry Archive: Good/9.)

Water supplies, baths and closets

Water supplies for the Pavilion were plentiful and easily accessible. Beneath the Steine and the Pavilion Gardens were abundant springs creating a high water table. During a recent excavation of an area just north of the original water tower an active well was found in a basement area, which had been created in the post-1850 period. The well, at the level of the ground of the new house's coal cellars, was some 12 feet (3.7 m) deep, with the water level only 3 feet (1 m) below the ground. The high water level was probably a factor in the way new basements were dug in Nash's building: they were excavated only where considered essential, for example at the north and south ends.

When the new north-end apartments were constructed basements were dug to create areas for essential services for the King's rooms and, in particular, for his bathroom. In 1819 Nash noted the problem of 'sinking the ground thereof 18 inches below the springs'[224] to create the basement rooms as well as the subterranean passage to the stables. To prevent flooding and water penetration he proposed using bricks, pounded chalk or his patent 'dihl mastic'.[225] Concerned about the problems of containing the water, Nash observed that, given the difficulty and uncertainty of these works, his estimates might be over budget.

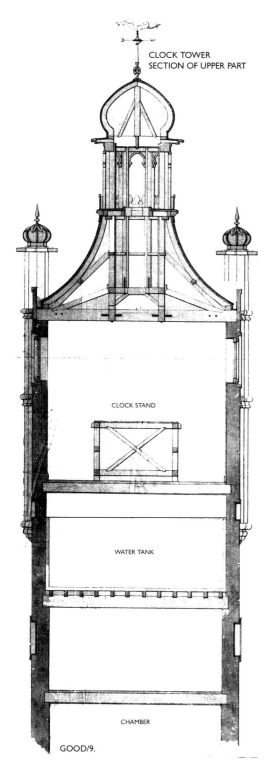

CLOCK TOWER
SECTION OF UPPER PART

CLOCK STAND

WATER TANK

CHAMBER

GOOD/9.

These springs ensured easily available supplies of water which could be pumped from adjacent wells. But only the King was provided with a fitted and fully plumbed bathroom.[226] Guests could bathe (as did members of the Royal Household) at one of the local town bath houses such as Mahomed's establishment or the Royal Baths. The availability of cheap labour made it more convenient to undertake one's ablutions on site and in privacy. The usual bathing equipment was metal tubs or slipper baths (thus named because they were shaped like a slipper or shoe) filled with hot water carried by hand by the plentiful servants and placed in the bedroom. Queen Victoria kept a gold and enamelled slipper bath for her personal use in Brighton. In the early decades of the nineteenth century guests in country houses would also use foot baths, described by Lady Dorothy Neville as a cross between a wine cooler and a soup tureen.[227] Poor personal hygiene was generally tolerated and unfortunate odours were concealed by perfumes, oils and fragrant waters.

The water closets (or flushing lavatories) throughout the Pavilion were supplied with water from cisterns. Water was pumped throughout the building through iron mains and lead pipes by a forcing engine in the water tower (fig.7), which was located in the kitchen courtyard to the south. Generally the seats of the water closets were made of mahogany and the backs panelled in cedar to conceal the pipes and mechanism. More rudimentary closets, in the servants' areas, were constructed of painted deal.

Closets at this period were made with two basic mechanisms: the valve water closet and the pan closet. The more expensive (and most pleasant) was the valve closet, devised and promoted by Joseph Bramah. In Bramah's closet a horizontal valve under the ceramic basin kept a level of water in the basin to minimise smells during use and to prevent smells arising from the soil pipe, drains and cesspool beneath. Apart from the expense of installation, the valve closet also needed regular maintenance.

The pan closet, unlike the valve closet, retained a little water in the basin or tipping pan itself. Though cheap to install it was unhygienic and smelly. The pan closet was difficult to clean and foul smells rose up from the pipes and drains when the pan was dropped to release its charge. (fig.9) Despite this, it continued to be used for servants into the 1880s. Many closet rooms in the Pavilion – including, for example, the closet in the King's bedroom – had no direct external ventilation. Consequently, the valve closet

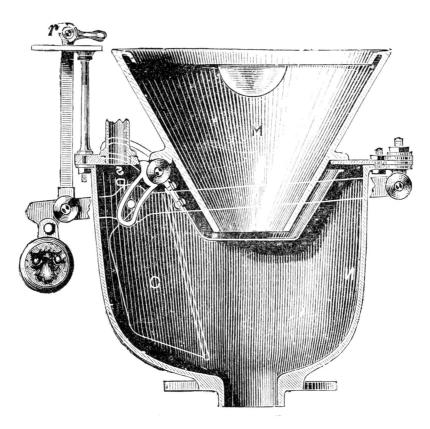

9. Pan closet. *Cross-section of a pan closet both when new (left) and when used (below). The copper pan held 3–4 inches (8–10 cm) of water, but after use the discharges clung to the sides of the pan and the main vessel. Every time it was used the smells of the soil and urine in the main vessel discharged up into the room. From* The Plumber and Sanitary Houses *by S. Stevens Hellyer, 1882.*

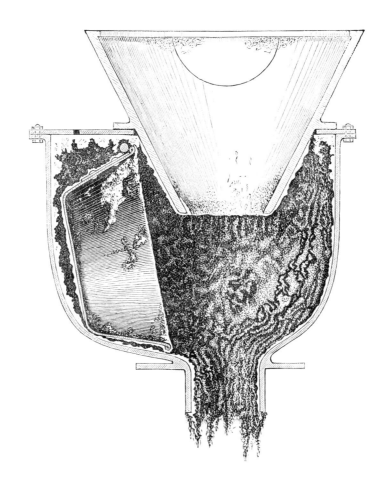

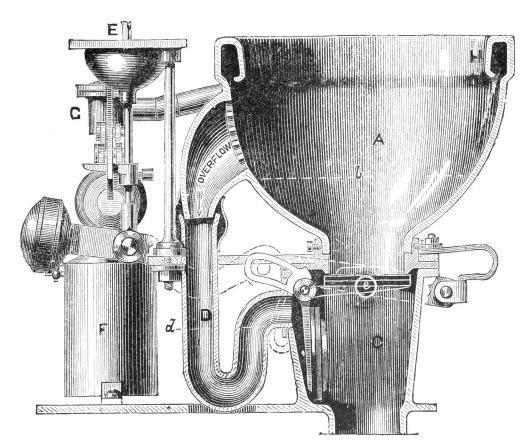

10. The valve water closet. *The invention of Joseph Bramah in 1778; the basin is kept two-thirds full of water by means of a flap-valve. Though expensive to install and maintain, it was hygienic and ideal for enclosed spaces with no external ventilation. From* The Plumber and Sanitary Houses *by S. Stevens Hellyer, 1882.*

was installed in most areas of the Pavilion, (fig.10) though accounts also record the installation of pan closets, probably only to be used by the servants.

The bedrooms in the Pavilion, if not provided with a water closet, were furnished with 'a night convenience' or a chamber pot, sometimes placed in a bedside 'pedestal' or cabinet or incorporated into bed steps. Stored in the Pavilion were various night conveniences such as the 'Box Night Convenience covered and lined blue Velvet' recorded in the Pavilion's 1828 inventory. Several three-tread satinwood bed steps, enclosing night conveniences, were available for use by guests. In addition, the accounts record the purchase of blue-printed ceramic slippers (slipper-shaped pots), chamber pots of various sizes and design, stool pans and bedpans. Slipper pots were also called 'coach pots' (as they were used on long journeys) or by the French name *bourdalou*, named after, it was claimed, a French cleric renowned for very long sermons. (fig.12) Such wares were made with transfer-printed design by a number of pottery firms such as Spode and Ridgeway. Ladies' under-garments at this period had separate legs, not joined at the crotch, allowing for discreet use of a slipper pot whilst travelling or at the opera.

Holland's Marine Pavilion was furnished with a limited number of closets on the ground floor only. Nash's Pavilion was amply furnished with flushing water closets on ground, first and basement floors. The more important guest rooms, such as those of the King's brothers, the Duke of York and the Duke of Clarence, had their own private

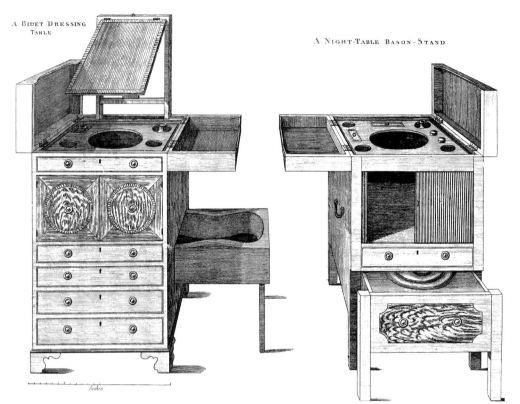

A BIDET DRESSING TABLE

A NIGHT-TABLE BASON-STAND

11.a. *A bidet dressing table, and a night table basin-stand. These convenient pieces of furniture for bedrooms combining several functions were designed by Thomas Sheraton in the 1790s.*

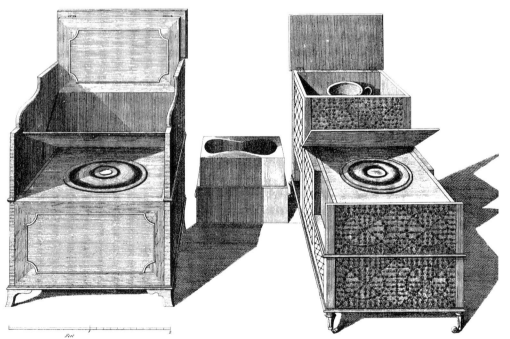

11.b. *Two bed steps, also designed by Thomas Sheraton. These bed steps, providing easy access to the bed, also neatly concealed a bidet and a chamber pot. From Thomas Sheraton's* The Cabinet Maker and Upholsterer's Drawing Book, *published in 1794.*

12. (right) Slipper pot and (below) *bourdalou,* Spode *printed earthenware. Ladies on journeys or at the opera and theatre used these pots, more usefully shaped than the standard chamber pot. © The Spode Museum Trust.*

closets supplied with water from cisterns or reservoirs on the roof. All the waste was carried away to the sea in a specially constructed sewer. The central dome over the Saloon, flanked by two towers, was also supplied with water and a soil pipe. This area, a cluster of odd-shaped small rooms within the dome, was probably used by 'above stairs' servants.

The generous provision of closets in the Pavilion contrasts with Chatsworth House, the old-fashioned but grandest of the Duke of Devonshire's country residences. Chatsworth was sumptuously decorated with a dining room capable of seating a hundred guests. Though renowned for lavish entertainment it was, in the late eighteenth century, fitted with only three water closets to service the entire family, servants and numerous guests. By contrast the modest-sized Pavilion had over thirty water closets and the Ladies Retiring Room, near the Banqueting Room, had its own private water closet for female dinner guests.

To foreign visitors this new technology was intriguing and noteworthy. In 1810, the French *emigré* Louis Simond toured England on a visit from his adopted home in the United States. He was impressed by the common sewers in the streets of London and described a new facility he had seen in the houses of the rich which he noted 'are called water-closets'.[228]

Ice houses

With no forms of modern refrigeration available in the early nineteenth century, ice houses played a vital role in ensuring the provision of ice and of cool larders throughout the year. The Pavilion was serviced by at least two ice houses, one located in the south-west corner of the grounds and another nearby in North Street.

Since the 1790s, the Marine Pavilion had been supplied with ice from the ice house in North Street, built on land acquired by Weltje for the Prince of Wales. It was referred to as 'a new erected building … called an Ice House with Tea Room and Summer House over'.[229] Subsequently, in 1822, a new ice well was built, as an annotated drawing in the Royal Archives records: 'proposed new Ice Well to be made instead of the present two … situated in the upper part of North St, Brighton'.[230] It would seem that this new ice well was finished by December as accounts recorded that the gardener, John Furner, filled the 'new ice wells compleat', having collected twenty-three cartloads of ice from ponds at Falmer.[231]

In *Rural Residences*, published in 1818, John Papworth commended the benefits of the ice house. In addition to servicing the needs of the confectioner:

13. The ice house in the Pavilion Gardens rediscovered by workmen excavating the ground to build an electricity substation in the 1950s.
The Brighton Herald,
10 December 1955.

14. The ice house *at Felbrigg Hall in Norfolk. Of similar design to the Pavilion's ice houses, the brick-domed construction, with a 9-metre pit, was built c. 1820. Reproduced by courtesy of The National Trust.*

the ice-house forms an excellent larder for the preservation of every kind of food that is liable to be injured by heat in summer; thus fish, game, poultry, butter, &c, may be kept for a considerable time: indeed, in London they are used for such purposes by persons who deal largely in either fish or venison; and for the table, where coolness is desirable, the use of ice in summer is a great luxury.

He also suggests the use of ice as a form of air cooling:

By the proper introduction of ice into apartments in close and sultry days, streams of cool and refreshing air are produced that no other means can obtain; for the air is cooled by the ice being urged forward by the warm air, continued currents are created, that prove as salutary as agreeable.[232]

Ice creams, iced confections and iced drinks were fashionable in Regency England, and this demand encouraged the more extensive development of ice houses in the cities, as well as at country residences. Two key factors were good drainage and appropriate soil: chalk allowed a pit to be dug entirely underground, as in the case of the Pavilion's ice house, a domed and bricked structure (fig.14). A similar type of construction can still be seen in the grounds of Felbrigg Hall in Norfolk.

Ice houses were usually supplied with ice from local ponds and streams or specially constructed ice ponds. The first cargo of imported fresh-water ice from Norway arrived in London in May 1822. It was transported in *The Spring*, a vessel chartered by a Mr William Leftwich. The journey was recorded in a Norwegian newspaper some three months later. Despite 20 per cent duty imposed by Customs, Leftwich realised a large profit:

> as people in London had not seen ice before between May and November … As soon as
> the pastrycooks and fishmongers heard that a whole cargo of this priceless article had
> arrived, they came forward in crowds. The discharge of the ice and its sale to thousands of
> eager buyers offered a lively scene, the like of which, as regards its novelty and
> strangeness, had never been seen.[233]

The collection of ice was the responsibility of the gardener, John Furner, and his staff. An account for the quarter ending 5 July 1822 refers to 'expenses to and from London to see Mr Stonehouse respecting a vessel load of ice to Brighton'.[234] This may have been a cargo from Norway, which could by then provide ice supplies all year round. By the mid-nineteenth century North America and Norway dominated the import trade to Britain, providing purer, cleaner ice, less dangerous to the health of its consumers.

George was fond of ice cream and iced confections as well as iced drinks. The kitchen offices, south of the Great Kitchen, included a dedicated ice room furnished with lead-lined ice storage bins. This room was adjacent to the confectionery, where ice moulds and utensils were stored for use by chefs. Ice bins were also placed in the wine cellars beneath the Banqueting Room, storing ice ready for use in wine coolers at dinners.

Fire prevention

The timber and iron construction of the Pavilion and the extensive use of candles, oil lamps and gas meant that the threat of fire was always a concern. An engine, fixed in a cast-iron frame, was located beneath the octagonal water tower at the south end of the Pavilion and supplied water to the various internal and external fire cocks. In the Engine House within the stable complex was stored a large fire engine with leather hose pipes, and a second smaller fire engine. Fire buckets, made of leather and filled with sand, were used for minor incidents. They were strategically placed in large numbers within the building in the servants' corridors, hung high on iron hooks.

The fire engines in the Pavilion were supplied and maintained by Thomas Simpson & Sons.[235] Most fire engines of this period consisted of a wood frame (oak or fir) on which was mounted hand-operated air cylinder pumps, which could draw water in from the fire cocks and then pump it out at the fire itself (fig.15). The engines were moved either by horse or by a team of men.

15. Six-inch barrel fire engine, *made of wood with cast-iron supports, engraving based on fire engine designs made by the London firm of W. J. Tilley. In the foreground can be seen a length of leather hose. Published in* On the Construction of Fire Engines ... *by James Braidwood, 1830.* © The British Library

A standard engine was supplied with six coils of leather hose, each 40 inches (102 cm) in length. An innovation of the early nineteenth century was the replacement of the thread-sown leather hose pipe (which tended to leak) by copper rivet hose. The quality and strength of leather used was vital and skin from the softer parts of an animal (neck, shoulders and belly) was to be avoided. Strips of leather were laid under a 3-inch by 1-inch (8 x 2.5 cm) iron bar (with rounded corners), then stretched, and the seams were riveted to form a hose. Should there be a leak whilst in use 3–4-inch (7.6–10.2 cm) strips of sheepskin were tied over the damaged area as a temporary measure.

Maintenance of both the Pavilion's engines and leather hose was essential and the accounts record the purchase of tallow and oil by Thomas Simpson for this purpose. To retain the flexibility of the leather the hose, after use, was partially dried and then rubbed with tallow, beeswax or oil. Once completely dry the leather was oiled, waxed or greased again and coiled ready for use. The fire engines were decorated with the royal coat of arms, as were the riveted leather sand buckets.

There are, however, no recorded incidents of fire in the Pavilion during its period of royal occupancy.

8 A controversial palace: reviled and restored

The Georgian perspective: 'a childish bauble'

The Royal Pavilion has always provoked strong reactions from guests, visitors, journalists and writers. The exotic extravagance of the structure and decorations, and the immense financial resources dedicated to its realisation, were legendary even in the Regency period. Lord Byron, familiar with the King's architectural (and other) excesses, gibed in *Don Juan*:

Shut up – no, <u>not</u> the King, but the Pavilion
Or else t'will cost us all another million![236]

As Nash's oriental splendour emerged from scaffolding (1817–1820) the wits and anti-monarchists revelled in the opportunity presented by such a curious structure: 'a childish bauble … in the form of the Kremlin' exclaimed the *Morning Post* in 1818: 'Strange that in the nineteenth century our Princes should go to the most barbarous times, and the most barbarous people for models for their Palaces!'

The Pavilion's style, described as Chinese, Turkish, Gothic, Moorish or in imitation of the Kremlin – caused both confusion and amusement amongst observers. Karl Frederick Schinkel, the eminent neo-classical German architect, who visited Brighton in 1826, described the exterior as reminiscent of 'the Moorish style of royal tombs in India'; the interior was simply 'magnificent'.[237]

Schinkel was initially refused admittance by the Lord Steward, the Marquis of Conyngham, following the King's instructions that no one could visit his Palace. On hearing that the request was from Schinkel, the King allowed him to visit the Pavilion as well as Windsor. Schinkel was particularly impressed by Nash's use of cast iron, both structurally and decoratively, as well as the technological innovations and gadgets. He devoted, uniquely, some three pages of his journal to the Pavilion, with his impressions and drawings of details such as the steam outlet system in the kitchens and cast-iron bannisters. Though admiring the design of Porden's stables, with its vast glass and iron dome, he was critical of its function and noted: 'Too hot inside, really crazy: it was designed to be a green house.'[238]

For radicals and political opponents of the King, the Pavilion quickly became a symbol of the abuse of power, the waste of public funds and social injustice. Writing on the effect of war and taxes in 1819, William Hazlitt described examples of productive and unproductive labour. The former adds materially to the necessities of life. As an example of the latter he writes 'if I hire a livery-servant, and keep him fine and lazy and well-fed to stand behind my chair while I eat turtle or venison, thus is another instance of unproductive labour'.[239] By his definition unproductive labour funded from taxes, from the public purse, was totally unacceptable, even if it had provided employment. The Pyramids of Egypt and the Pavilion at Brighton, both costly royal monuments, were cited as examples. His point is valid and such sums as were expended at the Pavilion could have been much better used for social benefit. However, the cultural and economic value of the Pavilion to Brighton, then as now, was always recognised by those responsible for the management of the town.

William Cobbett, political writer and reformer, visited Brighton in 1822. His description of Nash's completed structure has become almost as famous as the building itself. He only saw the exterior and ridiculed the design as follows:

> Take a square box … Take a large Norfolk-turnip, cut off the green of the leaves … put the turnip on the middle of the top of the box. Then take four turnips of half the size, treat them in the same way, and put them on the corners of the box. Then take a considerable number of bulbs … put all these, pretty promiscuously, but pretty thickly, on the top of the box. Then stand off and look at your architecture. There! That's 'a Kremlin!'[240]

Joseph Farington, RA, on seeing the Pavilion in 1818, more astutely recognised Nash's inspiration, noting the resemblance between the Pavilion and 'some of the Palaces represented in Daniell's *Oriental Scenery*. However, he continued, 'its singularity is ill suited to its situation', as it was sited amongst conventional buildings which were 'of a common ordinary English form & appearance'.[241]

The King admired the Scottish novelist Sir Walter Scott, who brilliantly stage-managed his historic visit to Scotland in 1822. In addition to literature and Scottish history, they shared an interest in the new gas technology. Scott, however, was not impressed by Porden's or Nash's architectural achievements. To a letter to a friend in Brighton he added a footnote: 'Will you do me a favour set fire to the Chinese Stables and if it embrace the whole of the pavilion it will rid us of a great eyesore.'[242]

Some, with much irony, purported to appreciate this 'most original and unique structure in Europe' and saw in the oriental style a political appropriateness for the future monarch: 'it may be presumed that the Regent, who must be led to consider himself as virtual sovereign of the East, deemed it respectful to his eastern dependencies to exhibit in conformity with their notions of architectural perfection'.[243]

Oh we must now leave this place; it may do for the Royal family, but not for a fashion—able one

What shocking Savages!!

Wot time was we to be on the Rail-Road again?

PROBABLE EFFECT OF THE PROJECTED RAIL-ROAD TO BRIGHTON.

William IV and Queen Adelaide

2. Probable effect of the projected rail-road to Brighton, late 1830s. The London to Brighton railway opened in 1841. The elegant couple, shocked by the arrival of an unsavoury-looking family ('shocking savages,' the lady remarks), decide they must leave Brighton: 'It may do for the Royal family, but not for a fashionable one.'

The King's younger brother, William, Duke of Clarence, continued to favour the Pavilion (and Brighton) when he acceded to the throne in 1830. William had been a regular visitor to Brighton during his brother's lifetime and the Yellow Bow Rooms (south) were dedicated for his use. As King, he sought the approbation of his people, and being an affable, domestic and good-natured individual, he achieved both popularity and approval.

One of his first acts as King was to dismiss George IV's cooks and French servants, as a gesture of patriotism and an indication that the extravagant days of his brother were over. To make this policy clear to all in Brighton, William IV issued a directive that meat for his establishment must not cost more than sixpence a pound and fowl no more than 5 shillings a couple.[244] In George IV's day tradesmen had benefited from the culinary and alcoholic opportunities of visits to the Palace, and were daily seen leaving in a serious state of intoxication. The new King gave orders that in future all tradesmen who had business at the Palace would be given only bread, cheese and porter.

Former close associates of George IV poured scorn on such apparently trivial decrees. Princess Lieven felt monarchy had gone to William IV's head, and it was 'a weak head'. She decried the sacking of French cooks and servants: 'the cook business was the first act of his reign – on the very day of the late King's death'. But she acknowledged that the new King loved court ceremony and made himself visible to his subjects. After years of his brother's reclusive behaviour William IV's new attitude met with popular approval: 'the mob adores him' she continued, and 'he goes about openly and treats everyone familiarly'.[245] His clear commitment to Brighton reassured local interests.

The Pavilion's accommodation, designed for a King who lived apart from his wife, was not suitable for a married sovereign. There were additional domestic requirements for William IV's wife, Queen Adelaide. Her household included her Mistress of the Robes, six Ladies of the Bedchamber, six Bed Chamber Women, six Maids of Honour, two Keepers of the Robes, an Assistant Dresser and Sempstress [sic], nine Gentlemen Ushers (with various responsibilities), and six Pages of the Backstairs, as well as administrative staff, physicians, surgeons and staff to manage the Queen's stables. Initially some fifty beds were rented in the town for their servants, but within a year or so new building works began on the estate. These included servants' dormitories and more stables with additional rooms for footmen and stable staff, as well as new gatehouses to the north and south of the gardens to enclose the estate.

The Queen's preference for simplicity and informality, combined with William's generosity and sociability, ensured that the Pavilion was still used for entertainments, though they were not characterised by the glamour or extravagance of former decades. The atmosphere was homely, the food dull – 'cold pâtés and hot champagne', as one guest observed – and behaviour sensible and appropriate to court life.

Charles Greville experienced social life in the Pavilion under both monarchs. He described the new Queen as a prude who would not allow women to come *décolletées* to her parties. George, on the other hand, had 'liked ample expanses of that sort' and would not let them be covered.[246] One feels that Queen Adelaide was somewhat overwhelmed by the opulence of the Pavilion. In 1833 the immense dragon chandelier in the Banqueting Room was removed and put in store as she feared it might fall on her dining guests.

Following William's death in 1837, the aspirations of the town were again reassured by the arrival of the new monarch, the young Queen Victoria, who came to Brighton only a few months after her accession.

Queen Victoria and the Pavilion

Queen Victoria, however, felt little sympathy for Brighton. The style of the Pavilion and its inevitable association with her profligate and unpopular elder uncle made her uncomfortable. When she made her first visit to the Pavilion in 1837, this gesture of royal approval thrilled the people of Brighton. Queen Victoria recalled in her journal the friendly and enthusiastic reception she received, and noted the elaborate decorations of the Pavilion. Her initial reaction was cool:

> The Pavilion is a strange, odd, Chinese looking place, both outside & inside. Most of the rooms are low, & I can only see a morsel of the sea, from one of my sitting room windows, which is strange, considering how close one is to the sea.[247]

Queen Victoria returned again to the Pavilion in December 1838 and seems to have enjoyed her second visit more. She recorded in her diary: 'The Pavilion, lighted up, looked cheerful … & my impression of it, was not so cheerless as last year.' [248] She did not return again until 1842, when her visit (10 February – 8 March) coincided with the second anniversary of her marriage to her beloved Albert.

On this occasion the Hon. Georgina Liddell, Maid of Honour, accompanied the Queen to Brighton. She was not enthralled by the royal estate. She later described her impressions:

> I have been walking in the Pavilion garden, which is odious; so low and damp, without a
> glimpse of the 'deep and dark blue ocean'; one might as well pace round and round
> Berkeley Square [in London]. I suppose it *is* sea air, but so mixed with soot and smoke it
> loses half its value.

She continued, 'the whole place was a strange specimen of royal eccentricity, and a most uncomfortable, dull residence, so I never wondered at the Queen's getting rid of it'.[249]

Throughout Queen Victoria's period of residence in Brighton a policy of financial stringency prevailed. The Office of Woods and Forests (formerly the Office of Works), which was responsible for the structure of the Pavilion, consistently instructed its Clerk of Works, Joseph Good, to prepare estimates for the maintenance of the buildings 'with the most rigid and severe economy'. In 1839 Good was ordered to limit the works at the Pavilion 'to keeping the outside and roofs in good repair and the prevention of injury to the interior by rot occasioned by confined air or damp'.

The arrangements of the Chamber (or first) Floor had to be adapted for the 1842 visit to accommodate the Queen, Prince Albert and two children, the Princess Royal and the Prince of Wales. A plan of the Chamber Floor, probably executed before the 1842 visit, shows the reallocation of rooms and certain proposed structural alterations. Baroness Lehzen, the Queen's confidante, now less in favour since the Queen's marriage, was moved to apartments in the south-west tower, so providing rooms for Prince Albert near the Queen.

Victoria retained her modest bedroom known as the Chamber over the Entrance Hall, with the wardrobe maid's room to the east and the wardrobe to the north. Above, in the four tiny attic rooms, resided the Queen's dressers. Her bedroom was linked by a jib door and steps to the dressing rooms of herself and Albert.[250] The original bedroom of George, Prince of Wales, on the east front became their sitting room;[251] the South Gallery served as a breakfast and lunch room. A partition to the north end of the South Gallery created a servants' passage and access to the royal sitting rooms. The children were accommodated in the Yellow Bow Rooms, with the nursery kitchen and dining room in the north-west tower. The Prince's valet occupied rooms in the dome above the Saloon, with his dressers located in the northern range of rooms.

Victoria recalls in her diary how Prince Albert was struck with the strangeness of the Royal Pavilion. She noted that he 'was in great admiration of the Dining and Music Rooms, which are so splendid and richly done up and furnished, in every detail'. Possibly, as a result of his enthusiasm, the magnificent central dragon chandelier in the Banqueting Room was reinstated later that year. After concern was expressed by the Office of Woods and Forests regarding the safe replacement of the chandelier, Good carefully examined the ceiling of the Banqueting Room. He recommended the installation of nearly two tons of iron bracing in the roof to provide vital support for the chandelier, which, in itself, weighed just under a ton.

As the Queen's family grew rapidly in the early 1840s, the Pavilion failed to provide her with the space and privacy she needed. The height of the walls enclosing the gardens was increased and the railings were boarded on the inside to inhibit the inquisitive. The Queen felt unable to walk in the town or by the sea without being annoyed by crowds of onlookers. A local newspaper report in 1845 recorded her displeasure with the unfortunate behaviour of 'errand boys' rudely peering at her beneath her bonnet. The report continues, 'but if the Queen cannot enjoy a walk without being subject to annoyances from which the meanest of her subjects are free it is not to be wondered that Brighton is so seldom selected for the royal residence'.

The new railway from London to Brighton, which opened in 1841, marked the beginning of mass tourism. (fig.2) This was one reason why Queen Victoria decided to sell the Royal Pavilion to the Town Commissioners of Brighton and build Osborne, a secluded family home on the Isle of Wight that would become the personal creation of

FANCY FAIR IN THE PAVILION, BRIGHTON, FOR THE BENEFIT OF THE BRIGHTON DISPENSARY.

4. A 'Fancy Fair' being held in the Music Room. The Crace chandeliers, removed by Queen Victoria, have been replaced with Apsley Pellatt gas-lit globe hanging lamps. Christopher Wren Vick redecorated the room, and John Thomas designed the stone chimneypiece. From the Illustrated London News, *22 March 1851.*

her beloved husband. Another reason was her desire to dissociate herself and the monarchy from George IV and from the building so closely associated with his extravagance and dissolute lifestyle.

In the late 1840s all interior decorations, fittings and furnishings, including copper piping from the King's bath, were dismantled, sold or removed to store in Kensington Palace. Even the plants from greenhouses and the garden implements (such as rakes, hoes and brooms) were auctioned locally in 1848. In 1850 after a long public debate, the Pavilion was sold for some £53,000.

Many of the finest elements of the Pavilion's furniture and decoration were reused in Buckingham Palace in Edward Blore's new wing, concentrated in three rooms – the Chinese Luncheon Room, the Centre Room and the Yellow Drawing Room. Queen Victoria described the first of these new decorative schemes in her *Journal* in 1849:

We breakfasted as we already dined last night, in the new room that has been made for us … a fine large lunch room, very handsomely fitted up with furniture &c., from the Pavilion at Brighton, including the Chinese pictures, which were on the Dining-room walls there, the doors with the serpents &c. which had belonged to that room. A dragon has been painted on the ceiling to harmonise with the rest.[252] (fig.3)

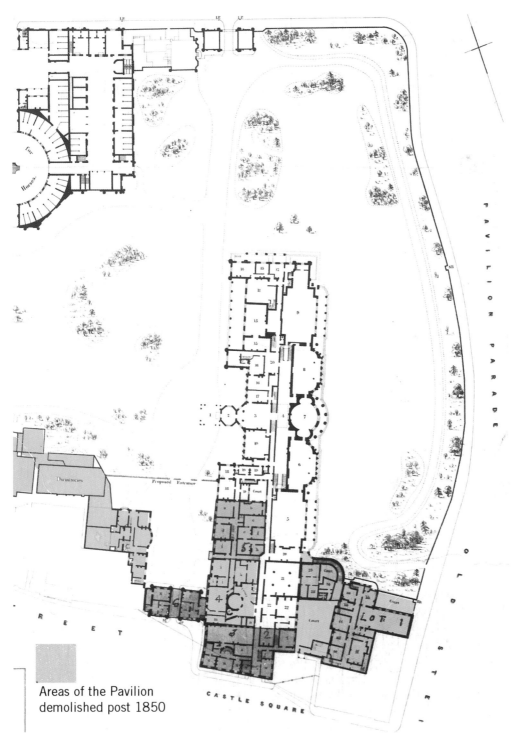

5. Plan of the Royal Pavilion in 1849, showing the areas (in shades of pink) that were demolished and sold in lots to developers by Brighton's Town Commissioners. The demolition of the South Gate House and the Royal Chapel allowed the creation of two new streets – Pavilion Buildings and Palace Place.

Areas of the Pavilion demolished post 1850

The influence of the architectural style of the Pavilion in the period up to its municipal ownership was limited to imitations (or selective borrowings) mostly applied to seaside architecture. There was no flowering of fashionable orientalism in the 1820s, 1830s or 1840s.[253] The most significant impact of the Pavilion was not in England, but in the United States. The American showman P. T. Barnum, following visits to Brighton in the 1840s, determined to build a fabulous palace in oriental style in Bridgeport, Connecticut. Iranistan (or Oriental Villa as Barnum translated the name), was said to be loosely based on the Pavilion. The designs were commissioned by Barnum, executed by a London architect and translated into reality by an American builder. This domed extravaganza, sadly destroyed by fire in 1857, would appear from surviving illustrations to owe more to Humphry Repton's proposed ideas for the Pavilion available in *Designs for the Pavilion at Brighton*, published in 1808, and Thomas Daniell's *Oriental Scenery* than the actual building realised by John Nash.

Brighton in the 1850s

Brighton retained its fashionable and racy reputation despite the impact of two rather domestic and homely monarchs. It was to Brighton that the novelist William Thackeray sent the lovelorn Amelia Sedley and the reluctant George Osborne for their honeymoon after their secret marriage. Here Rawdon Crawley, William Dobbin and Jos Sedley enjoyed themselves, and the relentless Becky Crawley tried to re-establish herself with her former patroness, spying on her bathing machine through her telescope from the balcony of her sea-front hotel. Although *Vanity Fair* was first published in 1848, it was set some thirty years earlier, in the Regency period. With some irony, Thackeray paused in his story to expand on the charms of Brighton's ocean, 'smiling with its countless dimples, speckled with white sails, with a hundred bathing-machines' that enraptured the Londoner. Then he likened the town of Brighton to 'a clean Naples with genteel Lazzaroni [vagabonds] … brisk, gay and gaudy, like a harlequin's coat'.[254]

In the late 1850s, the Duke of Buckingham favourably reviewed the reign of George IV and his achievements, attributing the complete transformation of Brighton, 'an insignificant fishing village', to George's love of his favourite residence and his patronage of the town. He continued, somewhat more accurately:

> his taste and enterprise gave there an impulse for building, which in due time transformed
> its huts into palaces, and its dirty thoroughfares into fine terraces, and elegant squares. All
> the attractions of architecture have since been lavished on the place, and the
> recommendation of fashion has insured for it every benefit that could be conferred on a
> marine resort, within a few hours distance of the metropolis.[255]

Before the Pavilion was sold to Brighton in 1850 its magnificent rooms had been completely stripped and left in a dilapidated state:

> Scarcely more than the bare walls remained, for the chimneypieces had been torn down;
> the chandeliers, the organ, and even the grates removed; the Music Room stripped of its
> beautiful Chinese paintings, and the whole place dismantled and disfigured, as though its
> doom had been fixed.[256]

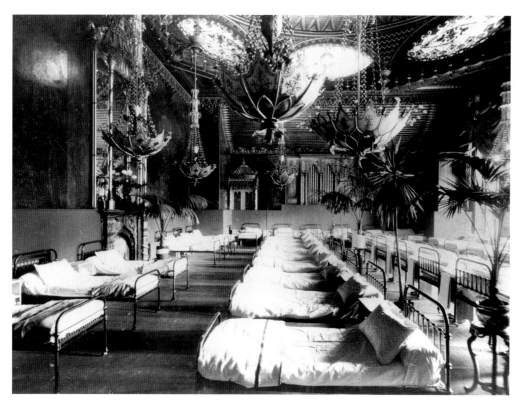

6. (left) The Music Room during the First World War, used as a hospital for Indian soldiers. The entire complex, including what became known as the Dome and the Corn Exchange (the King's former stables and riding house) was closed and converted into a military hospital.

7. (right) The Music Room during the Second World War, used by Brighton Borough Council as a venue for administrative war work.

The Town Commissioners, aware of the economic and symbolic importance of this former palace, established a committee to oversee the refurbishment of the Pavilion. The committee was somewhat disconcerted to discover that fixtures and fittings, part of the freehold, had been removed by the Queen's officials. A survey carried out in July 1850 recorded wallpapers and canvases, doors, painted glass, fixed columns and marble chimneypieces had been removed, in their view illegally. Over forty marble chimneypieces, including the three used by Prince Albert's personal staff in the Saloon 'bottle' or dome, were ripped out and removed along with their grates and hearth stones. Recourse to the Lord Chamberlain's Office resulted in referral to the Office of Woods and Forests. Many of the superb marble and ormolu chimneypieces had already been cemented into Buckingham Palace. Their return was not a realistic aspiration, a fact the Town Commissioners had to accept. New stone chimneypieces, designed by John Thomas, were installed as replacements. Within a year of purchase, however, the main ground-floor rooms had been completely redecorated in an approximation of Crace and Jones's designs and opened to public view.

The Pavilion, the symbol of Brighton, and to many a symbol of its prosperity, has remained in the care of the local authority since 1850, and undergone extensive structural and interior restoration works. This could not have been possible without the support of successive monarchs from Queen Victoria to the present Queen, who have supported its restoration and returned numerous original furnishings, fittings and *objets d'art*.

Municipal ownership: 'a temple of vanity'

8. (far right) The Chamber over the Entrance Hall, originally used by the young Queen Victoria as part of her private apartments. It was gutted and converted in the post-1850 period into a large double-height museum exhibition space.

The post-1850 history of the Royal Pavilion is one of continuous redecoration and restoration and forms a fascinating study of Victorian attitudes to period refurbishment.[257] So the long process of restoration and refurbishment began, which still continues today. Successive members of the Crace firm, notably J. G. Crace (Frederick Crace's son) and J. D. Crace (Frederick's grandson), contributed to the refurbishment in the latter half of the nineteenth century. Queen Victoria returned many items (chandeliers, wall paintings, fixtures and fittings) in 1864; these were items still in store, which had not been reused in Blore's new wing in Buckingham Palace. The town received further gifts in 1899 and many fittings and features were reinstated in their original positions.

Sadly a decision was taken after the town purchased the Pavilion estate to demolish a large part of the buildings to the south and sell them off in lots to developers (fig.5). Presumably this was done to generate income to offset the cost of purchase and redecoration. The Royal Chapel, the kitchen and household offices south of the Great Kitchen, the Clock Tower and most of the new buildings commissioned by William IV were pulled down, and the size and shape of George IV's original estate changed. As a result two new public thoroughfares were created, Pavilion Buildings and Palace Place.

Recent historians generally denigrate the Victorian phase of the Pavilion's history. Undoubtedly by today's standards Victorian restoration works tended to be crude and insensitive. In the 1890s, however, they were much admired by contemporaries, and as a result civic pride in the Royal Pavilion was maintained, thus ensuring its future. Enthusiastic reports in the local papers followed each project. Whilst J. D. Crace's restoration to the Music Room was still in progress in 1898, the *Brighton Herald*

9. The Chamber over the Entrance Hall transformed in the 1950s into a mid-Victorian-style bedroom to commemorate Queen Victoria's residency (1837–1845) in the Pavilion. It was furnished in a somewhat feminine style with gilt and lacquered furniture, a metal half-tester bed with pink furnishings and a predominantly pink Aubusson carpet.

commented that 'ere long the Music Room will become one of the most beautiful rooms in the Kingdom, and one of which the town may well be proud'.[258]

The Royal Pavilion can claim to be amongst the earliest municipally owned houses to be preserved and opened to the public. Byelaws, published in 1851, allowed ratepayers free admission on five days a year during April to August. Otherwise the admission fee was sixpence (remaining the same from 1851 to the 1920s). Admittance was between 12.00 and 4.00 p.m., provided no functions (such as fêtes, bazaars, baby shows, exhibitions, charity balls or conferences) were being held inside. In this period the Pavilion was frequently used for social or civic events and consequently never furnished to reflect its original function. (fig.4)

The members of the Pavilion Sub-Committee permitted all kinds of events. In May 1853 the King's Bedroom was given over to an exhibition of fleas, for which the town received 25 per cent of the gross receipts. In January 1880 a Mr William Balchin was allowed to install a cascade of water on the north staircase for a ball for the officers of the 16th Lancers.[259] The Pavilion Gardens, enclosed during royal ownership, were now opened to the public, providing in the centre of a town 'an agreeable place of recreation'.[260] Finally, the gardens, abundantly planted with shrubs, trees and the avenue of elms, were made accessible to residents and visitors.

Victorian guide books to Brighton and the region were far from enthusiastic about the design of the Pavilion: 'an unintelligible pile of buildings ... to any person of true taste it must appear as anomalous and insipid in idea, as ridiculous, too, in absurdity, as the Kremlin of Moscow'.[261] The controversy regarding the Pavilion's 'style' continued throughout the nineteenth century. When the sale of the Pavilion was under discussion in 1846, Punch (under the heading of 'Rubbish for Sale') suggested it should become

10. The same bedroom in Queen Victoria's apartments restored in the 1990s using original archive material, new physical evidence and the 1846 Denews inventory. The original interior architecture, comprising two floors – her bedroom, wardrobe and maid's room with four attic rooms for servants above – was reinstated. The actual repairs and alterations done prior to her arrival in 1837 were modest: the original yellow India wallpaper was repaired and cleaned and the draperies and bed furnishings were renewed in green gros de nap, a finely ribbed silk. A simple patterned Brussels carpet covered the floor, with rosewood and mahogany furniture taken from other rooms in the Pavilion.

a tea emporium; then, 'with a few paper lanterns, and a real native at the door, we feel confident a deal of business in selling Tea … might be done'.[262]

In the early 1880s Moncure Daniel Conway recorded his travels, including a visit to Brighton to see the Pavilion. Here he saw a vigorous revival of the 'barbaric element in English taste'; the building he likened to a physiognomical monument of George IV, 'the fop who had come to prefer figment to fact'.[263] But Conway praised the current and varied public use of this former 'temple of vanity'. It seemed to him that the excessive spending and reckless extravagance of the King could only now be justified as his palace had been made into an agreeable, instructive and socially useful public institution.

11a. The Yellow Bow Room (north): decorated in the 1950s as a fictional drawing room for Mrs Fitzherbert, furnished with some of her own satinwood furniture, an Aubusson carpet and Coles striped Regency-style wallpaper.

The twentieth century: 'a place of real enchantment'

A number of factors made possible the reinstatement of the Royal Pavilion as a building of international importance in the inter-war years. Firstly, the enthusiasm and support of Queen Mary for the refurbishment of the Royal Pavilion was of vital importance. During the First World War, when the Royal Pavilion was used as a hospital for Indian soldiers (fig.6), the interiors were altered, damaged and inevitably neglected.[264] In 1920 a programme of restoration began under the guidance of the Pavilion's enlightened director, Henry Roberts. Funded by a settlement made by the government for the damage done to the building during the war, attempts were made for the first time to reveal the brilliant colours of the original interiors. Numerous layers of overpainting and discoloured varnish applied by the Victorian decorators were removed. Although there was still little opportunity to furnish the rooms (as they were still used primarily for functions), they were wherever possible conscientiously restored.

Queen Mary visited the building on many occasions and returned a number of original items that had remained in store. In 1920 she donated the eight Spode ceramic

11b. The Yellow Bow Room (north): restored in the 1990s to the original vivid Regency scheme with a chrome yellow version of the King's favourite dragon paper, with applied Chinese export paintings and satinwood furniture (see also p. 59).

and ormolu lampstands which originally stood in the Banqueting Room. In the 1930s the pilaster ornaments from the Saloon were returned, and these were reinstated, along with the original doors and some Chinese papers that had been given by Queen Victoria and remained in store in the Pavilion since the nineteenth century. Indeed, Queen Mary's involvement extended to selecting the precise shade of blue for the reproduction wallpaper installed in the Banqueting Room in 1933.

Stylistically the eclectic, decorative character of the Regency struck a sympathetic chord with the decorative modern styles of the 1920s and 1930s. Both borrowed liberally from exotic and historic sources, both relished the decorative and surface qualities of precious materials. Chinoiserie as a style became fashionable in the 1920s, whether on gramophone cabinets, furniture or wallpapers. The contemporary vogue for things Chinese found popular expression in the design and decoration of cinemas, providing that vital ingredient of fantasy for the public. The Curzon cinema in Brighton, built in 1930, was a typical example.

Collecting Regency (and Empire) decorative objects became fashionable in these decades, and was associated with a group of notable connoisseurs, such as the playwright Edward Knoblock, Sir Albert Richardson (some of whose Thomas Hope pieces are now in the Pavilion) and Edward James. Decorators such as Mrs Dolly Mann used Regency furniture in their schemes, and Osbert Lancaster coined the term 'Vogue Regency' to describe the fad for Regency-style interiors.

A turning point in the critical history of the Pavilion came in 1935 with the publication of *Brighton* by Osbert Sitwell and Margaret Barton. Perhaps for the first time in the twentieth century, the beauty and romance of the Pavilion were fully appreciated and celebrated in prose that itself embodied the poetry of Nash's supreme creation. That the Pavilion was Nash's most significant work the authors were in no doubt:

> not even Windsor, although the work there was conceived on so gigantic a scale, ranks as
> a higher achievement than the Pavilion; for to this singular dwelling undoubtedly attaches
> something of the dream-like quality which often is found to infuse great poetry …[265]

Ten years later Osbert's brother, Sacheverell Sitwell, felt the romance and spirit of the Pavilion: 'let us lose ourselves among the bamboos and Mandarins', he urged, 'we surrender our prejudices, completely, in the corridor, a place of real enchantment'.[266]

The poetic perceptions of the Sitwells were in stark contrast to those of the architectural establishment, with their preferences for classicism, modernism and vernacular styles. Sir John Summerson, writing in 1935, was unequivocal:

> To-day the Pavilion is a curiosity which rouses only a vague, transient wonder in the visitor.
> Its ornaments are scarcely more extravagant than those of the roundabouts at Hampstead
> … for singularity of form it has long ago been surpassed by the Crystal Palace and the
> White City; and for richness it compares unfavourably with the Granada Cinema at Tooting.

He concluded, 'it is simply a minor historical monument'.[267]

12. (above) 'Gilding the lily': the Long Gallery in the 1950s smothered in floral arrangements (and insect life) supplied by Brighton Borough Council's Parks Department.

13. (right) The Long Gallery used as a location for fashion photography for Vogue's Christmas edition of 1958, taken by one of the Pavilion's admirers, Norman Parkinson. © Reproduced by courtesy of the Fiona Cowan Archive and Vogue.

THE ROYAL PAVILION, BRIGHTON

BRIGHTON AND HOVE

FULL INFORMATION FROM DIRECTOR OF PUBLICITY, BRIGHTON, OR TOWN CLERK, HOVE

FREQUENT ELECTRIC TRAINS FROM LONDON   **BRITISH RAILWAYS**

THROUGH TRAINS FROM THE WEST, NORTH & MIDLANDS

14. (left) Poster
promoting Brighton
and Hove and British
Railways, designed by
Heskett Hubbard in
the 1960s. The
Pavilion's rendered
surfaces, as well as
those of adjacent
buildings, are
all painted
duck-egg blue.

Noël Coward in his romantic comedy *Conversation Piece*, published in 1934, lamented from the perspective of the old fishing community the demise of Brighton as a fishing town, destroyed by the Prince Regent and the 'Doxys and Dandys and Regency Randys'. The satirical tradition continued:

The Pavilion
Cost a million
As a monument to Art,
And the wits here
Say it sits here
Like an Oriental tart!
The dashing 'beau monde'
Has ruffled our pond,
And even the turbot
Know Mrs Fitzherbert.
We're richer than ever before
But Brighton is Brighton no more.[268]

Despite threats to its very existence during the inter-war years (calls to pull it down and build a conference centre), the Royal Pavilion flourished and became one of the most visited historic houses in England. The establishment of the Regency Society of Brighton & Hove in the late 1940s provided a vital impetus to the movement to furnish the interior as a royal palace. Annually during the summer months, special temporary exhibitions of original or Regency furniture were organised, with loans from The Queen and notable collectors of Regency decorative arts.

The Regency Society also provided, at a key moment in the Pavilion's history, a lobbying body of experts and enthusiasts to support the then director, Clifford Musgrave, and to modify the Council's policy of using the Pavilion as a civic centre for functions, catering, conferences and events. Through their influence they held in check some rather excessive proposals – such as, for example, the plan in 1951 to paint the exterior of the Pavilion pink. Unable to decide between pink and duck-egg blue, various samples were painted on the stuccoed walls by the King's apartments for the perusal of the Pavilion Sub-Committee. Fortunately they succumbed to the advice of John L. Denman from the Regency Society and agreed to paint the exterior in a more tasteful 'light off-white warm cream colour'.

Eight years later, however, notions of authenticity were quashed and the rendered surfaces were all painted duck-egg blue to blend with the copper tent roofs (fig.14). And pale duck-egg blue the Pavilion remained until the 1980s when it was painted broadly in accordance with Nash's picturesque scheme, where rendered surfaces blended seamlessly in colour with the Bath stone. Still today, some visitors remember the duck-egg blue and complain of the dull, though correct, stone colouring.

15. (left) The Music
Room with a model
wearing a Bill Blass
designed chiffon
dinner dress, standing
on the Victorian
fireplace. Photography
by Gene Laurents for
the American
magazine Look
(25 January 1965).

During the 1950s and 1960s cleaning and restoration of the ground floor began in earnest, as did the refurbishment of the first-floor bedrooms, creating fictional 'historic' rooms associated with royal personages. To our eyes these interiors, such as Mrs Fitzherbert's Drawing Room, furnished with Coles' striped Regency wallpaper, an Aubusson carpet and some of her original satinwood furniture, appear typically 1950s in style. (fig.11a) These rooms, originally called the Yellow Bow Rooms, have all now been authentically restored using contemporary accounts, original plans, inventories and new physical evidence. For a building of its period, the Pavilion is extremely well documented, but this information, though readily available, was not used in these mid twentieth-century restorations. (fig.9,11a)

Support from Her Majesty Queen Elizabeth II has been crucial in the refurbishment of the Pavilion. In 1955 a large number of items of furniture and decorative objects were returned by Her Majesty on loan to the Pavilion and many have been reinstated in their original locations. The annual Regency exhibitions and the progressive restoration ensured the Pavilion's place as a historic attraction of international importance.

Though the English have tended to view the Pavilion with somewhat puritanical eyes, American visitors are usually overwhelmed by its visual fantasy and opulence. In 1964 the fashion editor of the New York magazine Look[269] approached the Pavilion with a proposal to create fabric designs based on the Pavilion, to be made into garments by contemporary designers and promoted through the Fifth Avenue department store Lord & Taylor.

Designers such as Bill Blass used the fabrics, which were created by William Poole and inspired by designs and features in the Pavilion. For the photoshoot Vidal Sassoon created the hair styles. The models were freely draped around the Pavilion – standing on the Music Room chimneypiece (fig.15), or on the top of the hot closet in the Great Kitchen – in a manner that would render incoherent today's curators, let alone Health and Safety officials.

From the records that survive it seems that the Pavilion received no financial benefit from this project from either the magazine Look or Lord & Taylor. No doubt they were grateful for the international publicity. Some twenty-five years later a more commercial approach predominated and a licensing agreement with the fabric designers and manufacturers Brunswig & Fils of New York brought invaluable and regular royalty income to support the restoration of the Pavilion's interior.

In 1966 a lavish eight-page photo spread in American Vogue combined 'the enchanting contemporary sprite', the French actress Leslie Caron, with the 'poetic fantasy' of the Pavilion. On the roof, in the Long Gallery or provocatively posed in the King's bedroom, she modelled fashionable striped harem pyjamas and short nightdresses in chiffon, crêpe, cotton and nylon.[270] (fig.1)

Controversy always seems to follow the Pavilion. A solution of the mid-1960s to the problem of the progressive decay of the stonework, including the Bath stone minarets, was to reproduce them in plastic (or fibreglass). This suggestion, put forward by the Chairman of the Regency Society, was canvassed in the press. It was supported by the poet and conservationist John Betjeman, with the proviso that they must actually look

like stone – not like 'one of those plastic toys'. Cheaper to produce and lighter in weight, they would not decay. (fig.16) The Pavilion's director, Clifford Musgrave, was positively enthusiastic, saying 'in the next 100 years I envisage the whole of the roof – including the domes – being rebuilt in plastic.'[271]

Several fibreglass minarets were installed, and though coated with a stone compound, stood out, whitish-grey in colour, failing to weather as natural Bath stone. Proposals in the late 1970s to remove the fibreglass minarets and replace them in costly Bath stone were opposed by the Victorian Society, which put forward the somewhat spurious argument that if fibreglass had been available to Nash, he would have used it. Fortunately, such views did not prevail, and the decaying stonework was either restored or replaced with Bath stone as part of a major £10 million structural restoration programme during the 1980s funded by Brighton Council with support from English Heritage.

Dry rot, a problem even in the 1820s, was rampant and the corrosion of the iron frame and iron cores of the minarets caused serious damage to the fragile structure and decaying stonework. To retain the picturesque exterior appearance Nash had built all the rainwater down-pipes into the walls of the building. These became blocked, causing

16. A fibreglass minaret being delivered to the Pavilion, c. 1970. At the time this seemed an innovative and cheap option; each original Bath stone minaret weighed about 12 tons.

hideous fungal growths and wet and dry rot. Nash's building was constructed over, and incorporated, Holland's building, thus creating a complicated structure to restore and maintain. For Brighton Council, then a small borough council, with significant areas of social deprivation to address, this programme of works was a major financial commitment.

For over a decade the building was swathed in scaffolding, hoardings and blue plastic, but with some difficulty always remained open to the public. At that time not everyone in the town supported this use of ratepayers' money or the high level of expenditure. Indeed, my first task as the new Keeper of the Pavilion in 1985 was to remove some massive graffiti painted across all the hoardings, which read 'the most expensive Council house in Brighton'.

The reinstatement of Nash's garden scheme began in parallel with the structural restoration, in the early 1980s. It took some twenty years to complete.[272] During the nineteenth century, the gardens had become split (north to south) by a wide tarmac road, complete with pavements, that linked the William IV Gate and the India Gate, thus creating the 'Eastern' and 'Western' Lawns. This road combined the functions of a free car park and a short cut from Church Street to East Street. (fig.17) Twentieth-century features included neatly mowed lawns resembling cricket pitches and regiments of bedding plants, including raised plant displays creating 'Welcome to Brighton' in large, floral letters.

Nash's picturesque scheme with its sinuous gravelled paths, undulating grassed and shrubbed areas has taken years to establish itself and to achieve maturity. The most controversial aspect of this restoration (apart from the banning of cars) was the length of the grass. At one time in the mid-1990s when the turning circle, paths and western beds had been reinstated, complaints were received almost weekly about the length of the grass. In Nash's scheme the feeling of naturalness was partly achieved by the hand-scythed long grass that merged into the shaped shrubberies, with no rigid edging. Accusations were made of Council neglect and poor management. Signs, guide books and articles continuously proclaimed the message of Regency principles of gardening. When that failed to achieve the desired conversion, the more practical observation that manual or electric mowers[273] did not exist in the 1820s achieved some success. Nowadays, with the support of the garden volunteers, led by the head gardener, the restored Regency gardens are a source of delight to historic garden enthusiasts, gardeners, general visitors and local residents.

The restoration of the original interior schemes of Frederick Crace and Robert Jones, as approved by George IV in the 1820s, is slowly nearing completion. Recent restorations, and in some instances reconstructions, are as authentic as is possible in the light of documentation, physical evidence and materials available.

The interior layout of the first floor had been considerably altered in the late nineteenth century to create spaces for functions, conferences and museum displays. In the 1990s the interior architecture was reinstated and key areas, such as the Yellow Bow Rooms, the North and South Galleries and Queen Victoria's apartments, were restored.

A disastrous fire, an act of arson, nearly destroyed the Music Room in 1975. So began over a decade of careful restoration, to be interrupted by the damage caused by the great storm of 1987. The Pavilion's delicate interior is cared for by a team of dedicated conservators, decorative artists and technical staff. Given its fragility and its highly decorative surfaces, it needs constant maintenance and restoration by highly skilled staff.

The Pavilion, in its various guises, has been a landmark in Brighton for over two centuries. Though its long-term architectural influence is negligible, it has captured the imagination of many artists, designers and film-makers. When the *Observer* launched a poll in 1989 to determine the public's opinion of the best and worst of British architecture, the Royal Pavilion was voted the best in the south east (and the Brighton Centre, the worst). It was put forward by the internationally renowned photographer Norman Parkinson. For Parkinson the Pavilion epitomised fantasy, and the exciting and unpredictable – all of which, in his view, were a source of constant delight. During his career he used the Pavilion as a location for a number of shoots including a session for *Vogue* in 1958. (fig.13)

Aspects of the interior have inspired contemporary designers such as Hans Hollein in his Austrian Tourism Office in Vienna (1978), which reveals inspiration drawn from the Great Kitchen's palm tree columns. A number of film-makers have chosen to use

17. View (from the north east) of the Royal Pavilion grounds, taken in the 1960s, showing the broad tarmac road that linked the William IV Gate to the Indian Gate, cutting the garden into two distinct areas.

18. The same view, taken in 2002, after the restoration of the gardens to their Regency design.

the extraordinary interiors as locations, even when irrelevant to the original texts. Recent examples have been Sir Ian McKellen's interpretation of *Richard III* (1996) and Neil Jordan's adaptation of Graham Greene's novel, *The End of the Affair* (2002).[274]

The Pavilion is the result of a talented architect and a supremely confident and demanding patron. Like Gothic Strawberry Hill at Twickenham, or Surrealist Monkton House at West Dean, it represents an innovatory and eccentric strand in English architecture. Ridiculed for much of its existence, the Pavilion's place and importance in our cultural history is secure. In a debate in February 1997 in the House of Commons on the state of architecture in England, the importance of good architects and the confidence and bravery of patrons (or clients) in the public and private sectors was stressed. Denis MacShane (MP for Rotherham) urged civic leaders not to be frightened of the vulgar philistine criticism that greets any innovative design. He continued, 'I have no doubt that, when the then Prince of Wales built the wonderful Brighton pavilion 200 years ago, some wiseacre described it as a "monstrous carbuncle". Today it is a joy to behold unlike the supremely forgettable façade of the extension to the national gallery.' Though his analogy and references may be confused, his message about the need for courage and conviction in commissioning contemporary architects is clear.

19. (left) The scaffold, covered with blue plastic, that shrouded the north end of the Pavilion to allow the structural restoration to continue all year round, moved during the violent storm in October 1987. A large stone ornament was dislodged and fell though the Music Room tent roof and Music Room ceiling, recently restored following an arson attack. The new hand-tufted replica carpet had been laid earlier that year.

20. (left) The stone ornament damaged the decorative coving and the new carpet. It proved too large to remove through the French windows. However since there was already a large hole in the ceiling and roof the ornament was lifted out by crane, the same way it came in.

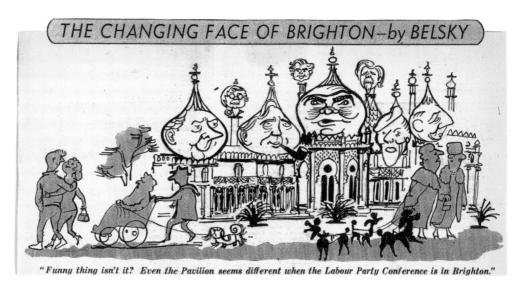

21. (right) Still a subject for satire: cartoon published in the Daily Herald (1 October 1957) during the Labour Party Conference in Brighton. Key personalities depicted are Hugh Gaitskell (far left), Harold Wilson and Denis Healey.

22. (right) The 'Kremlin' allusion reinterpreted: Tony Blair in Brighton for the TUC Conference in September 1995. Here Blair's proposed modernising agenda is set against an image of totalitarianism. © Peter Brookes/ The Times, London 13/9/95.

And even Sir John Summerson was to revise his scathing opinion of the Pavilion, published in the 1930s, describing the building nearly half a century later as a 'felicitous materialisation of the careless, humorous, audacious genius of its architect'.[275] Today the Royal Pavilion can be more easily understood, as one of the great European royal pleasure palaces evoking images of Empire and the exotic, unmatched in its variety of styles and sheer inventiveness. It remains a monument to the taste, determination and creativity of George IV.

Notes

1   *Sussex Weekly Advertiser,*
    24 April 1820.
2   Harvey and Darton (publisher),
    *Sketches of Young People or a Visit to
    Brighton,* London, 1822.
3   George, Prince of Wales, is referred to
    in the text with the appropriate title
    according to the historical context. He
    was Prince of Wales until 1811, when
    he became Prince Regent following his
    father's illness. In 1820 he acceded to
    the throne as George IV; he died
    in 1830.
4   A. Aspinall (ed.), *The Correspondence
    of George, Prince of Wales,
    1770–1812,* London, 1963–1971,
    vol. 3, letter 1384.
5   Grove House, substantially pulled down
    to allow the building of the north end of
    Nash's Pavilion, was purchased by the
    4th Duke of Marlborough in 1790, at
    which point it was renamed
    Marlborough House. It retained this
    name until the Duke sold it to the
    Prince Regent in 1812. This large red
    brick house is sometimes confused
    with stuccoed Marlborough House
    (which still exists) on the Steine which
    was sold by the Duke of Marlborough
    in 1786 to a Mr Hamilton. The former
    house was occupied by the Prince of
    Wales for a short period in 1795 whilst
    his Pavilion was being redecorated.
6   The Earl of Bessborough (ed.),
    G*eorgiana, Extracts from the
    Correspondence of Georgiana,
    Duchess of Devonshire,* London,
    1955, p. 289.
7   The Earl of Ilchester (ed.), *The Journal
    of Elizabeth, Lady Holland
    (1791–1811),* London, 1908,
    vol. 1, p. 97.
8   Jane Austen, *Pride and Prejudice,* first
    published 1813, London, 1963,
    p. 195. Austen (1775–1817) began
    writing the novel that would be entitled
    Pride and Prejudice in October 1796,
    although it was not published
    until 1813.
9   *Brighton Gazette,* 14 November 1822.
10 James Peller Malcolm, *Anecdotes of
    the Manners and Customs of London
    during the Eighteenth Century,* London,
    1810, vol. 2, p. 423, excerpt from 'A
    Review of the State of Society in 1807'.

11 E. M. Butler (ed.), *A Regency Visitor,
    The English Tour of Prince Pückler-
    Muskau, Described in his Letters
    1826–1828,* London, 1957, p. 165.
12 Ibid., p. 169.
13 R. Sickelmore, *The History of Brighton
    from the Earliest Period to the Present
    Time,* Brighton, 1823, p. xxxi.
14 C. Wright, *The Brighton Ambulator,*
    London, 1818, p. 171. '*Sans-Culotte*'
    literally means 'without knee-breeches',
    a garment associated with the
    aristocracy, hence the expression came
    to mean in the 1790s a French
    revolutionary or radical (who wore
    pantaloons or long trousers to express
    solidarity with the working classes).
    During the Regency period women did
    not wear knickers or underwear in the
    modern sense – though some adopted
    pantaloons, which fashion and taste
    dictated should not be visible.
    Traditionally a postillion (or post-boy)
    rode astride the lead horse pulling a
    carriage, obviating the need for a
    coachman. Usually there was one
    postillion per pair of horses.
15 *Sussex Weekly Advertiser,*
    27 November 1820. *Sine die,* literally
    'without a day', means postponed
    indefinitely.
16 *Sussex Weekly Advertiser,*
    15 January 1821.
17 *John Bull,* 13 January 1822, p. 451.
18 *Brighton Gazette,* 11 December 1823.
19 See chapter 5.
20 John Gore (ed.), *The Creevey Papers,*
    London, 1970, p. 257.
21 *Brighton Gazette,* 12 February 1824.
22 L. G. Robinson (ed.), *Letters of
    Dorothea, Princess Lieven, during her
    Residence in London 1812–1834,*
    London, 1902, p. 225; letter to her
    brother dated 8–20 July 1830.
    Princess Lieven was the wife of the
    Russian Ambassador, Count Lieven,
    and a loyal friend to the King.
23 See Henry D. Roberts, *A History of the
    Royal Pavilion,* London, 1939, and
    John Morley, *The Making of the Royal
    Pavilion,* London, 1984.
24 John A. Erredge, *History of
    Brighthelmston,* Brighton 1862, vol. 5,
    p. 108; unidentified newpaper cutting
    dated 27 July 1806.
25 For further information on the role of
    the Crace firm in the history of the
    decoration of the Royal Pavilion, see
    Megan Aldrich (ed.), *The Craces, Royal
    Decorators 1768–1899,* London, 1990.

26 See *Carlton House: The Past Glories of
    George IV's Palace,* London, 1991.
27 *Crace Accounts 1802–1822,* Royal
    Pavilion Archives, p. 40.
28 Aspinall (ed.), *Correspondence, op.
    cit.,* see note 4, vol. 3, letter 1006.
29 Ibid., vol. 3, letter 1017.
30 *The Times,* 3 September 1795.
31 Aspinall (ed.), *Correspondence,
    op. cit.,* see note 4, vol. 3, letter 1034
    (dated 1 September 1795).
32 Amanda Foreman, *Georgiana, Duchess
    of Devonshire,* London, 1998, p. 297.
33 The Earl of Bessborough, *op. cit.* , see
    note 6, p. 219. A mawkin (or malkin)
    was a scarecrow or a guy.
34 M. Charles Nicoullaud (ed.), *Memoirs
    of the Comtesse de Boigne
    (1815–1819),* London, 1907,
    vol. 2, p. 133.
35 Castalia, Countess Granville (ed.), *Lord
    Granville Leveson-Gower (first Earl
    Granville): Private Correspondence
    1781 to 1821,* London, 1917, vol. 2,
    p. 120. Letter dated 9 October 1805.
36 Ibid, p. 120.
37 Philip Whitwell Wilson (ed.), *The
    Greville Diary,* London, 1927,
    vol. I, p. 123.
38 Aspinall (ed.), *Correspondence,
    op. cit.,* see note 4, vol. 3, p. 271,
    letter 1193.
39 John Gore (ed.), The Creevey Papers,
    London, 1963, p. 58. Creevey's papers
    were first published in 1904, edited by
    Sir Herbert Maxwell. Creevey died
    in 1838.
40 Ibid., p. 41.
41 Ibid., p. 54.
42 Lady Theresa Lewis (ed.), *Extracts of
    the Journals and Correspondence of
    Miss Berry from the Year 1783 to
    1852,* London, 1865, vol. 2, p. 490.
43 Ibid., p. 490.
44 Poem by Peter Pindar, published
    London, 1816. Quoted in *Florizel's
    Folly* by John Ashton, London, 1899.
45 Master Ellar was a renowned
    horseman.
46 A firkin was a vessel or barrel
    containing 9 gallons.
47 J. Greig (ed.), *The Farington Diary by
    Joseph Farington, RA,* London,
    1922–1928, vol. 2, p. 270; entry for
    20 July 1804.
48 C. Wright, *op. cit.,* see note 14, p. 41.
    The complex ceased to be used for
    horses in the 1850s. The interior of the
    domed stables (now known as the
    Dome Concert Hall) was radically

altered in the 1930s, losing most of its original features.

49 A. Aspinall (ed.), *The Letters of King George IV, 1812–1830*, Cambridge, 1938, vol. I, p. 8, letter 517 (dated 17 January 1815).

50 Mrs Warrenne Blake (ed.), *An Irish Beauty of the Regency: The Unpublished Journals of the Hon. Mrs Calvert, 1789–1822*, London, 1911, p. 74.

51 A. Aspinall (ed.), *The Letters of George IV, 1812–1830*, vol. 2, p. 158.

52 *Sussex Weekly Advertiser*, 30 June 1817.

53 *John Bull*, 2 July 1821, p. 225. Hydrophobia: a morbid aversion to water.

54 *Sussex Weekly Advertiser*, 20 July 1818.

55 *Sussex Weekly Advertiser*, 16 November 1818.

56 *Crace Accounts 1802–1822*, Royal Pavilion Archives, p. 9.

57 Ibid., p. 12.

58 Louis J. Jennings (ed.), *The Croker Papers. The Correspondence and Diaries of the Late Right Honourable John Wilson Croker, LLD, FRS*, London, 1885, vol. I, pp. 126–7. Nash's original plans and drawings for the Pavilion have never been traced.

59 *The Monthly Magazine*, 1 November 1819. The letter to the editor is signed *W.P.*

60 Peter Quennell (ed.), *The Private Letters of Princess Lieven to Prince Metternich 1820–1826*, London, 1937, p. 22, entry dated 19 March 1820.

61 Nicoullaud (ed.), *op. cit.*, see note 34, vol. 2, p. 133. The Comtesse (1781–1866) came to London with her father in 1816, returning to France in 1819. A sharp observer of social life, she wrote several volumes of memoirs.

62 Jennings (ed.), *op. cit.*, see note 58, vol. I, p. 249.

63 Pretyman Papers, East Suffolk Record Office (562). For this visit a canopy bed with crimson drapery was specially designed and constructed by local craftsmen and a local needlewoman in great haste.

64 Nicoullaud (ed.), *op. cit.*, see note 34, vol. 2, p. 248.

65 Ibid., pp. 134–5.

66 Ibid., p. 249.

67 Ibid., p. 249.

68 Ibid., p. 249.

69 Ibid., p. 257.

70 Ibid., p. 252. Given her somewhat grand and cool manner, Lady Hertford (the current mistress and companion of the Prince), was given the nickname by some of 'the Marchioness'.

71 Gore, *op. cit.*, see note 39, pp. 232–3.

72 Erredge, *op. cit.*, see note 24, vol. 5, p. 117.

73 Lewis Melville, *Brighton: Its History, Its Follies and Its Fashions*, London, 1909, p. 105; Frederick Harrison, *The Story of Brighton, Hove and Neighbourhood*, Brighton, 1931, p. 108.

74 Jennings (ed.), *op. cit.*, see note 58, vol. 1, p. 249.

75 Quennell (ed.), *op. cit*, see note 60, p. 145.

76 Whitwell Wilson (ed.), *op. cit.*, see note 37, vol. 1, pp. 114–15. Charles Greville (1794–1865), the grandson of the Duke of Portland, was appointed Clerk-in-Ordinary to the Privy Council, which gave him ample opportunity to observe the social and political world of George IV, William IV and Queen Victoria. An expert on horses and bloodstock, for some five years he managed the Duke of York's stables.

77 Henry Reeve (ed.), *The Greville Memoirs*, London, 1874, vol. 1, pp. 46–7.

78 Ibid., p. 49.

79 Quennell (ed.), *op. cit.*, see note 60, p. 150. Perhaps the word 'disgusting' is less strong in meaning than today – more akin to 'offensive'.

80 Butler (ed.), *op. cit.*, see note 11, pp. 73–4.

81 *The Times*, 27 January 1827. The King only arrived in Brighton on 23 January – so this report is somewhat exaggerated. He left on 7 March.

82 Robinson (ed.), *op. cit.*, see note 22, p. 91.

83 Lord Byron, *Don Juan*, 1823/4, canto 11, LXVII. Ormolu: eighteenth-century French term for gilded metals (or surfaces).

84 C. Wright, *op. cit.*, see note 14, p. 45.

85 Robert Kerr, *The Gentleman's House*, 1864, reprinted New York/London, 1972, p. 186.

86 Jennings (ed.), *op. cit.*, see note 58, vol. 1, p. 127.

87 Ibid.

88 'Royal Patronage of Music', *The Quarterly Musical Magazine and Review*, vol. 1, no. 1, 1818, p. 158.

89 Jennings, *op. cit.*, see note 58, p. 250.

90 Erredge, *op. cit.*, see note 24, vol. 5, p. 105.

91 *Baxter's Stranger in Brighton and Directory*, Brighton, 1824, p. xxiv. The organ now in the Music Room is not the original, but that which formerly stood in the Royal Chapel.

92 Aspinall (ed.), *Letters of George IV, op. cit.*, see note 51, p. 482. In a letter to his mother dated 22 August 1814, George describes Princess Lieven charming the company at the Pavilion 'with her uncommon beautiful talent on the Piano Forte'.

93 Quennell, *op. cit.*, see note 60, p. 124.

94 *Requisitions Book: Abstract of Accounts for the Lord Chamberlain's Department*, quarter ending 5 April 1820. Royal Pavilion Archives.

95 Jennings (ed.), *op. cit.*, see note 58, vol. 1, p. 250.

96 A. Carse, 'The Prince Regent's Band', *Music and Letters*, 1946, vol. 27, pp. 147–55.

97 Erredge, *op. cit.*, see note 24, p. 116, unidentified cutting, 8 January 1822.

98 *Brighton Gazette*, 22 January 1824.

99 *Brighton Gazette*, 12 February 1824.

100 A picture of the lives of band members and personalities emerges through fragments of evidence from contemporary newspaper reports, material in the Public Record Office, family histories and even St Nicholas's Church baptisms registers. As musicians, they were deemed 'the finest in Europe' and were generally called 'the gentlemen of the private band'. The majority, however, lived at modest addresses in Brighton; for example, George Best lived at 36 Gardener Street, Robert Medhurst at 2 Sion Hill and John Tucker at 24 High Street. Jackie Frisby researched the various members of George IV's private band. Her research files are held in the Royal Pavilion Archives.

101 *Brighton Gazette*, 16 August 1821.

102 *Quarterly Musical Magazine and Review*, vol. 1, 1818, p. 159.

103 *Brighton Gazette*, 23 August 1821.

104 *Brighton Gazette*, 15 August 1822; with thanks to Eileen Hollingdale for the reference.

105 RA GEO/29064–29065.

106 Virginia Hinze, 'The Recreation of John Nash's Regency Gardens at the Royal Pavilion, Brighton', *Garden History*, Summer 1996 (vol. 24, no. 1), pp. 45–53.

107 *Brighton Gazette*, 7 June 1821.

108 [Prince Pückler-Muskau,] *Tour in England, Ireland and France in the Years 1828 and 1829, by a German Prince*, London, 1832, vol. 2, p. 208.

109 Aspinall (ed.), *Letters of George IV*, *op. cit.*, see note 51, vol. 3, letter 1246 (dated 20 June 1826).

110 F. Max Müller (ed.), *Memoirs of Baron Stockmar*, London, 1872, vol. 1, p. 122.

111 Christopher Hibbert (ed.), *Louis Simond, An American in Regency England: The Journal of a Tour in 1810–1811*, London, 1968, pp. 37–8. In pre-decimal money £1 = 20 shillings, 1 shilling = 12 pence.

112 John Burnett, *Plenty and Want, A Social History of Diet in England from 1815 to the Present Day*, London, 1979, p. 35.

113 RA GEO/29064–29065.

114 The National Archives (NA) (formerly the Public Record Office), Lord Chamberlain's Papers, LC 3/21, 'An Establishment of Our Expenses of Our Chamber …', January 1823. The rough equivalent of £1 in 1823 is estimated at £33 in 2003.

115 NA, Lord Steward's Papers, LS 2/49, Accounts of Salaries Chargeable to the Civil List for 1823.

116 Household Establishment 25 December 1811 (L.114/51), by courtesy of the Duke of Devonshire, Chatsworth House. See also J. Jean Hecht, *The Domestic Servant Class in Eighteenth-century England*, London, 1956, chapter 6, for comparative salaries.

117 NA, LS/13/295, Allowances in Lieu of Pitcher Wine (5 April 1815 – 6 April 1816). Loose papers. These dates would seem to commemorate military events in the Peninsular War when Britain was at war with France and the United States.

118 NA, LS/13/205, Allowance for Platters to the Prince Regent's Servants at Brighton (5 April – 6 July 1816). Loose papers.

119 NA, LS 8/222, Account for the Quarter to 5 January 1824.

120 Robinson (ed.), *op. cit.*, see note 22, letter dated 16–28 May 1830.

121 For a full discussion of the organisation of the Royal Household in the early decades of the eighteenth century, see John M. Beattie, *The English Court in the Reign of George I*, Cambridge, 1967.

122 Charwomen were hired for menial domestic tasks on a daily basis, as needed. They were not waged servants.

123 Le Comte A. de la Garde, *Brighton, Scènes détachées d'un voyage en Angleterre*, Paris, 1834, p. 204. In this text the housekeeper is called Madame White. Sarah Whittle is recorded as housekeeper from 1817 to 1831, and Mrs Lovatt (or Lovett) from 1837 to the mid-1840s.

124 *Memorandoms* [*sic*], manuscript notebook of the housekeeper at the Royal Pavilion, 1837–1845 (No. 2300.3, SB.9.MSI), Royal Pavilion, Libraries & Museums, Brighton & Hove City Council.

125 Reeve (ed.), *op. cit.*, see note 77, vol. 2, p. 3. *Tracasseries*: quarrels or disputes.

126 Pavilion inventory, *c.* 1828, Royal Pavilion Archives. It lists the furnishings of the pages' rooms as follows: a cast-iron register stove, brass wire fire-guard, cut iron fender, set of plain fire irons. A dimity festooned window curtain, with buckram head brass rod and pulley, two brass blind rods and brackets. A plain mahogany post tent bedstead, canopy laths, lath bottom, dimity furniture, palliasse, bordered hair mattress, flock and hair mattress in white case, feather bed and bolster and white cased pillows, three blankets. A mahogany chest of three drawers with sliding fall-down secretary top. A mahogany chest of five drawers. A swing dressing glass in a reeded frame. A mahogany box top bidet on taper legs. A old mahogany sweep front dressing table. A dressing table with low ledge to match. Four common chairs, painted buff and black lines, cane seats. A grey drugget and a hearth rug, red and black border.

127 Mrs Vernon Delves Broughton (ed.), *Court and Private Life in the Time of Queen Charlotte: Being the Journal of Mrs Papendiek*, London, 1887, vol. 1, p. 181.

128 Ibid., vol. I, p. 299.

129 Ibid., vol. 2, p. 17.

130 NA, LS/13/194 Ordinances, Rules, Orders, Instructions for the well governing of Our Household. The Board of Green Cloth, 1822, Public Record Office, LS 13/194.

131 *Sketches of Her Majesty's Household* …, London, 1848, p. 108. 'Bag' here presumably refers to a type of wig called a 'bag-wig' in which a black satin bag was used to enclose the queue of the wig (usually made of horse hair). As the nineteenth century progressed, liveried servants stopped wearing wigs and began powdering their own dressed hair.

132 Apart from short visits to London, the King stayed in the Pavilion as follows: 25 December 1820 to 2 May 1821; 21 November 1821 to 17 April 1822; 26 October 1822 to 16 April 1823; 6 December 1823 to 12 February 1824; 23 January to 7 March 1827.

133 *Brighton Gazette*, 24 October 1822. See chapter 7.

134 Ibid., 17 October 1822.

135 See NA, LC/ 30, Thomas Saunders's account for the quarter ending 5 July lists the jobbing works undertaken following the King's departure for Carlton House in London on 19 April 1820: '4 Men taking up beating and putting down Carpets Druggetts Oil cloths &c – Taking down & putting up Beds Window Curtains Roller blinds &c – Examining & shifting the Feathers beating Beds Bolsters & Pillows – Examining & Repairing Mattresses – Examining sorting Blankets & placing Do to their proper Beds – Uncovering & Covering Furniture in apartments cleaning Repairing & Removing Furniture – &c &c … 4 Women unpicking Remaking & Repairing Beds, Window Curtains Roller blinds Sofa & Chair Covers &c & Repairing Bed Ticks Mattresses Bolster, & Pillows – sewing on Marking on the Blankets. Repairing Carpets & Druggets &c &c … Beating Carpets, druggets to Bed Rooms best apartments Castle Square Building & Marlborough Row Houses – West front &c.'

136 NA, LC/22/35, quarterly account from S. Weaver, to 6 April 1822.

137 Butler (ed.), *op. cit.*, see note 11, p. 160.

138 NA LC/11/24, quarterly account for William Stark, to 5 January 1817, describes a drying closet with a double body and two hollow shelves all heated by steam; the base of the closet and the shelves were lined with tin.

139 NA, LC/11/43. To achieve these tasks, the following extra staff were employed: 339$\frac{1}{4}$ days men (presumably skilled)

@ 5/6 per day, 78³/₄ day labourers @ 3/6 per day, and 19 day women @ 3/- per day. The present hand-knotted replica Music Room carpet (which has half the knotting density of the original Axminster) requires some forty men to lift, roll and remove it. The original, considerably heavier, must have needed an army of manual staff to take it up for dancing or cleaning.

140 Jutsham *Receipts and Deliveries*, vol. 3, 15 December 1823, The Royal Collection Trust.

141 For accounts for 1823 see NA, LS/2/49, Expenditure of the Lord Steward's Department, 1823, and LS/8/282, Creditors' Accounts.

142 John Ashton, *Social England under the Regency*, London, 1890, vol. 2, p. 330.

143 Aspinall (ed.), *Correspondence*, *op. cit.*, see note 4, vol. 7, letter 3038 (from the Prince Regent, dated 21 May 1811).

144 Richard Russell, *The Oeconomy of Nature in Acute and Chronical Diseases of the Gland*, Oxford, 1755, p. 214.

145 A. Relhan, *A Short History of Brighthelmston, with Remarks on its Air, and an Analysis of its Waters*, London, 1761, pp. 2–3.

146 Aspinall (ed.), *Letters of George IV*, *op. cit.*, see note 51, p. 222, letter 718 (from Brighton, dated 16 December 1817). *Solomongrundy*: slang for a mixture, from the dish 'salmagrundi' a combination of meat, herring and condiments; equally *Olla* or *Oglio*: a medley, a mixture.

147 Thomas J. Graham, *Modern Domestic Medicine*, London, 1840, p. 451.

148 A. Aspinall (ed.), *Letters of the Princess Charlotte, 1811–1817*, London, 1949, p. 224.

149 Rudolf Ackermann (publisher), *Repository of Arts, Literature, Commerce, Manufactures, Fashion and Politics*, London, 1809–1828. Extant examples appear to be standard chairs with the mechanism added to effect movement.

150 The Hon. Mrs Hugh Wyndham (ed.), *Correspondence of Sarah Spencer Lady Lyttleton 1787–1870*, London, 1912, p. 128.

151 Sir Herbert Maxwell (ed.), *The Creevey Papers*, London, 1904, vol. 1, p. 272.

152 Francis Bickley (ed.), *The Diaries of Sylvester Douglas (Lord Glenbervie)*, London, 1928, vol. 2, p. 339.

153 Pavilion inventory, Royal Pavilion Archives.

154 T*he First Indian Author in English* by Michael H. Fisher, Oxford, 1996, provides a full account of Sake Deen Mahomed's fascinating life (1759–1851) in India, Ireland and England.

155 de la Garde, *op. cit.*, see note 123, pp. 279–80.

156 I am grateful to Matthew Winterbottom of the Royal Collection Trust for showing me this account for June 1825 in the Royal Archives (RA 31757).

157 Graham, *op. cit.*, see note 147, p. 65.

158 Ibid., p. 51.

159 Aspinall (ed.), *Correspondence*, *op. cit.*, see note 4, vol. 8, letter 3257 (dated 23 November 1811).

160 NA, LC/11/55, quarter ending 5 April 1827.

161 Francis Bamford and the Duke of Wellington (eds.), *The Journal of Mrs Arbuthnot 1820–32*, London, 1950, vol. 1, p. 431, entry for 21 December 1825.

162 The Earl of Bessborough (ed.), *Georgiana*, *op. cit.*, see note 6, p. 262.

163 NA, LC/11/55, quarter to April 1827. As early as 1794 a valetudinarian bedstead was purchased from J. J. Merlin for Carlton House.

164 Jutsham *Receipts and Deliveries*, vol. 3, 22, 24 and 31 January 1827.

165 Aspinall (ed.), *Letters of George IV*, *op. cit.*, see note 51, vol. 2, letter 1051 (dated 7 December 1822, from the Pavilion in Brighton).

166 Sir Henry Halford, *Essays and Orations*, London, 1833, p. 110. The lecture entitled 'On the Treatment of Gout' was given in June 1831.

167 Gore (ed.), *op. cit.*, see note 39, p. 150.

168 Maxwell (ed.), *op. cit.*, see note 151, vol. 1, p. 297.

169 Aspinall (ed.), *Letters of George IV*, *op. cit.*, see note 51, vol. 2, p. 546.

170 Ibid., vol. 3, p. 432.

171 Ibid., p. 432.

172 Lord Byron, *Don Juan*, 1823/4, canto 7, CXXVI.

173 Granville (ed.), *op. cit.*, see note 35, vol. 2, p. 375. Rough translation: Princes move swiftly not only for love but also for cooks – anyhow they are not very scrupulous in things when it affects their pleasure.

174 Anon., *Almack's A Novel*, London, 1826, vol. 3, p. 48.

175 Ibid., vol. 3, pp. 325–9.

176 Marie Antonin Carême, *French Cookery*, translated and edited by William Hall, London, 1836, p. 76.

177 Ibid., p. 76.

178 Ibid., p. 77.

179 Lord Byron, *Don Juan*, 1823/4, canto 15, LXVI.

180 Ibid., LXXII. A punning opportunity not to be missed: *goût*: French for 'taste' and the English 'gout'.

181 Nicoullaud (ed.), *op. cit.*, see note 34, vol. 2, p. 252.

182 Wright, *op. cit.*, se note 14, p. 43.

183 The inventory of the Royal Pavilion of 1828 (Royal Pavilion Archives) lists the equipment in all the kitchens and ancillary areas; accounts for equipment supplied by William Stark are retained in the Lord Chamberlain's papers in the National Archives. See also an article on the kitchens in *Country Life*, 'Steam Cuisine' by Jessica Rutherford, 14 December 1989, pp. 41–3.

184 Kerr, *op. cit.*, see note 81, p. 207.

185 RA 26310, Memorandum, watermarked 1822, Royal Archives. I should like to thank Sir Geoffrey de Bellaigue for drawing this document to my attention.

186 J. Trusler, *The Honours of the Table*, London, 1788, p. 6.

187 The Hon. Charles Langdale, *Memoirs of Mrs Fitzherbert*, London, 1856, pp. 133–4.

188 RA MRH/Menu Book/Brighton/1819.

189 See chapter 7, p. 148.

190 Bickley (ed.), *op. cit.*, see note 152, vol. 2, p. 120.

191 Thomas Cosnett (publisher), *The Footman's Directory*, London, 1825, p. 87.

192 Hibbert (ed.), *Louis Simon, op. cit.*, see note 111, p. 35.

193 François de La Rochefoucauld, *A Frenchman in England*, 1784, translated by S. C. Roberts, Cambridge, 1933, p. 29.

194 Ibid., p. 31.

195 Ibid., pp. 31–2.

196 I am grateful to Lord Leicester for showing me this cupboard at Holkham Hall, Norfolk. Up to the outbreak of the Second World War this room was used as an informal dining room.

197 See chapter 7, p. 138.

198 Jennings (ed.), *op. cit.*, see note 58, vol. 1, p. 125.

199 J. M. Rutherford, 'Lighting in the Royal Pavilion 1815–1900', *Country House Lighting*, 1992, Temple Newsam Country House Studies, vol. 4, pp. 28–34.

200 [Pückler-Muskau, Prince,] *op. cit.*, see note 108, vol. 1, p. 208.

201 Jane Austen, *Emma*, first published 1816, Harmondsworth, 1996, p. 299.

202 Maria Edgeworth, *Tales of Fashionable Life*, London, 1809, vol. 1, p. 10.

203 Jennings (ed.), *op. cit.*, see note 58, vol. 1, p. 127. Hancock & Co. was a celebrated lighting emporium in London.

204 Argand lamps, patented in 1784 by Ami Argand, were colza-oil lamps; the burners were gravity fed with oil from a reservoir located about the level of the burners.

205 *Crace Accounts*, 1802–1822, p. 105, Royal Pavilion Archives.

206 Ibid., p. 85.

207 Matthew Williams, *A Historical Sketch of the Origins, Progress and Present State of Gas Lighting*, London, 1827, p. 177.

208 For over two centuries publications have so frequently recorded that in the 1820s the Music Room and Banqueting Room chandeliers were lit by gas that the term 'gasolier' has crept into recent literature on the Pavilion. In fact these rooms were lit only by gas from the exterior, at high levels, and the chandeliers themselves were lit with candles. In the post-1850 period the Pavilion was illuminated by gas.

209 M. Meade-Fetherstonhaugh and O. Warner, *Uppark and its People*, London, 1964, p. 80. I should like to thank James Lomax for showing me this reference.

210 Letter from J. Taylor to J. Watier at Carlton House, dated 29 September 1818; Collections of British Gas (South Eastern).

211 Minutes of the Committee of Management of the Brighton Gas Light & Coke Company, 20 December 1820; East Sussex Record Office (GBRI/2).

212 Ibid., 14 December 1821; East Sussex Record Office (GBRI/2).

213 *Brighton Gazette*, 17 January 1822.

214 NA, LC/11/31, account for quarter to 5 April 1821.

215 Ibid.

216 NA, LC 11/32, account to 5 July 1821.

217 Jennings (ed.), *op. cit.*, see note 58, vol. I, pp. 248–9. The chapel was subsequently demolished in the latter part of the nineteenth century.

218 NA LC/11/71, account for quarter to April 1831. Noble's bills appear in the quarterly accounts in the 1820s in the Lord Steward's papers. It would seem that from c. 1830 this role was transferred to the Lord Chamberlain's Department.

219 J. W. Hiort, *Practical Treatise of the Construction of Chimneys*, London, 1826.

220 Butler (ed.), *op. cit.*, see note 11, p. 71.

221 *Requisitions Book*, Royal Pavilion Archives.

222 Quennell (ed.), *op. cit.*, see note 60, p. 148.

223 NA Works/19/1/2, letter from Dr Reid dated 12 December 1842.

224 RA GEO/33931, estimate of works to be done in 1819.

225 'Dihl mastic' was a patent stucco developed to create a stone-like render. It proved not to be waterproof, and the Pavilion's tent roofs had to be recovered with copper as early as 1827.

226 See chapter 5, p. 105.

227 Ralph Neville (ed.), *Leaves from the Note-books of Lady Dorothy Neville*, London, 1907, p. 125.

228 Hibbert (ed.), *Louis Simond, op. cit.*, see note 111, pp. 35–7.

228 R. G. Martin, 'Ice Houses and the Commercial Ice Trade in Brighton', *Journal of Sussex Industrial History*, no. 14.

230 RA/GEO 34045.

231 NA, LS/8/222. Bill supplied by Furner for the quarter ending December 1822.

232 John Buonarotti Papworth, *Rural Residences*, London, 1818, p. 89.

233 S. P. Beamon and S. Roaf, *The Ice-houses of Britain*, London, 1990, p. 46.

234 NA, Lord Steward's Accounts, LS 11/9/XC 000445, p. 274.

235 An example of an 1820 Simpson manual fire engine from Windsor Castle is in the collections of the National Museum of Science in London.

236 Lord Byron, *Don Juan*, 1823/4, canto XIX.

237 D. Bindman and G. Riemann (eds.), *Karl Friederich Schinkel, The English Journey, Journal of a Visit to France and Britain in 1826*, New Haven and London, 1993, p. 108.

238 Ibid., p. 110.

239 P. P. Howe (ed.), *The Complete Works of William Hazlitt*, London, 1932, vol. 7, pp. 220–2 (political essay entitled 'On the Effects of War and Taxes' first published in 1819).

240 William Cobbett, *Rural Rides*, edited by Pitt Cobbett, London, 1885, pp. 92–3.

241 Greig (ed.), *op. cit.*, see note 47, col. VIII, p. 197.

242 H. J. C. Grierson (ed.), *The Letters of Sir Walter Scott*, London, 1934, pp. 410–13; letter to J. B. S. Morritt, dated 6 February 1826. In 1823 Scott illuminated his house, Abbotsford, in the Scottish borders with gas.

243 *The Monthly Magazine*, October 1819.

244 *Brighton Gazette*, 17 October 1830.

245 Robinson (ed.), *op. cit.*, see note 22, letter dated 8–20 July 1830. George IV died on 26 June 1830.

246 Reeve (ed.), *op. cit.*, see note 77, vol. 2, p. 106.

247 RA VIC/QVJ/1837: 4 October.

248 RA VIC/QVJ/1838: 18 December.

249 Georgina, Baroness Bloomfield, *Reminiscences of Court and Diplomatic Life*, London, 1883, vol. 1, pp. 42–3.

250 This room is now called the William IV Room.

251 These apartments on the first floor were used by the Prince of Wales before Nash designed his new ground-floor apartments. In the 1820s they were used as guest rooms.

252 RA VIC/QVJ/1849: 10 June. For further information about the incorporation of Pavilion furniture and fittings into Blore's new East Wing, see Geoffrey de Bellaigue, 'Chinoiserie at Buckingham Palace', *Apollo*, May 1975, pp. 380–91.

253 For further information: Patrick Conner, *Oriental Architecture in the West*, London, 1979.

254 W. M. Thackeray, *Vanity Fair*, London, 1869, pp. 235–6.

255 The Duke of Buckingham and Chandos, *Memoirs of the Court of England*, London, 1856, vol. 2, p. 411.

256 Charles Fleet, *A Handbook of Brighton*, Brighton, 1854, p. 54.

257 For further information, see Jessica Rutherford, 'Redecoration and Restoration: The Crace Firm at the Royal Pavilion, Brighton, 1863–1899', *The Craces, Royal Decorators*

1768–1900, M. Aldrich (ed.), London, 1990, pp. 167–79.

258 *Brighton Herald*, 13 August 1898.

259 Proceedings of the Pavilion Committee, vol. 1, p. 226 (12 May 1853) and vol. 11, p. 36 (15 December 1879). Royal Pavilion Archives.

260 Moorecroft's *Brighton Guide*, Brighton, 1866, p. 35.

261 George Meason, *The Official Illustrated Guide to Brighton and South Coast Railways*, London, 1853, pp. 52–3.

262 *Punch*, 22 August 1846, vol. 11, p. 76.

263 Moncure Daniel Conway, *Travels in South Kensington with Notes on Decorative Art and Architecture in England*, London, 1882, pp. 137–9.

264 For details of the use of the Pavilion estate buildings as a military hospital for Indian soldiers, and then as a hospital for limbless soldiers, see Roberts, *op. cit.*, see note 23.

265 Osbert Sitwell and Margaret Barton, *Brighton*, London, 1935, p. 230.

266 Sacheverell Sitwell, *British Architects and Craftsmen*, London, 1945, p. 257.

267 John Summerson, *John Nash Architect to King George IV*, London, 1935; 2nd edition 1949, p. 169.

268 Noël Coward, *Conversation Piece*, London, 1934, Act II, Scene III, p. 71.

269 See Royal Pavilion Archives for correspondence between the magazine and the then director of the Pavilion, Clifford Musgrave.

270 *Vogue*, American edition, 15 April 1966. Leslie Caron, then married to theatre director Peter Hall, had visited the Pavilion in January 1960, with her young son. The *Herald* (9 January 1960) recorded her visit.

271 *Brighton Gazette*, 5 February 1965.

272 For detailed information on the reinstatement of the gardens see Mavis Batey, 'Regency Setting Restored', *Country Life*, 26 April 1984; Virginia Hinze, *op. cit.*, see note 106.

273 The first manual cutting cylinder lawn mower was patented by Edwin Budding (1795–1846) in 1830. He was inspired by the cutting cylinder tools used in textile factories to give a uniform finish to carpets or cloth and recognised the potential of this equipment for cutting grass.

274 *Kiss and Kill: Film Visions of Brighton*. Exhibition catalogue, published by the Royal Pavilion, Libraries & Museums, Brighton & Hove City Council, 2002.

275 John Summerson, *The Life and Work of John Nash, Architect*, London, 1980, p. 109. Sir John Summerson first published on Nash in 1935; forty-five years later he revised the early study which contained, as he acknowledged, some errors and misjudgements.

Bibliography

Perhaps no other historic building has been the subject of as many publications as the Royal Pavilion. Only three years after its completion John Nash published the lavishly illustrated *Views of the Royal Pavilion at Brighton*, dedicated to his patron George IV. In 1838 E. W. Brayley wrote a commentary to the reprinted edition of Nash's *Views*. This became a standard text used by writers long after the Pavilion had been stripped and despoiled in the late 1840s. More recently, in 1991, Nash's *Views* was reprinted with an introduction by HRH The Prince of Wales and a commentary by Gervase Jackson-Stops. In the latter part of the nineteenth century, the Brighton historian J. G. Bishop dominated the subject with lively, anecdotal stories about the Pavilion (and its inhabitants), many of which were more lively than accurate.

In the early 1920s Henry Roberts was appointed the first director of the Royal Pavilion. He wrote the first authoritative history of the building, from the late eighteenth century to his own time. It was published in 1939 and was dedicated to HM Queen Mary, a loyal supporter of the Pavilion and its restoration. Roberts's successor, Clifford Musgrave, moved into more lyrical and literary mood with *Royal Pavilion, An Episode in the Romantic* (1951), reflecting his generation's more romantic interpretation of Nash's extraordinary palace. The early 1980s were marked by two publications on the history of the designs and aesthetic of the Pavilion: the beautifully written *The Royal Pavilion* (1983) by John Dinkel, and John Morley's *The Making of the Royal Pavilion* (1984), a fully illustrated study (with catalogue) of all the known designs of the Pavilion, whether executed or not.

The interest today in George IV and the Regency period is acknowledged by a number of recent publications that follow on from Christopher Hibbert's excellent volumes of the 1970s: in 1998 Saul David's *Prince of Pleasure* and Venetia Murray's *High Society, A Social History of the Regency Period,* in 1999 E. A. Smith's *George IV* and in 2001 Steve Parissien's *George IV.*

The history of the Pavilion is extremely well documented. Records of works done by the Crace firm of decorators in the Marine Pavilion and Nash's later building exist in typescript form and the Royal Archives at Windsor Castle hold some fascinating archival material. The most important documents remain in the National Archives, in particular the Lord Chamberlain's and Lord Steward's papers. The MSS documents and notebooks in the Royal Pavilion archives include an inventory compiled in the late 1820s, probably after the King's decision to leave Brighton in 1827.

The use of the Pavilion by William IV and Queen Victoria is equally well documented in the Public Record Office, local newspapers and, by 1846, in Denew's inventory of the Pavilion held by the Royal Collection. As an object of curiosity and a former royal residence, the Pavilion continued to be a topic for comment by numerous diarists, commentators and satirists over the last three centuries. Its post-1850 municipal history is well recorded in volumes of Pavilion Sub-Committee minute books and material in the Plan Registry archive.

Selected archives

Royal Pavilion Archives (Brighton & Hove City Council): *Inventory of Contents* c.1828 (referred to as Pavilion inventory); *Requisitions Book: Abstract of Accounts for the Lord Chamberlain's Department*; *Memorandoms* [*sic*], manuscript notebook of the housekeeper at the Royal Pavilion, 1837–1845 (No. 2300.3 SB.9.MSI); Plan Registry: records of works done on the Pavilion Estate (mostly post-1830); *Crace Accounts* 1802–1822, a typescript of ledger entries from the books of Crace & Sons; acquired by Messrs Cowtan & Sons when they took over the Crace firm in 1899; *Proceedings of the Pavilion Committee*: minute books from 1850.

National Archives (formerly the Public Record Office): The Works Papers; Lord Chamberlain's Papers (LC) and the Lord Steward's Paper (LS). References in the footnotes are abbreviated to NA with document reference.

Royal Archives, Windsor Castle: Menu Book/Brighton/1819; George IV's Accounts, Queen Victoria's Journal (MSS). References

are abbreviated to RA in the footnotes with the document reference.

Royal Collection Trust, London: Denews 1846 Inventory of the Royal Pavilion (inventory probably compiled after Queen Victoria's decision to sell the Pavilion); Jutsham *Receipts and Deliveries*, 3 manuscript volumes of receipts and deliveries at Carlton House, 1806–1829.

East Suffolk Record Office: Pretyman Papers (562) relating to the Prince Regent's visit to Buckden Palace in 1814.

Printed sources

Ackerman, Rudolph (publisher), *Repository of Arts, Literature, Commerce, Manufactures, Fashion and Politics*, London, 1807–1828.

Adams, Samuel and Sarah, *The Complete Servant*, 1825; reprinted 1989, edited by Ann Haly, Southover Press, Lewes.

Aldrich, Megan (ed.), *The Craces, Royal Decorators 1768–1899*, London, 1990.

Anonymous, *Almack's A Novel* (3 vols.), Saunders & Otley, Public Library, London, 1826.

Ashton, John, *Florizel's Folly*, London, 1899.

Ashton, John, *Social England under the Regency* (2 vols.), London, 1890.

Aspinall, A. (ed.), *The Correspondence of George, Prince of Wales, 1770–1812* (8 vols.), London, 1963–1971.

Aspinall, A. (ed.), *The Letters of King George IV, 1812–1830* (3 vols.), Cambridge, 1938.

Aspinall, A. (ed.), *Letters of the Princess Charlotte, 1811–1817*, London, 1949.

Austen, Jane, *Emma*, first published 1816, Harmondsworth, 1996.

Austen, Jane, *Pride and Prejudice*, first published 1813, London, 1963.

Bamford, Francis, and Wellington, the Duke of (eds.), *The Journal of Mrs Arbuthnot 1820–32* (2 vols.), London, 1950.

Baring, Mrs Henry (ed.), *The Diary of the Rt Hon. William Windham 1784 to 1810*, London, 1866.

Barlow, Andrew, *The Prince and his Pleasure: Satirical Images of George IV and his Circle,* Royal Pavilion & Museums, Brighton, 1977

Baxter's Stranger in Brighton and Directory, Brighton, 1824.

Beamon, S. P., and Roaf, S., *The Ice-houses of Britain*, London, 1990.

Beattie, John M., *The English Court in the Reign of George I*, Cambridge, 1967.

Bernan, Walter, *On the History and Art of Warming and Ventilating Rooms and Buildings* (2 vols.), London, 1843.

Berry, Sue, 'Pleasure gardens in Georgian and Regency seaside resorts: Brighton 1756–1840' in *Garden History*, 28(2), 2000, pp. 222–30

Bessborough, The Earl of (ed.), *Georgiana, Extracts from the Correspondence of Georgiana, Duchess of Devonshire*, London, 1955.

Bessborough, The Earl of, and Aspinall, A. (eds.), *Lady Bessborough and her Family Circle*, London, 1940.

Bickley, Francis (ed.), *The Diaries of Sylvester Douglas (Lord Glenbervie)* (2 vols.), London, 1928.

Bindman, D. and Riemann, G. (eds.), *Karl Friederich Schinkel, The English Journey, Journal of a Visit to France and Britain in 1826*, New Haven and London, 1993.

Bishop, J. G., *The Royal Pavilion*, Brighton, 1900.

Blake, Mrs Warrenne (ed.), *An Irish Beauty of the Regency … The Unpublished Journals of the Hon. Mrs Calvert, 1789–1822*, London, 1911.

Bloomfield, Georgina, Baroness, *Reminiscences of Court and Diplomatic Life* (2 vols.), London 1883.

Braidwood, James, *On the Construction of Fire Engines and Apparatus …*, Edinburgh, 1830.

Brayley, E. W. A., *Illustrations of Her Majesty's Palace at Brighton*, London, 1838

Brighton Gazette.

Brighton Herald.

Buckingham and Chandos, The Duke of, *Memoirs of the Court of England* (2 vols.), London, 1856.

Burnett, John, *Plenty and Want*, A *Social History of Diet in England from 1815 to the Present Day*, London, 1966 (revised 1979).

Butler, E. M. (ed.), *A Regency Visitor, The Englist Tour of Prince Pückler-Muskau, Described in his Letters 1826–1828*, London, 1957.

Byron, Lord, *Don Juan*, 1823/4.

Carême, Marie Antonin, *French Cookery: Comprising L'Art de la cuisine française; Le Patissier royal; Le Cuisinier parisien*, translated by William Hall, London, 1836.

Carême, Marie Antonin, *L'Art de la cuisine française au dix-neuvième siecle Traité élémentaire et pratique*, Paris, [1833] 1847.

Carême, Marie Antonin, *Le Cuisinier parisien, ou l'Art de la cuisine française au dix-neuvième siècle*, Paris, 1828.

Carême, Marie Antonin, *Le Maitre d'hôtel français*, Paris, 1842.

Carlton House: The Past Glories of George IV's Palace, The Queen's Gallery, Buckingham Palace, London, 1991.

Cobbett, William, *Rural Rides*, edited by Pitt Cobbett, London, 1885.

Colvin, H. M. (ed.), *The History of the King's Works*, vol. VI, 1782–1851, London, 1973.

Conner, Patrick, *Oriental Architecture in the West*, London, 1979.

Conway, Moncure Daniel, *Travels in South Kensington with Notes on Decorative Art and Architecture in England*, London, 1882.

Cosnett, Thomas (publisher), *The Footman's Directory*, London, 1825.

Coward, Noël, *Conversation Piece*, London, 1934.

Cunningham, Hugh, *The Book of Fashionable Life: Comprising the Etiquette of the Drawing Room, Dining Room and Ball Room, by a member of the Royal Household*, London, 1845.

de Bellaigue, Geoffrey, 'Chinoiserie at Buckingham Palace', *Apollo*, May 1975.

de Bellaigue, Geoffrey, 'George IV: his Approach to Furniture', *Furniture History Society Journal*, 1985.

de la Garde, Le Comte A., *Brighton, Scènes détachées d'un voyage en Angleterre*, Paris, 1834.

Delves Broughton, Mrs Vernon (ed.), *Court and Private Life in the Time of Queen Charlotte: Being the Journal of Mrs Papendiek* (2 vols.), London, 1887.

Dinkel, John, *The Royal Pavilion, Brighton*, London, 1983.

Edgeworth, Maria, *Tales of Fashionable Life* (3 vols.), London, 1809.

Erredge, John A., *History of Brighthelmston* (grangerised collection of newspaper cuttings), Brighton, 1862.

Farrant, Sue, 'The Drainage of Brighton: Sewerage and Outfall Provision as an Issue in a Famous Seaside Resort c.1840–80', *Sussex Archaeological Collections*, 124, 1986.

Fisher, Michael H., *The First Indian Author in English*, Oxford, 1996.

Fleet, Charles, *A Handbook of Brighton*, Brighton, 1854.

Foreman, Amanda, *Georgiana, Duchess of Devonshire*, London, 1998.

Girouard, Mark, *Life in the English Country House*, Yale, 1978 (Penguin, 1980).

Gore, John (ed.), *The Creevey Papers*, London, 1963 (reprinted The Folio Society 1970 and Penguin 1985).

Graham, Thomas J., *Modern Domestic Medicine*, London, 1840.

Granville, Castalia, Countess (ed.), *Lord Granville Leveson-Gower (first Earl Granville): Private Correspondence 1781 to 1821* (2 vols.), London, 1917.

Greig, J. (ed.), *The Farington Diary by Joseph Farington, RA* (8 vols.), London, 1922–1928.

Grierson, H. J. C. (ed.), *The Letters of Sir Walter Scott*, London, 1934.

Halford, Sir Henry, *Essays and Orations*, London, 1833.

Harvey and Darton (publisher), *Sketches of Young People or a Visit to Brighton*, London, 1822.

Hecht, J. Jean, *The Domestic Servant in Eighteenth-century England*, London, 1956.

Hellyer, S. Stevens, *The Plumber and Sanitary Houses. A Practical Treatise on the Principals of Internal Plumbing Work …*, London, 1882.

Hibbert, Christopher, *George IV, Prince of Wales 1762–1811*, London, 1972.

Hibbert, Christopher, *George IV, Regent and King*, London, 1973.

Hibbert, Christopher (ed.), *Greville's England*, Folio Society, London, 1981.

Hibbert, Christopher (ed.), *Louis Simond, An American in Regency England: The Journal of a Tour in 1810–1811*, London, 1968.

Hinze, Virginia, 'The Recreation of John Nash's Regency Garden at the Royal Pavilion, Brighton', *Garden History*, Summer 1996 (vol. 24, no. 1).

Hiort, J. W., *Practical Treatise on the Construction of Chimneys*, London, 1826.

Howe, P. P. (ed.), *The Complete Works of William Hazlitt*, London, 1932.

Ilchester, The Earl of (ed.), *The Journal of Elizabeth, Lady Holland (1791–1811)* (2 vols.), London, 1908.

Jackson-Stops, Gervase, *Views of the Royal Pavilion*, reprint of Nash's *Views* (1827) with a commentary, London, 1991.

Jennings, Louis J. (ed.), *The Croker Papers. The Correspondence and Diaries of the Late Right Honourable John Wilson Croker, LLD, FRS* (3 vols.), London, 1885.

John Bull.

John Joseph Merlin The Ingenious Mechanick, The Iveagh Bequest, Kenwood and the Greater London Council, London, 1985.

Johnson, Samuel, *A Dictionary of the English Language*, 3 vols, London, 1827 (2nd edition).

Kerr, Robert, *The Gentleman's House*, 1864, reprinted New York/London, 1927.

Knighton, Lady, *Memoirs of Sir William Knighton* (2 vols.), London, 1838.

La Rochefoucauld, François de, *A Frenchman in England*, 1784, translated by S. C. Roberts, Cambridge, 1933.

Lamont-Brown, Raymond, *Royal Poxes and Potions*, Sutton Publishing Limited, United Kingdom, 2001.

Langdale, The Hon. Charles, *Memoirs of Mrs Fitzherbert*, London, 1856.

Leveson Gower, Sir George, and Palmer, Iris (eds.), *Hary-O The Letters of Lady Harriet Cavendish, 1796–1809*, London, 1940.

Lewis, Lady Theresa (ed.), *Extracts of the Journals and Correspondence of Miss Berry from the Year 1783 to 1852* (3 vols.), London, 1865.

Loudon, J. C., *Encyclopaedia of Cottage, Farm and Villa Architecture and Furniture* (2 vols.), first published 1848, reprinted by Donhead Publishing Ltd, 2000.

Mahomed, Sake Deen, *Shampooing; or, Benefits resulting from the Use of the Indian Medicated Vapour Bath*, Brighton, 1822.

Malcolm, James Peller, *Anecdotes of the Manners and Customs of London during the Eighteenth Century* (2 vols.), London, 1810.

Martin, Ron G., 'Ice Houses in Sussex', *Journal of Sussex Industrial History*, no. 24.

Martin, Ron G., 'Ice Houses and the Commercial Ice Trade in Brighton', *Journal of Sussex Industrial History*, no. 14 .

Matthews, William, *An Historical Sketch of the Origins, Progress and Present State of Gas Lighting*, London, 1827.

Maxwell, Sir Herbert (ed.), *The Creevey Papers* (2 vols.), London, 1904.

Meade-Fetherstonhaugh, M., and Warner, O., *Uppark and its People*, London, 1964.

Meason, George, *The Official Illustrated Guide to Brighton and South Coast Railways*, London, 1853.

Melville, Lewis, *Brighton: Its History, Its Follies and Its Fashions*, London, 1909.

Montgomery, J. M. (arr. by), *The Chimney-sweeper's Friend and Climbing-boy's Album*, London, 1824.

The Monthly Magazine.

Moorecroft's *Brighton Guide*, Brighton, 1866.

Morley, John, *The Making of the Royal Pavilion*, London, 1984.

Muhlstein, Anka (ed.), *Memoirs of the Comtesse de Boigne*, vol.11, 1816–1830, Turtle Point Press, New York, 2003.

Müller, F. Max (ed.), *Memoirs of Baron Stockmar*, London, 1872.

Munday, Harriot Georgina (ed.), *The Journal of Mary Frampton from the Year 1779 until the Year 1846*, London, 1886.

Murray, Venetia, *High Society, A Social History of the Regency Period*, London, 1998.

Musgrave, Clifford, *Life in Brighton*, London, 1970.

Musgrave, Clifford, *Royal Pavilion, An Episode in the Romantic*, London, 1951.

Nash, John, *Views of the Royal Pavilion, Brighton, 1826* (published 1827).

Neville, Ralph (ed.), *Leaves from the Note-books of Lady Dorothy Neville*, London, 1907.

Nicoullaud, M. Charles (ed.), *Memoirs of the Comtesse de Boigne (1815–1819)* (3 vols.), London, 1907.

Observations on the cruelty of employing Climbing Boys in sweeping chimneys, and on the practicability of effectually cleansing flues by mechanical means; with extracts from the evidence before the House of Commons etc., London, 1828.

Papworth, John Buonarotti, *Rural Residences*, London, 1818.

Porter, Roy, *The Greatest Benefit to Mankind, A Medical History of Humanity from Antiquity to the Present*, London, 1997.

[Pückler-Muskau, Prince,] *Tour in England, Ireland and France in the Years 1828 and 1829, by a German Prince* (4 vols.), London, 1832.

Pückler's Progress. The Adventures of Prince Pückler-Muskau in England, Wales and Ireland as told in letters to his former wife 1826–9, translated by Flora Brennan, London, 1987.

Punch.

Quennell, Peter (ed.), *The Private Letters of Princess Lieven to Prince Metternich 1820–1826*, London, 1937.

Raymond, John (ed.), *The Reminiscences and Recollections of Captain Gronow being Anecdotes of the Camp, Court, Clubs and Society 1810–1860*, London, 1964.

Reeve, Henry (ed.), *The Greville Memoirs* (3 vols.), London, 1874.

Relhan, A., *A Short History of Brighthelmston, with Remarks on its Air, and an Analysis of its Waters*, London, 1761.

Repton, Humphry, *Designs for the Pavillon at Brighton*, London, 1808.

Roberts, Henry D., *A History of the Royal Pavilion*, London, 1939.

Robinson, Lionel G. (ed.), *Letters of Dorothea, Princess Lieven, during her Residence in London 1812–1834*, London, 1902.

'Royal Patronage of Music', *The Quarterly Musical Magazine and Review*, vol. 1, no. 1, 1818.

Rush, Benjamin (ed.), *Richard Rush, Residence at the Court of London from 1819 to 1825*, London, 1872.

Russell, Richard, *The Oeconomy of Nature in Acute and Chronical Diseases of the Gland*, Oxford, 1755.

Rutherford, Jessica M. F., 'Lighting in the Royal Pavilion 1815–1900', *Country House Lighting*, Temple Newsam Country House Studies, vol. 4, Leeds, 1992.

Rutherford, Jessica M. F., 'Redecoration and Restoration: The Crace Firm at the Royal Pavilion 1863–1900', in *The Craces, Royal Decorators 1768–1900*, edited by M. Aldrich, London, 1990.

Rutherford, Jessica M. F., 'Steam Cuisine', *Country Life*, 14 December 1989.

Rutherford, Jessica M. F., *Victorian Chimneypieces in the Royal Pavilion*. Royal Pavilion & Museums Review, 1987, no. 2

Saxon, A. H., *P. T. Barnum. The Legend and the Man*, New York, 1989.

Sickelmore, R., *The History of Brighton from the Earliest Period to the Present Time*, Brighton, 1823.

Simons-Candeille, Mme, *Souvenis de Brighton, de Londres et de Paris*, Paris, 1818.

Sitwell, Osbert, and Barton, Margaret, *Brighton*, London, 1935.

Sitwell, Sacheverell, *British Architects and Craftsmen*, London, 1945.

Sketches of Her Majesty's Household … forming a Guide to Situations in the Sovereign's Domestic Establishment …, London, 1848.

Smith, E. A., *George IV*, Yale University Press, New Haven and London, 1999.

Stephenson, John, MD, and Morss Churchill, James, FLS, *Medical Botany*, London, 1829.

Strange, K. H., *The Climbing Boys*, London/New York, 1982.

Summerson, John, *John Nash Architect to King George IV*, London, 1935; 2nd edition 1949.

Summerson, John, *The Life and Work of John Nash, Architect*, London, 1980.

Sussex Weekly Advertiser.

Thackeray, W. M., *Vanity Fair*, London, 1869.

Thoms, William J., *The Book of the Court …*, London, 1838.

The Times.

Tredgold, Thomas, *Principles of Warming and Ventilating Public Buildings etc.*, London, 1824.

Trusler, J., *The Honours of the Table*, London, 1788.

Whitwell Wilson, Philip (ed.), *The Greville Diary* (2 vols.), London, 1927.

Williams, Matthew, *A Historical Sketch of the Origins, Progress and Present State of Gas Lighting*, London, 1827.

Wood, Heather, *Old Blocks for New: the Reprinting of the Dragon Wallpaper*. Royal Pavilion & Museums Review, 1993, no. 1.

Wright, Charles, *The Brighton Ambulator*, London, 1818.

Wright, Lawrence, *Clean and Decent*, London, 1960.

Wyndham, The Hon. Mrs Hugh (ed.), *Correspondence of Sarah Spencer Lady Lyttleton 1787–1870*, London, 1912.

Yarwood, Doreen, *The British Kitchen*, London, 1981.

Index

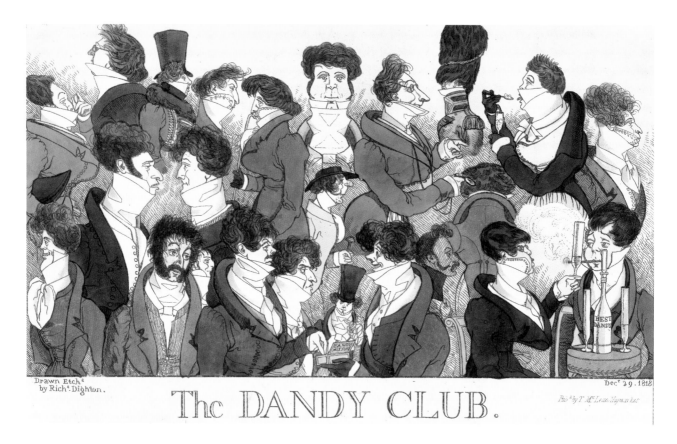

The Dandy Club by
Richard Dighton, 1818

OF THE ROYAL PAVILION
ART GALLERY & MUSEUMS

This publication is supported by:

The Friends of the Royal Pavilion, Art Gallery and Museums
Registered charity no. 275242

Patron: HRH The Prince of Wales
Chairman: the Rt Hon. Lord Briggs

For further information on the aims of the Friends and benefits of membership
please contact:

The Friends Organiser
The Royal Pavilion
4/5 pavilion Buildings
Brighton BNI IEE
Tel. 01273 290900/292789
Fax. 01273 292871
www.royalpavilion.org.uk
www.virtualmuseum.info